D0863869

OTHER BOOKS BY CHARLES J. JACQUES, JR.

Kennywood Park: Roller Coaster Capital of the World

Goodbye, West View Park, Goodbye

Cover photograph — The Wildcat.
(HERSHEYPARK)

M.S. Hershey

"He knew what it meant to be poor, he was more than acquainted with hard work, he experienced failure when starting out in business for himself after he learned his trade as a confectioner, but he also knew the sweetness of success and the great responsibilities that go with great wealth."
Alexander Stoddart

(Photograph by Charles J. Jacques, Jr)

HERSHEYPARK ®
The Sweetness of Success

by Charles J. Jacques, Jr.

Designed by Karen Morrison

Edited by Rick Shale

AMUSEMENT PARK JOURNAL

P.O. Box 478 • Jefferson, OH 44047-0478
(216) 576-6531

HARD COVER
ISBN #0-9614392-1-1

PAPERBACK
ISBN #0-9614392-2-x

Library of Congress Catalog Card Number 97-70318

TABLE OF CONTENTS

ACKNOWLEDGEMENTS

This book would not have been possible without the help of the following people:

Pamela Cassidy, archivist of the Hershey Community Archives, and her staff spent many hours helping me research the book. The archives has an extensive collection of photographs and written material on Hershey Park, which they graciously shared with me. Pamela Cassidy was also helpful with proper historical interpretations of M.S. Hershey and the town of Hershey in relationship to the park.

Harold and Dolly Sitler, who have been longtime friends and fellow carousel fans, shared their enthusiasm for and knowledge of the park and their wonderful collection of photographs.

Janet M. Maynard of the Hershey Public Library made available the library's collection of M.S. Hershey and Hersheypark material.

Although the Derry Township Historical Society is only five years old, its collection already includes many important items about the park. Thanks to Kathleen Lewis, president, and Joanne Lewis Viozzi, archivist.

The librarians, archivists, directors and others associated with the following groups were also helpful in locating historical information: Hershey Museum, Lebanon County Historical Society, Dauphin County Library System, Shippensburg University's Ezra Lehman Memorial Library, Henderson Memorial Library, National Carousel Association Archives, Herschell Carousel Factory Museum, Pennsylvania Room of the Carnegie Library of Pittsburgh, New York Public Library, and the Library of Congress.

James and Sandy Medic helped determine the number of pages in the book. William Mosso provided background material on Penn State and Hersheypark.

Samuel High III, former president of the Philadelphia Toboggan Company, was very helpful. The successor corporation to the Philadelphia Toboggan Company, Philadelphia Toboggan Coasters, Inc. has established a wonderful archives of material from the PTC. William Dauphinee is the chief executive, Thomas Rebbie, president, and Laura Grauer, archivist.

Significant information was gained from personal recollection provided by the following people: J. Bruce McKinney, Franklin R. Shearer, Harold Sitler, Dolly Sitler, Monroe Stover, Kenneth V. Hatt, John O. Hershey, Paul L. Serff, Robert B. Payne, Jeffrey W. Budgeon, Richard Hair, Gary Chubb, Neil Fasnacht, Teen Jacques, L. Eugene Jacques, Brad Cassady, and Ethel Schwartz.

Sandra Enterline, WITF-TV, producer of the documentary on Hersheypark. She conducted many interviews and generously permitted me to quote from them. She shared interviews of the following persons with me: Raleigh Hughes, Harold Brandt, Phil Funghi, Eunice Funghi, Mildred Fisher, Sarah Lutz, Joe Gosik, Mary Hubler, Betty Bartels, Milton Garland, Paul L. Serff, Tom Ribby, and Jim McCarthy.

Many thanks to the following people for providing old postcards, photographs and other graphics of the park: Richard L. Bowker, Barbara Fahs Charles, Paul L. Serff, Ralph E. Baylor, Eugene Krall, Jeffrey W. Budgeon, Chuck Woldarczyk, Brad Cassady, Gary Chubb, and Jim McCarthy.

Special thanks to Neil Fasnacht, who shared his wonderful collection of Hershey Park photographs, early postcards, and other graphics.

Mark Wyatt, editor and publisher of *Inside Tracks*, for his photographs including those from special events like the opening of TIDAL FORCE and The Wild Cat.

Wayne Stuber of Aerial Perspectives, who specializes in aerial photographs of roller coasters and parks.

Kathy Burrows, public relations coordinator, for her assistance in and around Hersheypark.

Brian Morgan, president of the National Carousel Association, for help in researching the Dentzel Carousel and Barbara Williams, archivist of the National Carousel Association, for researching the carousels of Hersheypark.

Mark Samels, executive producer of the WITF-TV documentary, for conceiving a book and documentary on Hersheypark.

Franklin R. Shearer, vice president and general manager of the park, for helping in many ways during the research and writing of the book. He opened many doors with a telephone call.

J. Bruce McKinney, chairman of HERCO, for writing a excellent preface to the book and making his staff available. He also gave me a wonderful three hour interview that was full of important stories and anecdotes about the park.

Karen Morrison designed a wonderful book. The pictures flow with the words because of Karen. She was able to include close to five hundred pictures in the book that illustrate the life and history of the park.

Rick Shale, Professor of English at Youngstown State University, edited the manuscript from its earliest stages through its final form. He helped make it a clearer, more consistent book. Shale also helped prepare the bibliography and index.

DEDICATION

This book is dedicated with love to my wife, Betty VanPelt Jacques.

PREFACE

Throughout its 90 year history, Hersheypark has undergone many changes. One element, however, has remained consistent– the quality of our product, which is second to none. Quality of product was paramount to Milton S. Hershey, the founder of Hersheypark, in establishing the community of Hershey and the businesses that support it.

Part of the legacy of Mr. Hershey, whether it be the rides, shows, or games at Hersheypark, is a continuation of the commitment to make our Park truly unique. But, most important to the success of Hersheypark are its employees–dedicated men and women working together, giving their time and energy, to make Hersheypark a place where they can proudly bring their own families. They are the quality that has always been the Hersheypark trademark. Their hard work has laid the foundation to enable Hersheypark to move into the future.

Mr. Hershey was a man who gave his personal fortune to establish a home and a school for underprivileged children, so they would be able to enjoy a better quality of life. I was one of the thousands of young people whose lives were profoundly changed by the school and home Milton Hershey created. As a proud graduate, I've had the great pleasure of watching the growth of Hersheypark both through the eyes of a young man and the eyes of an adult. When I was named General Manager of Hersheypark, I realized my own dream–having my chance to give something back in return.

In 1907, Mr. Hershey built Hersheypark as a simple "picnic and pleasure grounds" for his employees with swings, canoes, and a Bandshell. Over the years, the Park has grown and rides and attractions have been added. But, throughout all the years and all the changes, Hersheypark has retained its uniqueness and its importance within the community of Hershey. I'm very proud of that.

I feel that Hersheypark has just the right blend of everything–shows, rides, games, and beautiful scenery. The diversity of rides, entertainment, and family-oriented activities–from the state-of-the-art Wildcat coaster to a quiet bench beside Spring Creek–allows for our guests, whatever their age or interests, to fully enjoy themselves.

There are many moments that define Hersheypark. One of the most vivid memories I have is of the flood of 1972. Everyone who worked at Hersheypark, both full and part-time employees, pulled together to save buildings, rides, and even the animals in The Animal Garden. These people turned a potential disaster into the rebirth of a major amusement park. Everyone worked hard that year and many worked around the clock for a week prior to our 1973 Grand Opening. On that opening day, more than 22,000 guests visited Hersheypark. When the gates opened, the crowd was backed up to the parking lots. I'll always remember the pride I felt that morning as I looked at all those excited faces in the crowd.

As I reflect back over our rich past and look forward to an exciting future, I hope that Hersheypark will always hold onto its roots and continue to expand the vision of its founder.

In closing, I would like to thank Charles J. Jacques, Jr. for his dedication to this book. He has researched for countless hours in an effort to present an accurate record of the many people and events that have affected Hersheypark. I applaud his efforts in creating this documentary of our very unique Park.

J. Bruce McKinney
Chairman of the Board and CEO, HERCO, Inc.

M.S. Hershey in 1905.

CHAPTER 1

MANAGING THE ICE CREAM

"**I**t's my money," Milton S. Hershey was fond of saying when people questioned one of his decisions. It was his decision to create Hershey Park. It was also his decision and his money that determined how the park would be developed. As long as he lived, he controlled the park, and even after his death, one of his companies, Hershey Estates (later HERCO) continued to determine the park's future.

The site for Hershey Park was chosen July 7, 1903, when M.S. Hershey (Mr. Hershey preferred the initials M.S. rather than his name Milton) adopted a plan, which reserved 150 acres northeast of the town for a proposed park. This decision occurred very early in the development of the town of Hershey. (The name Hershey Park was changed to Hersheypark in 1971.)

Unlike other factory owners of his time, M.S. Hershey wanted to build a town where his employees could own their own houses. He avoided building a faceless company town with monotonous row houses. Even the names of the streets were charming, with the town's two main thoroughfares named Chocolate Avenue and Cocoa Avenue. Other streets had names like Granada Avenue, Java Avenue, Areba Avenue, Trinidad Avenue, and Caracas Avenue (places where cacao beans were grown).

Henry Hershey,
M.S. Hershey's father.
(HERSHEY COMMUNITY ARCHIVES)

Hershey lived in a period when people could control their own destiny. There were fewer government regulations, taxes, and rules. He was one of the old-style entrepreneurs who amassed a fortune and then gave it all away. He worked shoulder to shoulder with his employees and often led by example. Loyalty was what he most wanted from his employees. He realized that they had helped make him rich, and many things he did, including building an amusement park, were done to reward them.

Milton Snavely Hershey was born on September 13, 1857, in a fieldstone farmhouse near the village of Derry Church, Dauphin County, Pennsylvania. He was the son of Henry Hershey, whose forebears came from Switzerland and Germany in 1719, and Veronica (Fanny) B. Snavely. His father and grandfather had lived on the farm where he was born. Later Hershey would repurchase the old Hershey Homestead and incorporate it into his new town of Hershey. His family on both sides had been Mennonites for many generations.

America in the 1850's was predominantly a rural society. There were a few large cities, but the majority of the population lived on farms and in small communities. All of this changed during M.S. Hershey's lifetime; America was transformed from a country of farms and farmers into a nation of towns and cities and urban people. During his lifetime, the population of the country grew from about thirty million people to more than one hundred fifty-million people. Along with the growth came many obstacles but also many opportunities. Hershey was aware of the changes taking place. He overcame some obstacles, like lack of a formal education and stiff competition in the confectionery business, and he took advantage of the opportunities of the growth of candy distribution to the cities and a plentiful work force.

In 1866, when M.S. Hershey was nine, his family moved away from Dauphin County, Pennsylvania. His father bought a

Fanny Hershey, M.S. Hershey's mother.
(Hershey Community Archives)

forty-four-acre farm in the vicinity of Nine Points, a village sixteen miles east of Lancaster, Pennsylvania. M.S. Hershey grew up as a Pennsylvania farm boy, which meant he attended school only about four months a year. For various reasons he attended at least seven different schools in eight years, and his formal education never went beyond the fourth grade.

His parents were as different, as someone would later suggest, as chocolate and peanut butter. Fortunately for young Hershey, he inherited strong traits from both of his parents. He acquired his mother's common sense and his father's daring. His father was always searching for his fortune, whether it was in the oil fields of Pennsylvania or the gold and silver mining camps of Colorado. Henry Hershey fell further behind each time he attempted a new venture. Perhaps the best advice he gave his son was, "If you want to make money, you must do things in a large way."

His mother, who was more conservative and practical, gave her son some sound advice when he left home to take his first job: "Milton, you are now going out into the world to make a

M.S. Hershey as an apprentice for Joseph P. Royer in Lancaster, Pennsylvania.
(Hershey Community Archives)

The Lancaster Caramel Company, owned by M.S. Hershey in Lancaster, Pennsylvania.
(Hershey Community Archives)

man of yourself. My best advice to you is – when you tackle a job stick to it until you have mastered it." He never forgot those words, and he followed the advice of both of his parents.

When young Hershey was fourteen, his parents paid for his apprenticeship to a printer, who published a little pacifist German-language newspaper, *Die Waffenlose Waechter (The Weaponless Watchman)*. His employment as a printer's apprentice ended abruptly when he dropped his wide-brimmed Mennonite hat into a printing press, wrecking both the hat and the press. Years later, he told a newspaper reporter that he did it "accidentally on purpose."

Fanny Hershey wanted her son to learn a practical trade, making something, so young Hershey next sought employment in Lancaster with Joseph P. Royer, who had a confectionery shop that was located on West King Street, one of the principal thoroughfares of Lancaster. His mother paid down a certain sum of money and signed papers apprenticing her son. His father wanted him to do something more intellectual. Hershey stayed

Souvenir photograph of Catherine Hershey, M.S. Hershey, and Adeline Jackson from Coney Island, New York, circa 1890's.
(Hershey Community Archives)

four years at Royer's Ice Cream Parlor and Garden. He tried three jobs there, as a waiter, delivery boy, and superintendent of a big hand-operated ice cream freezer, before finding his life's vocation, working in the candy kitchen.

At nineteen M.S. Hershey was a full-fledged journeyman, able to ply his trade where he wished. His mother encouraged him to go into business for himself, and with a loan of $150 from his Aunt Mattie Snavely (his mother's sister), he moved to Philadelphia to start a candy shop. Fanny Hershey, as well as his Aunt Mattie, and his father, worked for M.S. Hershey in his early ventures. His first candy businesses did not work out well. He failed in Philadelphia and again in New York. In New York with his last money he sent his mother and Aunt Mattie back to Lancaster, and he was able to pay his creditors only forty cents on the dollar. However, he promised to pay them the remaining sixty cents as soon as he got his feet on the ground. Later he would say that he felt his creditors must have "laughed up their sleeves" at his offer to repay them someday.

Returning to Lancaster in 1886, Hershey tried again and succeeded, beyond anything he had felt possible. He started his new business on Church and Duke Streets, Lancaster. Caramels were popular confections then, and at first he sold two caramels for a penny. Children were always his best customers, and he never forgot it. Many things Hershey did later in life were to

Catherine Sweeney Hershey circa 1898.
(Hershey Community Archives)

The Hershey Band on the lawn at Hershey Park in 1907. New trees were planted all around the park grounds.
(HERSHEY COMMUNITY ARCHIVES)

make children's lives a little happier. In Lancaster, he made and then cut caramels with a caramel cutter before he purchased machinery to do the work. Within three years he paid back in full all of his former creditors.

One of his early employees, William Brinker, who started working for Hershey in 1890 in Lancaster, liked to tell the story of M.S. Hershey's wedding party. He had just married Catherine Sweeney in the rectory of St. Patrick's Cathedral, New York City, in 1898. He was forty-one, and his bride was twenty-five. By then Hershey had more than four hundred people on the payroll in Lancaster, and upon returning to Lancaster he gave his employees a chicken supper. He put in a new floor for dancing, and Brinker recalled, "Every employee came to the dance, and what a good time all of us had with round and square dances. After the opening dance, Mr. and Mrs. Hershey danced the rest of the numbers with other parties. It was a big night for all us."

Catherine Sweeney Hershey was an ideal helpmate for Hershey. They first met in 1897 in a confectionery store in Jamestown, New York, her hometown, when M.S. Hershey was calling on the trade. They never had any children, although both of them loved children. They liked to travel and they toured Europe and around the world. Catherine Hershey, whose health was not good, loved the seashore, and she spent weeks at a time in Atlantic City, New Jersey.

Hershey's company, the Lancaster Caramel Company, grew by leaps and bounds. He opened branches in Mount Joy and Reading in Pennsylvania and eventually plants in New York

City and Chicago. His western plant in Chicago was seven stories high and had 400 employees. His business grew to such an extent that his competitors wanted to buy him out. In 1900, at age forty-three, he sold his caramel business to the American Caramel Company of Philadelphia and New York for one million dollars.

He was now a millionaire, but once he reached that level, he had no intention of stopping. As part of the transaction, John E. "Judge" Snyder, Hershey's attorney, was able to secure for M.S. Hershey the right to continue to make chocolate. Hershey also kept his chocolate making machinery and leased a part of his former factory from the new owners. After the buyout, American Caramel controlled 95 percent of the caramel market, and it was not worried about Hershey's small chocolate business. Although caramels outsold chocolates then, Hershey felt that someday chocolate would outsell caramel, and of course he was right.

"Judge" Snyder, who was a slow, quiet-spoken Lancastrian, was one of the shrewdest attorneys in Pennsylvania. Hershey trusted him completely, and he was one of Hershey's principal advisers. Snyder became chief counsel for Hershey's businesses in the 1890's and remained in that capacity until his death in 1934. Perhaps one reason that Hershey and Snyder got along so well was that Snyder never put himself forward or took advantage of his position with Hershey.

Hershey tended to dislike professional men, lawyers in particular, but Snyder was an exception. For one thing Snyder was not a college graduate; he had learned the law by reading with an experienced lawyer, a preceptor. He was Hershey's personal attorney as well as the chief counsel for his businesses.

Following the sale, M.S. Hershey intended to expand his chocolate business in Lancaster, but two important things got in the way: First, he could not buy the property he wanted at a fair price, and second, he felt that Lancaster government officials had raised his taxes unfairly.

Therefore, in the winter of 1901, Hershey and Snyder traveled to Dauphin County to look at a possible plant site along Spring Creek in Derry Township. Since Hershey had grown up in the area, he was familiar with it, and he felt it would make the best site. Three years earlier he purchased The Homestead, the farm where he was born and where his father was now living. His father would die in 1903, shortly after the town of Hershey was founded. However, the decision to move his plant to Derry Township was made only after a careful study of many other possible sites including Baltimore; Yonkers, New York; and Kingston, New Jersey.

The land around the village of Derry Church was good dairy country. Spring Creek and the Derry Church spring offered a good water supply. He directed Snyder to purchase enough farmland for the factory, originally three hundred acres, and later more land for a town.

The first purchase, a railroad siding and quarry in the Derry Church area, was made on September 18, 1902. Surveying crews began work at once, and as each parcel was purchased, it was added to a huge survey map. M.S. Hershey continued to buy property and at the time of his death, he owned seventy-six farms and more than twelve thousand acres in three counties (Dauphin, Lebanon, and Lancaster) in Pennsylvania. His farms created a green belt around the new town, which helped preserve its rural nature.

Though Hershey's Mennonite mother viewed his plan for a park as frivolous, he was firm about providing a place where employees and townspeople could relax in their leisure moments. True to his words, M.S. Hershey officially dedicated Hershey Park on April 24, 1907. Hershey, who always liked to plan ahead, had most of the park's components in place long before the park opened. Even Fanny Hershey overcame her dislike for the park and personally visited it many times.

Hershey Park's initial appeal was its natural beauty and simplicity. The site, just north of the Philadelphia and Reading Railroad, was directly across the tracks from the chocolate factory and the town of Hershey. It had been farmed with some wooded groves along the meandering Spring Creek.

M.S. Hershey retained a landscape architect, Oglesby-Paul of Philadelphia, to draw up general landscaping plans for the town. Hershey had a great head gardener, Harry Haverstick, whom he had brought with him from Lancaster, to implement the plans. Haverstick planted new trees and shrubbery on the park's ground. It would take them years to reach maturity, but it was the beginning of the park's famous landscaping and gardens.

Hershey Park's main pavilion in 1905 before it was enclosed.
(Hershey Community Archives)

Harry Neff Herr, M.S. Hershey's chief engineer, was the only member of Hershey's inner circle who had a college degree.
(HERSHEY COMMUNITY ARCHIVES)

Catherine Hershey enjoyed working with gardens and landscaping. Haverstick said, "She was interested in the planting of trees and everything that made the properties look nice." M.S. Hershey gave definite instructions to his gardeners never to cut down a tree without his permission.

M.S. Hershey felt that landscaping was important at a time when the typical industrial town's houses were built on 25-foot lots, and most industries saw no need for any landscaping at all. The development of the town of Hershey and Hershey Park were controlled by Hershey's love of nature. Hershey Park would always be beautifully landscaped and maintained.

The entrance to Hershey Park was an open lawn, dotted with newly-planted trees and shrubs. Flower beds were planted along the edges of the lawn, which extended several hundred feet to the park's main pavilion and beyond.

The main pavilion was located on the hillside overlooking Spring Creek. It was a substantial structure, which cost Hershey more than sixty-two hundred dollars. It was built in 1904 and was used for dancing and roller skating, even before the park was officially opened. It was enlarged and extended the following year. A stage with drop curtains, including a colorful one that depicted Brazilians gathering cacao beans, and lighting were added. The structure could now be used as a theatre.

The town of Hershey had its own band that played in the park. At first it performed on the lawn under the trees, but soon a rustic bandstand (sometimes band shell) was built. In case of inclement weather the band would use the pavilion's stage.

The main pavilion was lighted with power supplied by the chocolate factory's power plant. There were also lights strung along the winding gravel pathways. At a time when many farms did not have electricity, the park made a wonderful, unforgettable sight at night.

Spring Creek, which was the focal point of the park, was dammed up to create a small lake for boating and canoeing. A

In 1907 many picnickers still came to Hershey Park in buggies.
(HERSHEY COMMUNITY ARCHIVES)

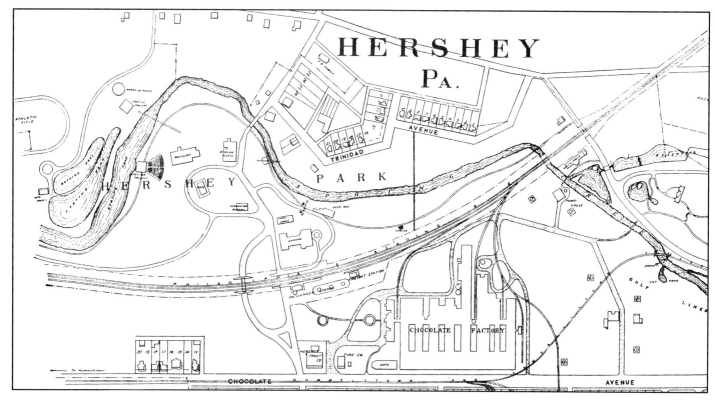

Map of Hershey Park in 1909.
(Hershey Community Archives)

romantic rustic bridge was built crossing Spring Creek, and picnicking was permitted along its banks, even before the park's official opening. Once the park opened, picnic tables and benches were purchased for use in the park's pavilion and around the grounds. Swings and slides were placed around the park for the children.

Later, other buildings, bridges, and overlooks would be built around the park. All of them were designed and constructed by James K. Putt, Hershey's ingenious head carpenter. Hershey told him what he wanted and Putt would build it. When Putt was constructing a new building, he would travel to Lebanon and Lancaster to hire as many carpenters as he needed.

Putt hated to work from blueprints. His nemesis was Harry Neff Herr, Hershey's 39-year-old chief engineer. As much as Putt disliked blueprints, Herr enjoyed them. Herr, who was the only college graduate among Hershey's top lieutenants, was a civil engineer. Herr and Putt would constantly argue over whether plans were needed for the new buildings in the park.

Herr was primarily responsible for laying out the roads, sewer and water lines, dams, and concrete bridges in the park and the town. At the peak of Hershey's building boom a playful item appeared in the *Hershey Press*, under "Herr's New Year Resolution." He was to "keep an exact and accurate account of all the sticks that I [Herr] put in the ground, and if at the end of the year, if it should so happen that I have not placed 10,000 sticks in and around Hershey, I shall have failed in my highest ambition."

The Hershey Improvement Company, predecessor to Hershey Estates and later HERCO, controlled spending on the park. Even the smallest screw or paint brush used in the park was listed in its books. M.S. Hershey tended to use the company as his own personal bank account. For instance, in addition to ledger sheets for each building in the park and each business in the town, there was a ledger sheet for M.S. Hershey's cigars, which he charged at the Hershey Department Store.

Most amusement parks at the turn of the century had a baseball field and athletic field. Hershey's first baseball diamond was located in town next to the Cocoa House. However as the town grew, there was fear that the ball players might break windows in the nearby houses, so the ball field was relocated across Spring Creek, in what became Hershey Park. A small wooden bridge was constructed so ballplayers and fans could get to the field. A grandstand and bleachers were built by Putt in 1906. The field was meticulously maintained and it was called the best baseball diamond in the area.

The Philadelphia and Reading Railroad ran through the property Hershey purchased. So in 1904 he made arrangements with the railroad to allow loading and unloading of freight cars at the factory. Hershey also requested that a passenger station be built to serve his new town. The railroad finally agreed to build a station after Hershey gave them land at the foot of Cocoa Avenue directly across from the park. The old station at Derry Church was abandoned.

The Hershey Band that helped manage Hershey Park in 1907.
(Neil Fasnacht Collection)

To connect the park to the town, without having to cross the railroad tracks, Hershey had Herr design a bridge to carry horse carriages, wagons, and people over the railroad track. Later a small passenger station was built on the north side of the tracks, which also served the park.

As Hershey Park developed, the Philadelphia and Reading Railroad provided special excursion trains to the park from Harrisburg, Lebanon, Lancaster, and beyond at reduced fares. Hundreds of church, community, and company groups took the train directly to the front entrance of the park. As many as fifteen to twenty railroad passenger cars would pull into the Hershey station bringing people to the park for a day of fun.

In addition to the trains, the park was served by the Hummelstown and Campbelltown Street Railway Company, whose name was changed in 1914 to the Hershey Transit Company. M.S. Hershey felt that his model town needed a trolley line to carry workers and transport milk to the factory, so in 1903, two days after the factory site was surveyed, Hershey applied for a charter for the trolley company. Herr laid out and supervised the construction of the twelve-mile line, which ran from Campbelltown east of the town of Hershey to Hummelstown located to the west. The line went into operation in the fall of 1904 at about the time the factory was completed. Hershey liked to ride on the trolley, sometimes boarding a trolley car as early as five o'clock in the morning to make sure everything was running properly.

The trolley line also served the park. In the early years it was one of the chief means of getting local people to the park. It cost just five cents each way. Extra cars were added for Sundays and holidays, and cars were borrowed from other trolley companies to help move large picnics to the park. Hershey purchased two small open-air cars, which were used during the summer. Hershey's trolley lines connected with other lines which served Harrisburg, Lebanon, and Elizabethtown.

At the turn of the century, amusement parks offered only a few simple attractions: dancing, skating, swimming, boating, and possibly a rifle range and a few rides. One of the most important attractions in any amusement park was a concert band. Almost every major town had at least one band. In the summer, these bands performed in outdoor band shells, and they played everything from classical excerpts to popular tunes of the day, but marches and patriotic numbers were their mainstays.

M.S. Hershey was familiar with these bands and their appeal. In the 1870's he retained a German band to play in front of his ice cream and candy store in Philadelphia to help attract business. Although he was not musically inclined, he enjoyed band music. In 1906 he engaged Jacob Hummel of Hummelstown, who came highly recommended, to organize a band for the town of Hershey. Hershey purchased most of the instruments, bought band uniforms, and encouraged his workers to join the bands. In fact, it might be said that the band was made up mostly of draftees from Hershey's chocolate factory.

Hummel, in addition to directing the band, served as a part time printer and part time policeman for Hershey Park. Having more than one job was common for a Hershey employee. M.S. Hershey believed that people ought to be kept busy, and everyone was encouraged to have several jobs. Some of M.S. Hershey's jobs were paid and some were "volunteer" jobs. However, Hummel seemed to have some trouble keeping his jobs straight. When a fight broke out at the baseball field, he attempted to break it up by using a clarinet as a night stick; it was pulled away from him, thrown against the bleachers, and smashed. Hummel was not a good policeman, and unfortunately, he was also a rather poor band director. The band never developed under his direction, so Hershey replaced him with Herbert Schultze from Philadelphia.

Part of the band's problem was that it was made up of volunteers who often could not play an instrument. One such woeful musician was Jakie Smaltz, a local character from nearby Sand Beach, Pennsylvania, who "tortured the bass horn." Fortunately for him, he was a much better mule driver and hauler, transporting ice, soft drinks, and picnickers' lunch baskets to the park from the railroad station or trolley stop.

At first there was not much need for a park manager since M.S. Hershey provided all of the services to the park and most of the activities were free. About the only activity that required some managing was operating the refreshment stand, which was located in the basement of the park pavilion. This duty was turned over to the volunteers of the Hershey Band, and since the band members were the only people who handled money, Hershey considered them his park managers.

In between performances, band members sold ice cream, cigars, chocolate bars, and soft drinks. On Labor Day of that first season, more than fifty gallons of ice cream were made, and yet no money was turned in at the end of the day to help pay for the cream, sugar, ice, and flavorings. "Too many men handling the money," complained Harry Lebkicher, Hershey's personal secretary and office manager, "and a lot of it stuck to their fingers; that's what it did."

Harry Lebkicher, M.S. Hershey's personal secretary and office manager.
(Hershey Community Archives)

Most people around the town of Hershey considered Harry Lebkicher a rather odd person. He was brusque and stingy. He would rather walk than ride, not for the sake of exercise but to avoid paying a fare. When he played Hausen Pfeffer at the Hershey Fire House, it was observed that "he would never bid his hand unless he had a full deck."

By 1907, Lebkicher, a 62-year-old bachelor, oversaw most of M.S. Hershey's personal spending, including expenditures on the park. Hershey never gave him a formal title, but everybody around town knew that he had great influence with M.S. Hershey. Lebkicher first met Hershey in Philadelphia in 1876, and he worked for him until that business failed. He encountered Hershey again in Lancaster in 1885 when Hershey needed money to get the railroad to release some of his candy making equipment. Lebkicher put up his meager savings and helped M.S. Hershey begin his successful caramel business.

Having the Hershey Band manage the park was really not that unusual for M.S. Hershey. After all, he ran Hershey as an unincorporated town without a mayor or council. When he started the Hershey Department Store, he wanted to make it a cooperative venture with employees owning shares, but there was not enough interest, so he opened it as a regular retail business.

As the first season drew to a close, M.S. Hershey, in hopes of improving the band, had Putt enclose and enlarge the main pavilion in the park, so that the band could practice during cold weather. Putt even installed a coal-fired boiler, which M.S. Hershey had salvaged from the chocolate factory in Lancaster. Lebkicher, who didn't think much of the band or their practices, complained that "It's a mighty expensive band practice, so it is, burning all that coal."

During the winter of 1907-08, a group of despondent bandsmen assembled weekly on the stage of the park pavilion. They were not very good and they knew it. They had been disgraced by the ice cream scandal. The new season was only months away, and they needed all the practice they could get.

CHAPTER 2

BILL MURRIE AND THE LANCASTER GANG

The baseball grandstands at Hershey Park were often crowded for big games when Hershey played teams from nearby towns.
(HERSHEY COMMUNITY ARCHIVES)

The opening of Hershey Park's second season, Decoration Day 1908, was announced with display cards and handbills. The day was celebrated with a baseball game between Hershey and Palmyra, a small town located nearby, which always had a good team. Hundreds of people walked to the park; others rode bicycles, while still others came by trolleys and trains. The grandstand and bleachers, which were decked out with American flags and patriotic bunting, were jammed. Even M.S. Hershey and his wife Catherine attended and cheered the team on to victory.

The manager of Hershey's baseball team that year was a six-foot, one-inch Scotsman by the name of Bill Murrie. He had red hair and a temper to match. He had some semi-pro baseball experience and was excellent at managing baseball players. He enjoyed Pittsburgh stogies, a habit

Hershey Baseball Team in 1905. Bill Murrie, manager of the team, is in a business suit in the center of the second row.

he learned while working for a confectionery company in Pittsburgh. His teams were good, beating teams from towns that were many times the size of the town of Hershey. When he was not managing the baseball team, he was running the Hershey Chocolate Company.

William Franklin Reynolds "Bill" Murrie started with the chocolate company on January 1, 1896, in Lancaster as a salesman and in his first week with the company he sold as much chocolate, two hundred barrels, as the factory could produce in a year. M.S. Hershey said, "If the man is good enough to outsell the plant, I want him to run the business." When Murrie joined the company, Hershey came off the road and retired as the company's chief salesman. In Lancaster, Hershey sat behind a partners' desk, running the caramel business from one side while Murrie looked after the chocolate business from the other side.

After the caramel business was sold, Murrie became the general manager in Lancaster, and when the new chocolate factory opened in Hershey in 1904, he became its first general manager. In 1908, the same year that his baseball team beat Palmyra at the opening of Hershey Park's second season, Murrie was named president of the Hershey Chocolate Company. It was a position he would hold for the next thirty-nine years. (M.S. Hershey was Chairman of the Board of the chocolate company and sole stockholder.)

Murrie ran the chocolate company, while Hershey devoted most of his time to building a town. However, these two interests were never completely separate during Hershey's lifetime, or even after his death. To this day, the amusement park and other nonfood businesses and the chocolate company are interrelated in many ways.

Murrie, whose frugality was legendary, liked to tell a story about his days as a semi-pro baseball pitcher on a team in Hagerstown, Maryland. He was afraid he might not be paid, so he asked the manager who was going to pay him. The manager told him that he need not worry about getting it because "the Pennsylvania Railroad was in back of the team." That sounded all right to Murrie, and he went into the pitcher's box and gave the opposing team "a good lacing." When the game was over, he went to the box-office to get his money. "I'm sorry, young man, but the treasury is flatter than a pancake," was the sad news from the manager. "Didn't you tell me that the Pennsylvania Railroad was in back of this team?" Murrie asked. "That's what I told you, young man," the manager replied. "Do you see those railroad tracks over there behind left field?" he pointed out. "Well, that's the Pennsylvania Railroad, and it's back of us, isn't it?" All Murrie got for his day's work was a sore arm.

Murrie learned some hard lessons in life, and making sure he was paid was one of them. He was a born leader, both on and off the baseball diamond. He was especially adept at picking

A rural scene in Hershey Park in 1908. The rustic bridge connected the entrance of the park to the baseball field on the north side of the creek. (HERSHEY COMMUNITY ARCHIVES)

good managers and delegating responsibility. Murrie, because of his thrifty ways, was one of the few persons in the town of Hershey, besides M.S. Hershey, who became really wealthy from the chocolate business.

All of M.S. Hershey's most trusted advisers, like Bill Murrie, Harry Lebkicher, John Snyder, Harry Herr, and Ezra Hershey (who was a second cousin and President of the bank and Treasurer of the chocolate company) had been with M.S. Hershey before he moved from Lancaster, Pennsylvania. This Lancaster Gang would control various parts of M.S. Hershey's business interests for more than forty years. Because of the interlocking nature of all of Hershey's businesses, each of them played a role in the development of the park.

At first, life was Spartan in the new town of Hershey, and this was one of the reasons that M.S. Hershey wanted to provide a park for his employees. The men were forced to leave their families behind. There were no houses in Hershey for there was very little town, and the only choice open to them was to board at the Haeffner House, a country hotel in Derry Church. M.S. Hershey saw the need for more suitable quarters for his employees, and he built a three-story limestone structure called the Cocoa House. It was located on the northeast corner of Chocolate and Cocoa Avenue. It was an all-purpose building that housed the bank, post office, and general store on the first floor and boarding rooms on the second floor.

The members of the Lancaster Gang were devoted to

Hershey and to his projects. They worked long hours building a chocolate factory, town, and park. But in the early years, when the factory whistle blew at twelve o'clock on Saturday, many of them headed for the train station to get back to Lancaster.

In 1908, Hershey Park competed with Paxtang Park, which was a small trolley park located just outside Harrisburg about nine miles from Hershey. Its attractions included a theatre, figure eight, merry-go-round, Japanese ball game, box ball alley, restaurant, ice cream cone and novelty stand, popcorn stand, shooting gallery, swimming pool, boat rides, and a small zoo. It also offered balloon ascensions and vaudeville that season.

Some large groups from the Harrisburg area traveled to York, Lancaster, or Philadelphia for their picnics. The Harrisburg Foundry & Machine Works traveled on the Philadelphia and Reading Railroad to Willow Grove Park near Philadelphia for their picnic in 1908.

The railroads promoted excursions during the summer months. The Pennsylvania Railroad offered excursions to Niagara Falls and the New Jersey seacoast. The more affluent traveled to Atlantic City, Ocean City, Wildwood, and Cape May.

Most families who went to Hershey Park spent the whole day in the park. They would leave early in the morning, sometimes sending someone ahead to claim a picnic table or shelter. People would carry their picnic lunches in large clothes baskets that were converted for that purpose. During the day they would often leave their picnic baskets unattended without any fear that they would be disturbed. In the morning, picnic committees would sponsor contests like running, spelling bees, and bag races. In the afternoon was the traditional baseball game.

After the park had opened in 1908, Lebkicher, somewhat out of character, suggested a fireworks display for the Fourth of July and Labor Day. He felt it would be a big attraction and would draw people who otherwise would not come to the park. M.S. Hershey thought it was a waste of money. Lebkicher countered, "We'll more than make up what some fireworks cost us by the fares we'll collect on the trolley cars."

Still Hershey would not give in. "I don't like the idea of burning up my money with fireworks," he said. "I can use the money to better purpose. If the weather is nice that day the people will come to the park anyway." Hershey's dislike of fireworks dated back to the time he was serving as an apprentice in Lancaster. One Fourth of July evening a falling skyrocket hit him on the head and left a scar that was noticeable for many years.

The Hershey Band, which had made some progress under the leadership of Schultze, gave two concerts each Sunday during the summer park season. Decked out in new uniforms purchased by Hershey, they still looked better than they sounded. It was said "what they lacked in numbers they made up in vim and persistence." After the first year's fiasco, Hershey, with the help of his 26-year-old cousin, Joseph Snavely, took over management of the park. Young Snavely was also named secretary-treasurer of the band and given a saxophone, which he later confessed he never learned to play.

In addition to helping Snavely manage the park, M.S. Hershey liked to experiment with making new flavors of ice cream for the park. All of his life, Hershey enjoyed trying new flavors. In between band concerts, Joseph Snavely, Jakie Smaltz, and Hershey would make ice cream. They made hundreds of gallons, which were sold in the park's refreshment stand. Smaltz was quite adept at turning the crank and licking the paddle clean, but Hershey was never able to concoct a really great new flavor.

M.S. Hershey provided ten weeks of free vaudeville in the park pavilion. The acts were booked through a Philadelphia agency. There were generally five acts, mostly comedians and acrobats, on an evening's program. People came from miles around. Business was good, even though the program was changed only once a week. Lebkicher, who had no experience with vaudeville, took charge of the bookings through the Rudy Heller Agency of Philadelphia. Lebkicher's idea of good vaudeville seldom coincided with Heller's, and therefore many arguments ensued between them.

One week the park's vaudeville featured a comedian whose jokes failed to evoke even a smile from the people of Hershey. Several weeks later he wrote an article for the *Philadelphia*

North American in which he told of his experiences while performing at Hershey Park. He said that "the people of Hershey had promised their parents, when they were children that they would never laugh at anything, and they had faithfully kept this promise." He finished the article with the following two-line poem:

Tell me truly, tell me please,
Is Hershey a town or a disease?

Some of the people in town wanted to sue the comedian for libel, but M.S. Hershey just laughed and had the article re-printed in the *Hershey Press*. Over the years, he was fond of repeating this story.

Interior of Hershey Park's main pavilion in 1908 when it was used as a theatre. The benches could be removed when it was used for dancing or roller skating.
(Hershey Community Archives)

Hershey Park's main pavilion after it was expanded and enclosed in 1907. On the right side is the cafe or fast food stand.
(Hershey Community Archives)

One of the chocolate salesmen who had recently been on the road thought that the park should have a merry-go-round (There is no difference in meaning between the words carousel and merry-go-round, and they can be used interchangeably.) He knew where the park could buy a good secondhand machine. He told Lebkicher who thought it was a good idea too, but M.S. Hershey was unimpressed. "That can wait," Hershey told him. But shortly after opening day he relented and agreed to buy one. The Hershey Improvement Company purchased a small, used merry-go-round and band organ from the Herschell Spillman Company of North Tonawanda, New York. It cost fifteen hundred dollars, while a new merry-go-round would have cost more than two thousand dollars.

The Herschell Spillman Company was one of the oldest merry-go-round companies in America. The company entered the business by manufacturing steam boilers, which were used on early portable carousels. At the turn of the century they manufactured small two and three row merry-go-rounds. They took many machines in trade, which they later resold.

M.S. Hershey and Lebkicher had different ideas on where the new merry-go-round should be set up. Lebkicher wanted it near the entrance to the park and not in some out-of-the-way place. M.S. Hershey wanted it on the far side of Spring Creek. He finally admitted to Lebkicher that he was thinking about adding a miniature railway to transport people into the park. This would make the merry-go-round accessible to everyone. The merry-go-round was delivered to the park in June 1908, and Putt and his men built a new pavilion to house it.

The merry-go-round was located across Spring Creek at what was then the far western edge of the park near the baseball field. The secondhand machine required some assembly, so Charles Glynn, the chocolate company's chief mechanic, came over and helped put it together. He also installed the band organ so that the ride would have music. There was not a job, whether for the trolley company, factory, park, or town, that Charles Glynn could not do.

Glynn had the merry-go-round set up and running the evening before the Fourth of July. After the band organ was

Hershey Park Ballfield. In the left center of the picture is the park's first carousel pavilion with awnings.
(Hershey Community Archives)

Hershey Park's multipurpose building, built during the winter of 1908-09.
(Hershey Community Archives)

tuned, it struck up a melody that could be heard more than three blocks away at the Cocoa House on Chocolate Avenue, and the town's people came to see what was going on. Even M.S. Hershey came over to watch the crowd ride the new machine. Lebkicher soon had John Snavely, who was running the merry-go-round, shut it down, because he wanted to save it for the Fourth. "There's no use overdoing a good thing, so there isn't," Lebkicher said. "They can ride all day tomorrow, if they want to. But they have to pay." On the Fourth it cost five cents to ride, and the total taken in that day was $87.05. Lebkicher was right; the merry-go-round was a great addition to the park. It earned $556 from the Fourth of July to the end of the season.

Hershey got its first golf grounds in 1908. It was much shorter than modern courses, and the rough was really rough. Hershey enjoyed a game or two of golf each year, and over the years a number of golf courses were built. For many years, Hershey Park actually managed a public course. The park's first tennis court was added near the entrance to the park that same year. Ezra Hershey especially enjoyed using the new court. Through the years, other tennis courts were added, and the location changed many times.

The Harrisburg Grocers Picnic, with six thousand in attendance, closed the 1908 season. Some of the local grocers closed their stores to go to the picnic. Not only was this picnic good for the park, but it was good for the chocolate company. The grocers were made aware of how good Hershey chocolate really was when free samples were handed out. A big program of thirty-one events was arranged, and sixty-eight prizes, ranging from a five-dollar gold piece and gold watch down to a little girl's box of chocolates, were given away.

During the winter of 1908-09, a large multipurpose structure was built near the entrance to the park. It was a three-story frame building almost 200 feet long. The park's printing office, which Joseph Snavely ran, occupied part of the first floor, with the rest of the first floor used for park purposes. There were two large rooms on the second floor, one used as a lodge hall and the other for band practices.

The park continued to gain in popularity with more people coming from Harrisburg, Lebanon, and Lancaster. Many came to see "the chocolate town" in the making, but even more were drawn to the attractions the park offered: baseball, tennis, boating, dancing, roller skating, band concerts, the merry-go-round, and free vaudeville.

PIC-NIC DAY AT HERSHEY PARK
HERSHEY CHOCOLATE CO. HERSHEY PA.

*Postcards were given away free with
every Hershey's Bar starting in 1909.
Entering the park, a shady nook
gazebo along Spring Creek, and the
park's main restaurant.*

(ALL FROM RICHARD BOWKER COLLECTION)

A SHADY NOOK IN HERSHEY PARK
HERSHEY CHOCOLATE CO. HERSHEY PA.

SCENE IN HERSHEY PARK
Home of the Hershey Chocolate Co., Hershey, Pa.

*Opposite page-
The up-and-down or Old
Chinese bridge.*

(RICHARD BOWKER COLLECTION)

CHAPTER 3

LIONS AND TIGERS AND MARES, OH MY

P rior to 1909, Hershey Park was a small park that primarily served the Harrisburg and Hershey area. *Billboard*, the weekly newspaper of the amusement park industry, reported on the park in June 1909:

> Hershey Park, near Harrisburg, Pa., has developed into quite an amusement center. It is twelve miles from Harrisburg, by rail or trolley, and plays a swell line of attractions. It is a veritable Hi Henry's dig up and not many of the professionals are aware of its existence.

The town of Hershey and Hershey Park would not remain relatively unknown for long. All this quickly changed that year when the chocolate company, which had grown from a small regional producer to a national brand in six short years, started printing postcard size views of Hershey as "Home of Hershey Chocolate Co., Hershey, Pa." and including one with each bar. Millions of chocolate bars were sold each year with scenes of Hershey Park. These cards, in both black and white and color, quickly became souvenirs and people all over the country now knew that there was a Hershey Park.

M.S. Hershey quickly realized the advertising value of his town, and he exploited it. He had a large pictorial window display prepared in attractive colors, which he then made available for

SCENE IN HERSHEY PARK—HERSHEY, PA.
Home of the Hershey Chocolate Co.

windows of stores that sold his chocolate products. The display included scenes of the chocolate factory, its two tall chimneys, each lettered Hershey; the town with its railroad station; the park and the green, flower-dotted lawns; the curving roads; and the winding Spring Creek. In the background were distant farms with Holstein cows grazing, and in the blue sky were the words, "The Home of Hershey's Cocoa and Milk Chocolate." M.S. Hershey marketed the Hershey experience as a total package. By 1911, sales of Hershey Chocolate topped $5 million annually.

James Putt designed and built a new, larger dance pavilion down along Spring Creek on the westerly edge of the park. Although enlarged and remodeled many times, this building would remain the park's dance pavilion (ballroom) into the 1970's. The dance floor was much larger than the previous one in the park's main pavilion, and it featured a large stage for the band or orchestra, as well as a balcony where more than five hundred spectators could sit and watch the dancers. Park Boulevard would be built in front of it.

The dance pavilion was described in a 1909 Hershey Park brochure as "a most handsome structure, and one of the largest to be found in any park in the entire country." These brochures were printed by Joseph Snavely in the small print shop located in the park. They were widely circulated in the Harrisburg and Hershey areas.

Adjoining the park's main pavilion, a new outdoor amphitheatre, "a model of excellence," was built. It had seating for 1,500 people upon the main slope of the park with seats rising in sharp tiers, so that every seat had an excellent view of the stage. Putt was pretty much given a free hand in its construction. A sign over the stage read, "Ye who enter here leave dull cares behind," and the free vaudeville entertainment was performed here. The amphitheatre had excellent acoustical qualities. Shortly before it opened, Lebkicher stopped by to check on the project. Putt was down on the stage, and Lebkicher yelled to him to talk, but not yell because he wanted to check the acoustics. Putt started to tell one of Bill Murrie's favorite stories. Lebkicher quickly interrupted him saying that he had heard it many times before, but the sound was fine.

At first, M.S. Hershey's mother Fanny disapproved of the new open-air theatre, but she finally had to admit to her son, "I guess the Lord approves of your having a theatre, because it didn't rain once all season while you were using it."

The 1909 season brought many other new attractions, including a pair of bowling alleys, which were located across

from the park's main pavilion (for years the area was called Bowling Alley Hill), and a photographic gallery, where a first class photographer, Harry Stoner, provided "work of the better kind at reasonable rates." Stoner purchased a new camera which took five different views, and he advertised it as "pictures that please" and "see yourself as others see you." He liked working for the park, because it gave him time for long hunting trips during the winter. The park also spent $377.32 on a new shooting gallery.

According to the books of the Hershey Improvement Company, Hershey Park made some money in 1909. The top three attractions were the bowling alleys (which were open year round), the refreshment stands, and the merry-go-round. Each of these took in between five and six hundred dollars. The shooting gallery made eighty dollars. The swimming pool, which was little more than a swimming hole, and boats on the creek had modest appeal taking in about forty dollars apiece.

The Harrisburg Grocers Picnic, three thousand strong, returned to Hershey Park on August 5, 1909. According to the *Harrisburg Patriot*, "about 1,500 persons [grocers and their families] went through the mammoth plant and souvenirs of sweet chocolate and postcards were handed to each one." Three special trains were run over the Philadelphia and Reading Railroad lines to the park, and two special trains brought the "tired, but happy picnickers home last evening."

M.S. Hershey liked to do the unexpected. He enjoyed ordering things for the park without telling anyone. Once he purchased a motor boat for the park. He told Lebkicher about it only after it arrived at the Hershey Freight Station. Lebkicher

The Hershey Park Amphitheatre and stage were built in 1909 by James Putt. At the far right is the park's main pavilion.
(HERSHEY COMMUNITY ARCHIVES)

Since the Hershey Park Amphitheatre was built on a hillside, the seating was tiered. When the theatre was later enclosed the vertical seating remained. Circa 1909.
(HERSHEY COMMUNITY ARCHIVES)

Hershey Park's bowling alleys, located in the multipurpose building, were used year-round. (HERSHEY COMMUNITY ARCHIVES)

complained that "Spring Creek is too shallow for a motor boat. Why it will get stuck in the mud every time it turns around, and it will cost us more to run it than what we will get out of it."

Lebkicher was right, and shortly thereafter the motor boat, which had been christened the Mayflower, was sold. But to Lebkicher's great delight, he got as much for it as Hershey had paid for it.

The early twentieth century was a much more formal time. Wherever M.S. Hershey went in town, he was shown the greatest respect by townspeople and his employees. In deference to his position he was no longer called Milton Hershey or even M.S. Hershey, but Mr. Hershey. The only exception was Harry Lebkicher who still called him Milton.

On November 15, 1909, an event took place that would have important ramifications for Hershey Park, the town, the chocolate company, and M.S. Hershey's other businesses. M.S. Hershey and Catherine Hershey signed a deed of trust that established the Hershey Industrial School for orphan boys. Their first gift to the trust was 486 acres in Derry Township. Later M.S. Hershey would give his entire fortune of Hershey Chocolate Company stock, worth sixty million dollars, to the school. This charitable remainder trust would perpetuate a connection between M.S. Hershey's businesses, including the park, and the town long after his death.

In 1910, the restaurant in the park was expanded by Putt, who built four separate alcoves in the four corners of the building. Each sold a different item: soda drinks, souvenirs, salt water taffy, and popcorn balls. The new construction and an expanded menu enabled the restaurant to increase its revenues to $2,837.83.

The vaudeville programs were no longer free. Standing room in the rear was still free, but chairs closer to the stage cost ten cents each. In 1911 motion pictures were added to supplement the vaudeville acts. Charles L. Maurer from Lancaster became the park's pianist and musical director.

The *Hershey Press*, a twelve-page tabloid size, weekly newspaper, was published for the first time on September 3, 1909, with M.S. Hershey as proprietor and his young cousin Joseph Snavely, as the editor. It was printed in the printing office, which was located in the park near the main entrance. It was a public newspaper that served Hershey, Hummelstown, Campbelltown, and Palmyra. Since Snavely was manager of the park as well as editor of the *Hershey Press*, the newspaper carried numerous articles on what was going on at the park. The first edition of the newspaper carried a story about Malcolm Murrie, son of Bill Murrie, the president of the chocolate company, who was injured in the park when he stepped down from a swing and broke his wrist. Later the paper reported that he had recovered.

The *Hershey Press* created a fictitious letter writer, Adam Knocker, who knocked things around the town of Hershey.

M.S. Hershey and Catherine Hershey in 1910.
(HERSHEY COMMUNITY ARCHIVES)

Hershey Park employees in 1913. Abraham T. Heilman, the park manager, is seated in the middle of the second row.
(HERSHEY COMMUNITY ARCHIVES)

Knocker called Hershey's trolley line, "the Cameltown trolley car," and said, "you don't know when it will come or how long it will go." The paper even poked fun at itself, when Knocker complained that "Hershey don't no more need a newspaper than a catfish needs mice."

Snavely gave up his job as manager of the park because of his duties at the *Press*. His successor was Abraham T. "Abe" Heilman, of Reading, who had managed Hershey's Reading branch plant until it burned down in the late 1890's. He stayed with the American Caramel Company after the buy out for a few years, before returning to work for M.S. Hershey.

Heilman's early career with M.S. Hershey had not always been easy. Heilman recalled an incident at the ill-fated Reading candy plant: "One day a kettle blew up," he said. "It went right through the ceiling. The girls panicked and a number were injured. One man, an inspector, was standing beside the kettle

---

Hershey Park Theater

Thursday, Friday and Saturday

Nelson & Nelson,
Comedy on Stilts

Madeline Burdette,
In Popular Songs

Lovitt-Nelson Troupe
Refined Acrobats

GENERAL ADMISSION 5c   RESERVED SEATS 10c

NEXT WEEK

Another Good Comedy Company

---

when it exploded. I rushed to see what had happened to him, and found nothing there but his shoes. A few minutes later I met him on a side street; not a scratch on him, but he had been scared crazy."

Bringing in Heilman, a first class manager, to run the park showed how much Hershey wanted the park to succeed. Heilman studied the amusement business and suggested improvements to M.S. Hershey. Hershey told him, "I want to get people and picnics here," and Heilman set to work.

Heilman persuaded the head of the Philadelphia and Reading Railroad to hand out color postcards showing views of the park to the passengers. He got the addresses of all Sunday Schools in the Hershey vicinity, sent them the same picture cards, and suggested that they get the youngsters to vote where they wanted to go for their next annual Sunday School picnic. And churches came from everywhere.

One important change Heilman made was to schedule regular dances in the park each week. Prior to this, dances had been held only sporadically in the park. He brought in a six-piece dance band, which played in the park's new dance pavilion. Admission was ten cents for ladies and fifteen cents for men. The *Hershey Press* commented that the band was not too bad "seeing that it was the first time that all of the members played together." Dancers were warned to keep shirts buttoned and sleeves rolled down. Dancing was an immediate success and it took in $437.25 in 1910.

After managing the park for a number of years, Heilman, who was one of Hershey's most versatile managers, returned to

Children's slide at Hershey Park circa 1910.
(HERSHEY COMMUNITY ARCHIVES)

the chocolate company. He became plant manager of the Hershey Chocolate Company before his career was over.

The park's original rustic bandstand was replaced by a new, larger one in 1910. The new twenty-four foot square bandstand was completed on March 17, 1910, when a flag was hoisted over it to the "lusty cheers" of Putt and his carpenters. It was used primarily for band and choral concerts of the Hershey Band and town choir.

The band made some progress under the leadership of Schultze, but not enough to suit M.S. Hershey, and in 1910 Schultze was replaced by Samuel J. Feese of Lebanon.

The new director, Feese, was both a first rate band director and pressman. He worked for Snavely in the *Press* office. He also was an excellent organizer and was able to develop the band into one of the best in the area. The untrained volunteer bandsmen like Jakie Smaltz were persuaded to give up their musical careers. Joseph Snavely tried to quit, but M.S. Hershey would not let him. Feese purchased all new instruments for the band through the Hershey Department Store, and he actively recruited experienced musicians from Harrisburg and Lebanon. These bandsmen, who received new navy blue uniforms, were paid, and Hershey finally had a band to complement his baseball team, which continued to win.

M.S. Hershey used to bring Catherine Hershey down to the park in the evenings, where they listened to the Hershey Band. Both of them loved band music, and these were some of the happiest times of their lives.

When he was by himself, Hershey poked into every corner of the park. He came to know the park employees and the people who came to the park. A story was told that Hershey made and sold onion ice cream in the park. He did this on a bet with a friend. He argued that you could get people to buy anything. It was decided to test this theory with onion ice cream. Hershey sprinkled generous quantities of Spanish onions over plain vanilla ice cream. A whole batch was sold, but the experiment was never repeated.

One of the park's most important rides, a narrow-gauge miniature railway, was added to the park in 1910. It was sometimes referred to as the scenic railway, electrical railway, or third railway line. It operated on the third-rail electric principle. The engine got its electricity from a hot rail between the regular two

The Hershey Band was led by Samuel J. Feese. He is standing in the front row holding his baton.
(HERSHEY COMMUNITY ARCHIVES)

While adults talk, a daredevil takes some children for a ride on a swing at Hershey Park. Circa 1913.
(HERSHEY COMMUNITY ARCHIVES)

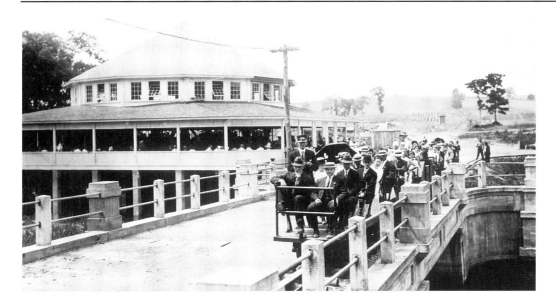

The miniature railway crossed Spring Creek on a Harry Herr-designed concrete bridge. To the left was the park's new merry-go-round pavilion with its Dentzel carousel.

(NEIL FASNACHT COLLECTION)

Hershey Park's famous miniature railway carried people into the middle of the park. The walkway along Spring Creek led to the park's new merry-go-round pavilion.

(HERSHEY COMMUNITY ARCHIVES)

rails. Direct current supplied by the chocolate factory's power plant was used, which was not as dangerous as using alternating current.

The 22-inch gauge railway was built by the Lancaster Iron Works, Lancaster, Pennsylvania. It was a one-of-a-kind ride. At the time it was built, the little railway was considered a technological achievement and was featured in an article in the *Electric Railway Journal* in 1910.

The *Hershey Press* followed its construction closely. The park had hoped to have it completed in time for the 1910 season, but due to construction delays, it did not run until September 5, 1910. Herr, the engineer, and Glynn, the mechanic, who were responsible for the construction of the ride, rode in the front seat on the inaugural ride.

According to the *Hershey Press*, M.S. Hershey originally intended to build the little railway "over the hills and far away." He planned on using it to connect the town of Hershey with Pat's Hill where Hershey planned to build a resort hotel someday. It was a distance of four or five miles. It soon became apparent that this longer version, which could be used only in the summer months, would be far too costly to build. Instead the line was constructed from the bridge which crossed the railroad, past the dance pavilion, across Spring Creek, to near the grandstands at the baseball field. Later the route would be shortened even further, stopping at the old swimming pool in the center of the park.

Herr soon found out that the little electric engine could not climb steep grades. To negotiate the valley he had to use fill, which he got from some new construction at the chocolate factory, and he had to blast through one rocky part of the route. This created a miniature gorge, which the park advertised as one

of the ride's scenic wonders.

There was no loop in the line, and it dead ended at both ends. Therefore, the line had only one train. The engine, with trolley-type electrical controls, was powered by two 10-HP motors and was located in the middle of the train with two flat cars on either side. The seats were built so that they could be tilted in either direction; thus, the passengers would always be looking forward. Two of the passenger seats were built on the locomotive itself. The train could carry between eighteen and thirty passengers on each trip and was capable of moving the four trailers at twenty m.p.h. The crew consisted of a motorman and a conductor, who collected the five cent fares and helped supervise the passengers.

The railway proved to be popular because it was more than an amusement ride; it was also a way of getting from one place in the park to another. People enjoyed riding through the park looking at the scenery.

Frantz Zinner feeding Bob the black bear in the bear pit at the Hershey Park Zoo in 1911.
(HERSHEY COMMUNITY ARCHIVES)

Spectators looking into the bear pit at the Hershey Park Zoo. Ladies would carry umbrellas even on sunny days.
(HERSHEY COMMUNITY ARCHIVES)

They were favorites of Bill Murrie, who would bring them chocolate bars when he visited them. Even Harry Lebkicher got into the act. According to the *Hershey Press*, Lebkicher purchased one buck and two does and a pair of raccoons and gave them to the "Zoological Gardens."

About the same time as the zoo was started, the park added Shetland ponies and a donkey. Children could ride either with saddles or in small carts around the park. Although not part of the zoo, these animals were maintained by the zoo employees. They became very popular attractions and remained in the park until the 1940's.

James Putt made a trip over to Paxtang Park to scrutinize their attractions. Upon returning, he reported to the *Hershey Press* that "Hershey has them all beat." Haverstick returned to his hometown, Wilmington, Delaware, and visited the gardens there to get new ideas for Hershey's gardens.

During the winter townspeople would ice skate on the park's frozen pond and creek. The best ice skater was William Brinker, who had moved from Lancaster with M.S. Hershey. Brinker would skate from the park to Hummelstown and back on the frozen Spring and Swatara creeks. Some hockey was played on the pond in the park, and the *Hershey Press* even mentioned hockey games as early as 1910.

A real swimming pool was constructed for the 1910 season. Eli Rhine dug out an area fifty feet by one hundred fifty feet down beside Spring Creek with his team of horses and a drag scoop. Then a cement bottom was made which went from three feet to six feet in depth. The first bathhouse, which had been a train waiting room, was remodeled and moved to the site.

Putt built a toboggan slide for the pool that was approximately forty feet high and one hundred feet long. People who used it had to carry a wooden slide or board up a flight of stairs and then ride the board down into the swimming pool. Monroe

The zoo, which opened in 1910, was located across Park Avenue from the park along Spring Creek. At first it was a rather modest affair with common native animals like deer, bears, raccoons, ducks, pheasants, and squirrels. The Hershey Improvement Company's books showed that the zoo's six squirrels cost four dollars, while the two bears, which were the most expensive animals, cost a little over one hundred dollars. But soon more exotic animals were added, including swans, Angora goats, peacocks, zebus, and lions. As more animals were added, Jim Putt built houses and pits for them.

The first zoo keeper, Frantz Zinner, was from Germany. Prior to managing the Hershey Zoo he worked for traveling wild animal shows in Europe and America. He liked to name his animals. He called the American black bears Bob and Maggie.

The swimming pool and, across Spring Creek, the newly enclosed Park Theatre (formerly the Amphitheatre).
(HERSHEY COMMUNITY ARCHIVES)

James Putt built a water slide for the pool that was forty feet high and one hundred feet long. On the hill above the bathhouse was the park's first merry-go-round pavilion.
(HERSHEY COMMUNITY ARCHIVES)

Stover, a long time Hershey employee, recalled that "it was busy all the time when the park pool was open."

During the winter of 1911-12 the amphitheatre was enclosed at a cost of $15,597.69. It became the Hershey Park Theatre. The tiered seating remained, which always gave the theatre an unusual appearance. By enclosing it the park enabled vaudeville and summer stock to be performed even in inclement weather. A summer stock company appeared at the park for the first time in 1912.

In 1912, M.S. Hershey bought for the park a new merry-go-round, which cost him ten thousand dollars. He acquired one of the best that money could buy, from William Dentzel of Philadelphia.

Dentzel, who was known as "the Carousel King," came from a long line of carousel manufacturers. The Dentzel family had been in the business since 1837 when members of the family manufactured their first carousel in Germany. Dentzel's father, Gustav Dentzel, came to America around the time of the Civil War and manufactured carousels in Philadelphia until his death in 1909. William Dentzel succeeded his father as head of the company. In 1912 the Dentzel Company was one of the largest manufacturers "of better, first class carousels in America." Dentzel specialized in manufacturing large carousels for use in amusement parks in his factory, which was located at 3635 Germantown Avenue, Philadelphia, Pennsylvania.

The old merry-go-round pavilion was too small for the new carousel, so Hershey had James Putt build a new pavilion. He built it directly across Spring Creek from the dance pavilion. The *Hershey Press* reported it was "an ideal situation as it can be reached by trolley and the third railway line, as well as by two different walks." Putt and a crew of eighteen carpenters built the

new pavilion in just ten days. The roof was made of cedar shingles and the rest of the structure from long leaf pine.

The new pavilion was more elaborate than the park's first merry-go-round pavilion. The new building was twenty-two feet high, octagon-shaped, and had thirty-six large windows, which provided plenty of light and ventilation. Although the new carousel was fifty-two feet wide, M.S. Hershey had Putt build the new structure eighty-six feet wide, so that people could sit around the carousel and watch it run.

The new carousel weighed 42,000 pounds and had an eighteen-foot center pole. Dentzel shipped the carousel motor, wooden animals, machinery, and structure by rail from Germantown to the park. There, Dentzel and his brother Harry, with the help of four other men, assembled the new carousel.

The platform was twelve feet, six inches wide. The outside row of large animals was stationary and included a lion, tiger, a deer, giraffe, and twelve horses of different designs, making a total of sixteen animals. The two inside rows were jumpers and included two ostriches, two rabbits, two goats, two bears, two pigs, two cats, two chickens, and two deer. There were also two large carved chariots with upholstered seats for people who did not wish to ride an animal. The carousel was a spectacular ride at night with more than four hundred lights on it.

To make the ride even more exciting, Dentzel supplied a ring board and a ring catcher. Riders on the outside row of animals could reach up during the ride and try to grab a ring, hoping to get the brass one that would give him or her a free ride. The ring machine remained very popular for many years. Some people got so good at it that they could grab as many as four sometimes five rings as the merry-go-round passed the ring arm. Rings were then tossed into the open mouth of a laughing

This was the Dentzel carousel believed to be from Hershey Park when it operated at Knott's Berry Farm, Buena Park, California, in 1976. If the merry-go-round was not Hershey Park's Dentzel carousel, it would be similar because it was built around the same period. (PHOTOGRAPH BY CHARLES J. JACQUES, JR.)

The Dentzel family always placed a lion on their carousels.
(PHOTOGRAPH BY CHARLES J. JACQUES, JR.)

The American Eagle horse was the lead horse on the Dentzel carousel. There was a step between the first and second row to accomodate the carousel's jumping mechanism.
(PHOTOGRAPH BY CHARLES J. JACQUES, JR.)

clown on the next turn around. The new carousel was definitely the highlight of the 1912 season.

Pennsylvania still had the blue laws, which restricted business on Sundays. The majority of the churches in the Hershey area frowned on most forms of entertainment on Sunday, so the carousel was not run on Sundays until the 1920's.

In an attempt to raise the cultural level of the community, M.S. Hershey paid twelve hundred dollars to stage "A Chautauqua Assembly for Hershey" in the park. It consisted of a series of concerts, lectures, motion pictures, and other entertainment for seven consecutive nights. Admission to the complete seven day series was two dollars and fifty cents with the proceeds going to the town's YMCA and YWCA. Ciricillo's Italian Band was featured. Lectures were given on topics like "The Right of a Child to Be Well Born: Heredity," and at nine o'clock each night, a moving picture with an accompanying address was given. One of the moving pictures was *Seeing America*, a travelogue.

A little controversy arose during the week. Several of the lecturers felt the crowd was too noisy and tried to quiet them. The *Hershey Press* came to the defense of the town stating that the audience was not too noisy. Perhaps the audiences were more accustomed to the cheers and jeers of vaudeville. Chautauqua meetings continued to be held sporadically at Hershey Park.

In just three years Hershey Park with Abraham T. Heilman as manager had become a much different place than it had been in 1909. Here was the park's May 1912 listing in *Billboard*:

Hershey Park: A. T. Heilman, mgr.; three trolley lines reach resort; 12 1/2 minute ride from Harrisburg and the same from Lebanon; direct electric current; park plays five vaudeville acts each week; it also plays bands and operates a dramatic stock company; does not sell or rent privileges; opening date, May 26; closing date, Labor Day; park is on a circuit; attractions, concessions, and devices in the park to date; merry-go-round, dance hall, theatre, restaurant, boating, swimming pool, bath house, shooting gallery, ball diamond, children's swings and slides, and shoot-the-chutes; average daily attendance 500; big day's attendance, 4th of July, 10,000; Decoration Day, 8,000; Labor Day 5,000.

Hershey Park had become the dominant amusement park in the Harrisburg area. M.S. Hershey was not satisfied and he wanted to make it the leading park in central Pennsylvania.

CHAPTER 4

A TIME TO CELEBRATE

A parade on Chocolate Avenue was part of Hershey's tenth anniversary celebration in 1913.
(HERSHEY COMMUNITY ARCHIVES)

In 1913, the deer was placed at the entrance of the park. It became the most photographed landmark in the park.
(HERSHEY COMMUNITY ARCHIVES)

During M.S. Hershey's lifetime, Hershey Park tended to reflect his personal ups and downs. Although it was owned by the Hershey Improvement Company, Hershey was, in fact, its sole proprietor. His fortunes controlled the fortunes of the park, both literally and figuratively. His moods dominated the outlook for the park. When he felt expansive and happy, the park grew. When he was unhappy or financially pressed, it tended to languish.

The town of Hershey celebrated its tenth anniversary May 30-31, 1913, and honored its founder, M.S. Hershey. A huge parade was staged with the Hershey Band's thirty-five members marching under the direction of Samuel Feese. Frantz Zinner's zoo float had his bears Bob and Maggie, a zebu, and other animals on it. Even Harry Haverstick's gardeners, twenty in number dressed in green coats and white pants, marched as "merrie greenwood men." They carried signs warning people about things like "chaps who crosscut it over the grass."

As part of the anniversary celebration, the park offered a spectacular attraction, a barnstorming aviator by the name of "Birdman McCalley." He was to present an air show in his 80 HP Curtis biplane. The park goers were promised, "daring stunts by McCalley including a 'spiral dip' and 'ocean roll.'" Unfortunately, the aviator broke his wrist at another air show shortly before he was to perform at the park. However, McCalley was able to find a substitute flyer, R.V. Morris. On his first landing, Morris lost control of the biplane, nearly running over McCalley, who was trying to help stop it, and his plane crashed into the shipping boxes in which the plane had been transported to the park. McCalley was not injured, but the crowd was disappointed and McCalley felt lucky to get out of town alive. The *Hershey Press* reported the whole incident, calling McCalley a hero. It also remarked how far aviation had come since the balloon ascensions and parachuting jumps made in the park just three years earlier.

In May of 1913 the park was advertised as the "most complete pleasure-grounds in the state, even down to a small zoological garden." It had rustic bridges, crow nests, and inviting little kiosks. "No need to go to Atlantic City to enjoy the pleasure of taking a dip," the park wrote. The new swimming pool, theatre, and dance pavilion attracted more and more patrons.

On June 19, 1913, the park placed a deer (sometimes called an elk) statue and a soldier statue near the entrance to the park. The deer would become the symbol of the park as thousands of people each year would take their picture in front of the statue. The soldier was one of Theodore Roosevelt's Rough Riders, and

this soon became its nickname. The Rough Rider was later removed and placed in the rose garden.

Abraham T. "Abe" Heilman, the manager of the park, opened the summer dancing season in 1913 with the first May Hop. It was held on the well-waxed floor in the new dance pavilion located along Spring Creek at the west end of the park. Matt J. Mannix, formerly music director at the Colonial Theater in Harrisburg, directed the five-piece Hershey Orchestra. Fad dances liked the "turkey trot" and "bunny hug" were banned.

In 1914, the park's second bandstand was replaced by a larger, more modern bandstand and an outdoor stage. This bandstand would be used by the park until 1977. The new structure was about twice the size of the former one. It had an arch that was forty-six feet high and a stage forty-eight feet wide that could accommodate up to sixty musicians. The building was supported on concrete columns, and the stage floor was five feet above the ground. "More than 20,000 can hear the music perfectly," the park claimed.

A beautiful artificial lake was constructed on the marshy ground between the swimming pool and Spring Creek in the center of the park. James Putt's men built an electric fountain on a rough limestone base in the westerly end of the new lake. It had a pump which sent many jets of water into the air. (This should not be confused with the Electric Fountain and Sunken Garden that were developed in the 1930's.)

Jim Putt, Hershey's master carpenter, added four little turrets to the restaurant's corners, which were used for selling food. (HERSHEY COMMUNITY ARCHIVES)

*The dance pavilion is on the left side of Spring Creek
and the new carousel pavilion is on the right side.*
(Neil Fasnacht Collection)

*Hershey Park's new dance pavilion was located
along Spring Creek on the western edge of the park.*
(Neil Fasnacht Collection)

Haverstick got a new greenhouse, his third, near the zoo. It doubled in the winter as a zoo house for the alligators and other tropical animals. By 1915, Haverstick and his gardeners had planted more than 100,000 trees, shrubs, and plants in and around Hershey. Harry Herr designed and built a new bridge, which was located near the new dance pavilion. Supported by concrete piers, it could carry both automobiles and trolleys over Spring Creek to the northern side of the park. Finally, a tasteful little fountain, "the boy and the boot," was erected at the easterly end of the swimming pool.

More than fifty special excursion trains carried picnic groups to the park in 1914. One of the largest was the Armstrong Linoleum Company which brought 2,500 workers from Lancaster in a special train with fifteen cars.

M.S. Hershey planned to build a summer resort hotel on Pat's Hill overlooking the park and town. In 1914, he had Haverstick's men plant more than twenty thousand trees and shrubs on the site. It was done in accordance with a comprehensive landscaping plan. Near the summit, Hershey built two concrete reservoirs with a capacity of one million gallons. They became the focal point of a new park, Highland Park. The entire area was landscaped and turned into a formal garden. Several small summer cottages were built for the use of M.S. Hershey and his guests.

The following year, 1915, M.S. Hershey built a trolley line that connected the park and Pat's Hill with the existing trolley lines in town. From the square on Chocolate Avenue it curled down the hill from the town, traveled past the dance pavilion, crossed over Spring Creek on Herr's new concrete bridge, went through the park, and then continued on to Highland Park on Pat's Hill. Two small single-track open cars shuttled back and forth between the park and the square hauling picnickers who had arrived on regular trolley cars. This service was free during the hours that the park was open to the public.

In 1914, a small man-made lake was constructed on the marshy ground between the swimming pool and Spring Creek. (HERSHEY COMMUNITY ARCHIVES)

In 1915, "the boy and the boot," was part of a fountain in the swimming pool. Later this statue would be moved to the Hershey Rose Garden. (CHARLES J. JACQUES, JR. COLLECTION)

The Hershey Band performs in the bandstand in 1914. Samuel J. Feese, the director, is seated in the foreground. (HERSHEY COMMUNITY ARCHIVES) *Crowds would sit on park benches and the lawns while bands performed in the bandstand.* (CHARLES J. JACQUES, JR. COLLECTION)

In 1915, a trolley line and the miniature railway ran in front of the park's new carousel pavilion.

(Hershey Community Archives)

The Philadelphia and Reading Railroad's station was located at the main entrance of the park. (Hershey Community Archives)

The Hershey Transit Company's trolleys converged on Chocolate Avenue. Trolleys brought thousands of people to the park each year. (Charles J. Jacques, Jr. Collection)

The *Hershey Press* reported that Hershey's summer resort hotel was going to cost more than one million dollars and was to be built in the near future. However, World War I and M.S. Hershey's financial difficulties following the war prevented its construction. The trolley line to Highland Park was abandoned in the 1920's and was rebuilt only when the hotel was under construction in the 1930's.

On November 30, 1914, the construction of a mammoth new tabernacle or auditorium was announced. The Church of the Brethren agreed to hold its annual conference in Hershey if a large assembly hall was constructed. In less than six months the huge hall was built.

The new Convention Hall, which cost M.S. Hershey more than sixty thousand dollars, could seat six thousand and could hold ten thousand. In addition to the cost of the hall, Hershey spent an additional fifty thousand dollars upgrading the roads and trolley lines in and around Hershey Park for the conference. (The new hall was made of steel and hollow tile on a concrete base. Its main auditorium was 71 feet high, 362 1/2 feet long, and 156 1/2 feet wide. There were four committee rooms 15 by 25 feet. The main entrance was 62 feet wide. The stage was 33 feet deep and 60 feet long. The building had 18 doors, each 6 feet wide. The choir loft, which was 14 feet wide and 86 feet long, could hold 250 people.)

The Convention Hall sat on a high knoll overlooking the town and the Lebanon Valley. It was illuminated at night and could be seen for miles by passengers on the Philadelphia and

Wide walkways and new roads were built to the Convention Hall. (Hershey Community Archives)

The 6000-seat Convention Hall was used for concerts, lectures, and large group meetings. Photograph circa 1915. (Hershey Community Archives)

An aerial view of Hershey Park in 1915. In the foreground are the carousel and dancing pavilions with many automobiles parked around them. (Neil Fasnacht Collection)

Reading Railroad. The building had four towers, in which M.S. Hershey had planned to install chimes, but the chimes were never added.

One of Hershey Park's special appeals to church groups like the Church of the Brethren was that it did not sell beer or alcohol. An early park brochure read, "No intoxicants are dispensed or permitted anywhere within the limits of the park; this is a feature that should commend itself to Sunday School and church organizations seeking an ideal place for an outing."

The same was also true for the town of Hershey; as *The*

Hershey Progressive Weekly reported in 1914, "there is no saloon or low place of resort in the town which is therefore entirely free from the bane of many manufacturing towns, the corner loafer. The whole moral atmosphere of the town, as well as its physical condition, is clean and wholesome."

The name Convention Hall was given to the new structure on April 29, 1915. The Brethren conference was an outstanding success. It was a celebration, and M.S. Hershey was honored from the platform during the assembly. He didn't want to make a speech, but he acknowledged the applause of the group. More

The interior of the Convention Hall at Hershey Park shortly after it opened in 1915.
(HERSHEY COMMUNITY ARCHIVES)

Visitor's Pass.
(NEIL FASNACHT COLLECTION)

HERSHEY CHOCOLATE COMPANY

VISITOR'S PASS **4647**

Admit M— *Albert Glassly and party (3).*
Lancaster, Pa.

TO VIEW HERSHEY CHOCOLATE FACTORY

JUL 18 ~~1916~~ 191   *Hershey Bureau*
                                          w.

This Pass is not transferable and is good only on the date written on the face and when signed

than ten thousand Brethren attended and somehow were able to find housing during the conference. Some stayed in the town of Hershey, while others traveled to adjoining towns, some as far away as Harrisburg and Lebanon. Heilman had a special cafeteria set up to feed the delegates during the day. The *Hershey Press* reported extensively on their meetings and activities.

As successful as the Brethren conference was, it also showed that the town of Hershey, population 2,000, was not large enough to hold other large conventions because of the lack of overnight accommodations. Other towns and cities were competing for religious, fraternal, and fire fighter conventions, and they had the hotels and rooming houses that were needed.

One lasting legacy of the Brethrens' conference was the formation of a Hershey Visitor's Bureau to help people find their way around the town of Hershey and to schedule tours of the chocolate factory. The bureau remained after the conference ended. It was another sign that the town of Hershey and the park were becoming important tourist destinations.

The Hershey Zoo was officially dedicated on May 26, 1916. Like its predecessor the park, the zoo's official opening took place many years after it actually came into existence. It had opened and even had been advertised as an attraction as early as 1910. By 1916, it had grown into the largest free private zoo in America. It had more than two hundred animals, birds, and reptiles from a snow white sparrow to a full-grown lion. A new bridge that crossed Spring Creek was built especially for the zoo.

The park's new bandstand was built in 1914.
(HERSHEY COMMUNITY ARCHIVES)

Special excursion trains on the Philadelphia and Reading Railroad brought thousands of guests to Hershey Park before World War I.
(Hershey Community Archives)

Women in white summer dresses and hats were a common sight in Hershey Park in the 1915.
(Hershey Community Archives)

M.S. Hershey's mother, Fanny Hershey, enjoyed walking about the park, up and down its hills and valleys, observing the crowds, sampling the eatables, and asking employees who they were and what they did. In time she came to feel that the park was hers.

One day a girl working in the candy kitchen noticed an elderly Mennonite woman moving about like a bee among the wild flowers, picking up candy and tasting it. She went to Mrs. Abraham Heilman, who was in charge, excited over her first experience with crime. Should they call the police? "Leave her alone," said Mrs. Heilman. "It's Mr. Hershey's mother."

The park experienced a high in 1913 and again in 1915. First it was the town's tenth anniversary and then the new Convention Hall coupled with the Brethren conference. These highs were almost artificially contrived by Hershey. He wanted them and he made them happen. His money had underwritten the tenth anniversary celebration, and Hershey had built the beautiful new Convention Hall. These extraordinary years would not be soon repeated. Intervening events beyond the control of M.S. Hershey would soon plunge his park, town, and chocolate company from the heights to the depths.

The Hershey Zoo and new bridge in 1916.
(Hershey Community Archives)

CHAPTER 5

TOMORROW WE GET OUR TOWN BACK

The Convention Hall was built on a knoll that overlooked the baseball field and grandstands.
By 1916 cars were parking along all of the roads in and around the park.
(HERSHEY COMMUNITY ARCHIVES)

By 1916, automobiles were replacing buggies as the patrons' favorite mode of transportation.
(Hershey Community Archives)

Even as M.S. Hershey was receiving applause at the Church of the Brethren conference for his marvelous new Convention Hall, he was mourning the death of his wife Catherine, who had died three months earlier at age forty-two. After her death everything seemed to fall apart.

Catherine S. Hershey died suddenly on a return trip from Atlantic City, New Jersey. She had not been well for years, but her death came as a shock to M.S. Hershey. They had traveled all over the world seeking some help for her illness, a respiratory disorder. The sea air seemed to help some, but she had gotten progressively worse over the years. She died in Philadelphia on March 25, 1915. M.S. Hershey, who kept his personal affairs private, would not permit his *Hershey Press* to report her death. After years of happiness and success in his life, Hershey was about to enter a period of grief, sorrow, and turmoil.

Following Catherine's death, Hershey seemed to lose interest in the town and the park. Plans for the hotel were shelved. A new community center, which had just been announced in 1915, would not be built until the 1930's. He turned his attention away from Hershey. In 1916 he purchased an old sugar mill in Cuba and began growing and refining sugar. This grew into one of the largest sugar-producing operations in the world. It seemed a relief to him to travel to Cuba, and he would stay for weeks. One thing he did for the town of Hershey was to send back tropical plants for his greenhouses.

Another setback occurred on December 2, 1915, when the Hershey Print Shop, located near the entrance to the park, burned to the ground. M.S. Hershey watched the building go up in flames and then had the entrance to the park expanded by planting more gardens and trees. James Putt built a large concrete base for the deer statue with the name "Hershey" on the front and "Park" on its side. After the fire the print shop and the *Press'* offices were moved to town in the building later occupied by the Hershey Department Store.

Hershey Park's swimming pool attracted both bathers and spectators. In 1916 there was no area set aside to sunbathe.
(Hershey Community Archives)

The automobile was fast replacing the trolleys and trains as the main way to get to the park. Traffic jams were common on weekends and holidays, and parking was getting to be a problem for the park. The *Hershey Press* reported: "Already it is seen that Hershey's visitors in 1916 will be very largely an automobile crowd. The number of machines increased daily coming from every direction and from many states."

That same year (1916), the park's main pavilion, which had been used for dancing and roller skating, was converted into the Hershey Park Cafe. It seated more than one thousand and featured an orchestra that played for people in the dining room. Its chicken and waffle dinners were said to be "the last word in eats."

That summer it was almost impossible to find a vacant room in Hershey's tourist homes, at the Hershey Inn, Hershey Men's Club, or the YWCA. On July 4, 1916, the largest crowd ever, estimated between twenty-five and thirty thousand, descended on the park. It was so hot on July 20 that it was

The park's cafeteria in 1916.
Ice cream remained one of the park's best selling items.
(Charles J. Jacques, Jr. Collection)

impossible to get into the bathhouse after 12 o'clock noon.

In August, Ralph Fiorer, a Hershey Transit policeman, who also worked for the park, caught three men who had stolen bathing suits from the bathhouse the previous year, and who "had the nerve to try and use them in Hershey's pool." The *Press* reported that Fiorer was kept busy that summer forcing "a score of objectionable characters out of the neighborhood."

The latest type canoes so popular with young people were added in 1916 to the flotilla on the creek, bringing the number of rowboats and canoes to thirty-five. One of the water craft on Spring Creek again used the name Mayflower. In 1918, the Old Chinese bridge, better known as the "up and down" bridge, which led from the rear of the Park theatre to the swimming pool, was removed and replaced with a twelve-foot driveway bridge. The bridge was designed and constructed by Hershey's master craftsman, James Putt.

In 1917, M.S. Hershey let Harry Haverstick go for a very unusual complaint – he worked too hard. Hershey had repeatedly warned Haverstick that he had to get his men to do more of the physical work. One day Hershey drove by and saw Haverstick digging while a group of his men stood around and watched. Haverstick just could not manage men. M.S. Hershey's own success had been built on delegating responsibility, and after many warnings Haverstick was fired. He was replaced by C.L. Schmidt, who was another excellent gardener.

There was fear that World War I would hurt the chocolate company, but instead it proved to be a boon to the company and production increased every year during the war. Once America entered the war, the government decided to send a Christmas gift package to every American soldier abroad. It included a half-pound chocolate bar. Hershey Chocolate Company received the contract, which was the largest order of chocolate ever given in America.

One of the reasons that the Hershey Chocolate Company made money during the war was because European production fell, and American-produced chocolate helped fill the gap. Prices rose, profits rose, and America grew prosperous. Americans had money to spend, and they spent part of it on chocolate. The one problem the chocolate company experienced during the war was the shortage of workers. More women were hired.

The shortage of workers hurt the park more than the chocolate company, and the park's hours were curtailed. The war meant the end of the Hershey Band because most of the band members joined the armed forces. Others were too busy working at their defense-related jobs to play in the band. Sunday band concerts continued with local and regional bands filling the gap. Following the war, the park continued to book local and regional bands for Sunday and holiday concerts. The Hershey Band was never reorganized, although occasionally one of the bands from Harrisburg was called the Hershey Band or Orchestra when it played in the park.

The railroads cut out all special train rates during the war. Limits were placed on travel by both train and trolley, and the park acknowledged in 1917 that "the war makes summer schedules uncertain." The theatre continued to present summer stock, interspersed with vaudeville and moving pictures. A number of stock companies, including the Pickert Sisters Stock Company, Brooklyn Stock Company, and the United Southern Stock Company, played in the theatre during the war, usually presenting two different plays a week. Each company would stay from three to six weeks. One vaudeville company, Broadway Follies, ran into trouble with park management. It brought a musical extravaganza with girls and comedians to the park that was closed after only one performance because the show was considered too risque.

Dancing continued to grow in popularity during the war. Dance bands and orchestras like Myer's Orchestra of Harrisburg played in the dance pavilion, which was decorated with American flags and bunting. The public wanted the new style jazz

Richland and Newmanstown Joint Sunday Schools'
EXCURSION
TO
HERSHEY PARK
SATURDAY JULY 7, 1917
RICHLAND, PA.
ADULTS TICKET   65 Cts.
Special Train Leaves Sheridan at 8.50 A. M.   Richland at 9.05
Returning, Leave Hershey 8.15 P. M.

In 1916, canoes were first added to the park's fleet of boats on Spring Creek. A pond had been dredged and a fountain added in a swampy area between the creek and the park's swimming pool.

(HERSHEY COMMUNITY ARCHIVES)

music. Another group which appeared regularly in the park was the Banjo-Saxo Orchestra of Harrisburg, which became almost the house orchestra for the park between 1919 and 1925.

In the 1910's and 1920's baseball, even at the amateur level, was segregated. Occasionally, Hershey's baseball team would play a black baseball team. In 1919, the *Hershey Press* reported that the Harrisburg Giants, "a crack colored organization," would play the Hershey team on the Hershey Park Field. "The local boys will have to exert themselves if they want to come off with a victory, as the colored boys have one of the fastest teams in this section." Hershey won with the final score four to nothing.

M.S. Hershey met William Wrigley on a trip to Europe in the mid-1910's and took an instant dislike to him. In 1915, Hershey entered the chewing gum market with Hershey's Easy Chew. During the war, Hershey could not get raw materials needed, and his chewing gum business failed. Hershey blamed Wrigley for its failure. To get back at Wrigley, who owned the Chicago Cubs, M.S. Hershey tried to buy the Philadelphia Phillies. The owners wanted too much money, $350,000, for a team that had few stars and played in a rundown ball park, Baker's Field. (Hershey liked the name Baker's because he had been denied the use of the name for his cocoa products in the 1890's by the Baker's Chocolate Company.) John "Judge" Snyder was able to talk M.S. Hershey out of the idea.

Toward the end of the war, Hershey was granted a privilege he never should have accepted, an unlimited credit account,

and he began to invest in the sugar futures market. He "bet" on sugar prices going up; when they collapsed, he faced financial ruin.

To make matters worse, his mother Fanny Hershey, who had served as his financial conscience, passed away on March 11, 1920. She had always feared that her son might lose his fortune, and he was at the time of her death very close to bankruptcy. As big as the Hershey Chocolate Company had become, there was a chance that M.S. Hershey might lose everything. He had not faced the possibility of default since 1885.

M.S. Hershey was forced to sign a note for fifty million dollars with National City Bank, and when he defaulted, the bank sent an administrator, R. J. deCamp, to watch over all of Hershey's businesses. DeCamp moved his offices into the Hershey Bank and took over the day-to-day operation of Hershey's companies. DeCamp, who knew nothing about farming, even controlled what was going on at the Hershey farms. Harry Lebkicher complained to Hershey, "Throw him out. You keep him around here very long and we won't have any cattle on the place." Hershey could not, even if he wanted to. Hershey told the boys at the factory, "Don't rock the boat, row it!"

DeCamp was "the kind of a man," a New York colleague commented, "who would walk in with spats, sit on his tail, and direct everybody, including Mr. Hershey." DeCamp undermined some of Hershey's basic policies, like delegation of responsibility and loyalty to his top employees. As a result M.S. Hershey hated everything about him from the spats he wore to the way he spelled his name.

Monroe Stover, who was working for Ezra Hershey at the bank at the time, remembered that "we almost felt like we had to ask Mr. deCamp if we needed to use a postage stamp."

Hershey Park did not escape deCamp's cost cutting measures. Although the park was only a minor pawn in the struggle, deCamp decided that no capital improvements should be made in the park as long as the financial crisis continued. The park had never made or lost a lot of money, but Hershey had spent generously on park improvements, landscaping, and roads. He could write part of it off as good will for his other businesses.

During the war, it had been hard to build or buy new rides, but in 1920, M.S. Hershey planned to expand the park and add some major new rides. Just about the time that National City Bank sent deCamp to town, the *Hershey Press* carried the following news article:

[April 1, 1920] It is the intention of the management [of Hershey Park] to install as soon as possible several new amusement features such as The Whip and an Electric Roller [Coaster]. These would have been erected some time ago, but for the fact that labor has been scarce. However, work will progress on them as rapidly as possible.

Purchasing new amusement rides was just the sort of transaction that deCamp could stop. They were not needed and no one was sure how quickly they would pay for themselves. A large wooden roller coaster cost between $35,000 and $50,000. A new 16-car stationary park model Whip cost approximately $6,000. It was manufactured by William Mangels of Coney Island, New York, who invented the ride in 1915. Mangels had a reputation of not selling to anyone, even family members, on credit. So cash was required to buy the ride. In ordinary times M.S. Hershey would have purchased the rides from his own funds, but in 1920 he did not have the money to do it. There would be no new rides for the park, at least not until Hershey regained control. So, for three long seasons, 1920, 1921, and 1922, Hershey Park stagnated. A period that had started with so much promise in 1916 came to a dismal close in the early 1920's with the park forced to "tread water."

Perhaps the people who lived in Hershey did not know how much control Hershey had lost in his day-by-day operation of the chocolate company, but they could read. When the new rides were not installed, they knew that the situation was serious.

The financial situation finally brightened in 1922. The boys at the chocolate company had made and sold enough chocolate so that M.S. Hershey could refinance his loan. He was able to send deCamp back to New York City. M.S. Hershey told a friend "tomorrow we get our town back."

Although M.S. Hershey still had to deal with some financial restraints, he regained control of Hershey Park, the chocolate company, and the town. The financial crisis also seemed to revive his interest in the park and town, and it would not wane again in his lifetime.

The children's playground, which now had all-steel equipment, was built along Spring Creek under the park's high level bridge. (Hershey Community Archives)

CHAPTER 6

THE PHILADELPHIA CONNECTION

Open front coaster cars on the final brake run of The Wild Cat. In the foreground is the tunnel that covered the coaster's first dip; in the background is the lift hill. (CHARLES J. JACQUES, JR. COLLECTION)

If Hershey Park's development was largely controlled by M.S. Hershey's moods and financial capability, then 1923 was going to be a banner year. Hershey's debt had been paid down, he had regained control of the park, and the town was about to celebrate its twentieth anniversary. He wanted to give the town and his employees, who had worked so hard to help him regain control of his businesses, an anniversary present. He chose to give them The Wild Cat roller coaster and the biggest celebration that the town had ever seen.

M.S. Hershey and his park manager, Abraham T. Heilman, knew that Hershey Park had to add rides to compete for picnics. The park remained the key to getting people to come to the town of Hershey. Attracting picnics was good for the town, businesses, and the chocolate company. But picnic groups were going where the excitement was.

Building a roller coaster in Hershey Park was not really a break with tradition. From the day it opened in 1907, the park was more than a typical small town park. In its first season, it had attractions like a theatre, dancing, roller skating, swimming, band concerts, boating, and baseball, and M.S. Hershey soon added a zoo, merry-go-round, and miniature railway. The first shoot-the-

The first name for Hershey Park's new roller coaster was The Joy Ride. Later the coaster would be renamed The Wild Cat.
Photograph circa 1923. (Charles J. Jacques, Jr. Collection)

In the loading station of The Wild Cat coaster, where tickets were sold from a small ticket booth in front of the ride.

(Charles J. Jacques, Jr. Collection)

chutes in the swimming pool was an exciting, daring ride for its day. When people wanted something new, M.S. Hershey was willing to give it to them.

The 1920's was the golden age for the roller coaster, and a number of builders crisscrossed the country trying to find parks that wanted one of their coasters. Hershey Park had to compete for business with many parks in central and eastern Pennsylvania that had roller coasters.

The park competed with two major parks: Willow Grove and Woodside in the Philadelphia area. These large, urban, trolley parks had dozens of rides and attractions in addition to several roller coasters each. Thousands of people each summer took excursion trains from the Harrisburg area to these Philadelphia parks.

Amusements were also offered in Atlantic City and elsewhere on the New Jersey coast. By the 1920's there were new highways leading to Philadelphia and the New Jersey shore, and

more people from central Pennsylvania were driving there for their entertainment.

The Philadelphia Toboggan Company (PTC) was one of the premier roller coaster construction companies in the United States. The company factory and offices were located in the Germantown section of Philadelphia. Founded in 1903 by Henry B. Auchy and Chester E. Albright, PTC also designed and built carousels, fun houses, and mill chutes. In the early 1920's the company built coasters for Willow Grove Park, Philadelphia; Rocky Glen Park in Scranton; Saratoga Park, Pottstown, Pennsylvania; and Schuylkill Park, Pottsville, Pennsylvania. By 1922 the company had built thirty-eight coasters.

George Smith, who was the general manager and chief salesman for PTC, contacted Hershey Park, offering to build the park a new coaster for $50,000. Instead of buying a coaster, the park granted PTC a fifteen-year lease with a five-year renewal option to build a new coaster in the park. Under the lease agreement the park received 25 percent of the profits. The lease and renewal option would terminate on January 1, 1943.

It is not known why M.S. Hershey did not insist on owning the coaster. Possibly he did not have the money to build it himself, but it was more likely that he did not want to assume the risk in case of an accident. In addition, since PTC owned the coaster, it also had to manage and maintain it.

The new coaster was designed by Herbert P. Schmeck, an engineer for PTC. It was the first coaster that he designed, although he had built a number of coasters for PTC as the construction manager. He and his wife moved to the town of Hershey, and they stayed there for six months until the coaster was completed in June of 1923.

M.S. Hershey wanted the coaster built on the level ground around Spring Creek, and to find enough room, Schmeck designed the coaster to bridge the stream so that he could use land on both sides. No steel was used to cross the creek. Instead Schmeck used a wooden arch, similar to arching used on covered bridges, built with four-by-six-foot wooden beams. It was built so close to the creek that the coaster was subject to periodic damage from spring floods.

The *Hershey Press* reported, "This was a huge and difficult task to accomplish in such a short time, but Mr. Schmeck was equal to the occasion, and he is to be congratulated upon the excellence of his work. The roller coaster is nearly one mile in length, and it has more dips and deeper dips than any of the like construction in America. There are longer roller coasters, but none that will give you more thrills, in such a short space of time."

Although the *Press* overstated the coaster's actual length (it was only 2,331 feet as measured by Schmeck on August 6, 1923), it nevertheless was a modern, high-speed, deep-dip coaster that was as exciting as any coaster in central Pennsylvania when it was built. The Wild Cat would serve the park well until 1945 when it was torn down and replaced by The Comet.

The Wild Cat was built of long leaf yellow pine, and Schmeck complained to his boss, George Smith, that it was the poorest grade of lumber he had ever seen. He also wrote that he couldn't hire any carpenters in the Harrisburg area for under a dollar an hour, and even then he was not able to get enough good men. Schmeck was a perfectionist, and he usually found something to complain about on every coaster job. He sought excellence and drove his men hard.

The coaster had a tunnel, which was painted white with green trim and a green roof, between the loading station and lift hill. Most of the buildings in the park were white with green trim and green roofs. Schmeck used one hundred goose neck lamps on the coaster's lift hill and around the loading station.

Smith advised Schmeck to do everything possible to get the coaster open by Decoration Day. John R. Zoll, who was in charge of Hershey's twentieth anniversary celebration, had writ-

ten Smith asking him to encourage Schmeck to get the coaster open in time for the town's twentieth anniversary celebration on June 16, 1923. Smith wrote Schmeck, "I am assuring him [Zoll] that the coaster will be in operation before the anniversary, and that we are hoping to have it for Decoration Day. Will you please see him to give him definite assurance?"

Unfortunately, May was the wettest on record. More than six inches of rain fell, and Schmeck's men had to work in the mud and flooded creek. Schmeck was saved in late May when M.S. Hershey lent him the extra carpenters he needed to get the coaster done for the opening.

On June 16, 1923, the youngsters of Hershey rushed to the park as word spread that the new coaster was running and the rides were free. Even the *Hershey Press* seemed to get caught up in the excitement when it described the reaction of the first riders to the new coaster: "it was necessary to dislodge a number [of riders] by the use of a crowbar, in order to give others a chance." No women were allowed to ride until the afternoon, and then Miss Marion Murrie, the daughter of William Murrie, "had the privilege of being the first to make the trip."

The *Press* continued, "Later in the afternoon after the cars had been broken in sufficiently to start, the turnstile began to click, and from that time on until late Saturday evening the pleasure-seekers almost swamped the ticket-takers in order to have a ride."

At first the new coaster was called "The Joy Ride," but within a short time the name was changed to the "The Wild Cat." The coaster's loading station was on the south side of Spring Creek not far from the park entrance and behind the Hershey Park Cafeteria. It was built on the edge of the hill overlooking Spring Creek, and gravity carried the coaster train out of the loading station across the creek through a tunnel to Derry Road, where the lift hill was located. The coaster was taken by chain to the top of the hill and then went down two giant hills that paralleled Derry Road. It made a wicked sharp right turn at the corner of Derry Road and Park Avenue; the train then traveled to a turnaround and back toward Spring Creek where it made another turn and passed under the lift hill before crossing the creek to the loading station. Houses had already been built along Derry Road, and the new coaster seemed almost to travel in their backyards. Schmeck was never completely satisfied with his design, and he made some changes to the coaster in the late 1920's and again in the mid-1930's.

Once the coaster was completed, there was a question of whether it should run on Sundays. The park's merry-go-round

Herbert P. Schmeck was the chief engineer for the Philadelphia Toboggan Company when he designed The Wild Cat in 1923. (CHARLES J. JACQUES, JR. COLLECTION)

had not been operated on Sundays. However, on Sundays the park generally had its largest crowds and since the coaster was such an important and costly ride, a decision was made to run the new coaster on Sundays. After the park ran the coaster on Sunday, June 17, 1923, the *Hershey Press* editorialized:

> If there is any harm in allowing people the opportunity of enjoying themselves by riding a Roller Coaster on a Sunday we fail to see it. Furthermore, we believe the merry-go-round should be run on a Sunday. Many are the kiddies that are disappointed because they cannot ride the hobbies. Surely there is no harm in delighting the heart of the children. The [band] organ should be subdued, and no one would be the worse, but a great many would be happier.

> We have these amusements in Hershey Park, so why not make use of them. There is no use of bucking the tide—the people are crying aloud for an opportunity of getting away from themselves—to enjoy themselves, and why shouldn't they be given the opportunity, especially if the amusements are clean and not harmful.

For the twentieth anniversary, M.S. Hershey did not want another parade. The *Hershey Press*, which usually reflected his views, wrote that "Instead of inviting in a carnival or organizing a circus, with a local parade with its hullabaloo and confusion, two celebrated musical organizations have been engaged for these two days." One was the 250-member Bach Choir of Bethlehem, Pennsylvania, and the other was Signor Guiseppe Creatore's fifty-member concert band. The *Press* continued, "Creatore's Band is the most brilliant musical organization playing before the public today. This band plays all the principal cities and parks of America and also plays for the Edison Phonograph Company."

Creatore, who was a very popular musician, and his large concert band were well received. He conducted his entire program without using a score, a remarkable achievement. Some people thought the director was a little eccentric in his leadership, but according to the *Press*, he "extracted the last atom of feeling from his musicians."

The anniversary celebration also included the Ella Kramer Stock Company performing a comedy, *The Three Wise Fools*, which had been produced in New York the previous year. The swimming pool was taxed to capacity. Hershey Park's dancing pavilion was jammed, and it was almost impossible to get on the merry-go-round. The miniature railway was filled every trip, and the giant roller coaster was unable to meet the demands of all who wanted a thrilling ride.

On the ball field the Hershey team took on a strong Lewistown team with its star pitcher "Smoky" Smith on the mound. The *Press* recounted that Zimmerman pitched for Hershey and the contest was "nip and tuck" with the final score seven to four in favor of Hershey.

The Bach Choir of Bethlehem gave three concerts in the Convention Hall on Saturday and Sunday, June 16 and 17, 1923. Only six thousand were able to get seats in the auditorium; so before each concert the Central Moravian Choir sang chorale tunes outside the Convention Hall for nearly a half hour so that thousands more could hear the traditional Moravian music. During the performances, the audiences gave standing ovations to the choir. For the closing number at the Sunday afternoon concert, the audience joined the choir in singing "The Star-Spangled Banner," which had not yet been made the national anthem. At the end of the song, a card prohibiting clapping was displayed, but the audience was overcome with emotion and broke into applause for

MONDAY, TUESDAY and WEDNESDAY

ELLA KRAMER STOCK COMPANY

CALL BELL PHONE 18-M

FOR RESERVE SEATS

SCANDAL

First Time at Popular Prices

THURSDAY, FRIDAY AND SATURDAY

"BEFORE BREAKFAST"

PEER OF ALL FARCE COMEDIES

the choir and its director.

The *Hershey Press* estimated that at least fifty thousand people attended the two-day event. The Pennsylvania State Police provided ten officers for traffic control to help back up the park's police force.

Fred Pronto's Orchestra was signed by the park to provide regular band concerts for the 1923 season. A policy of more jazz and fewer classics was announced. Park management used Pronto's Orchestra for the majority of Sunday concerts in the band shell, and his group occasionally played in the dance pavilion. His band was a favorite and appeared many times in the 1920's in the dancing pavilion and the outdoor bandstand.

For the 1924 season, the Banjo-Saxo Orchestra returned to the dance pavilion, which was redecorated into a "veritable Wonderland." Ella Kramer Stock Company returned to the theatre with such comedies and dramas as *Cat and the Canary, The Bat, The First Love, In Love With Love, The Clinging Vine,* and *Scrambled Wives.*

The merry-go-round was renovated, and new music rolls were purchased for the band organ. Russel Zentmeyer, who had run the machine for a number of years, remained in charge. The *Press* reported that Zentmeyer "gets all excited when he tells the wonders of his hobby horses, zebras, camels, etc." James Putt designed and built a new fifty-foot shoot-the-chutes for the swimming pool. "Whitey" Bistline was in charge of the miniature railway. Another improvement mentioned by the *Press* for the 1924 season was the widening of "lovers' lane."

In 1925 the Convention Hall was remodeled, and its acoustics were improved in time for a concert by Paul Whiteman and his 25-man orchestra. His program, called "An Experiment in American Music," included numbers by Victor Herbert and George Gershwin and was well received. Tickets for $2.20 and $1.10 could be obtained from John B. Sollenberger at the Hershey Trust Company as well as in retail stores in Lebanon and Harrisburg.

John B. Sollenberger, who grew up in the Hershey area, became M.S. Hershey's impresario. He was put in charge of booking entertainment, which included summer stock, vaudeville shows, moving pictures, concert bands and other attractions for the park and theatre in town. He also contracted for bands for the dance pavilion.

Sections of Spring Creek still maintained a natural look in the 1920's. (Charles J. Jacques, Jr. Collection)

Sollenberger was a risk taker who wanted to book the biggest and best. He knew that big name entertainment would help put Hershey on the map. He liked trying new and startling bands and acts, as well as new types of entertainment. Usually M.S. Hershey backed him up, but occasionally Sollenberger had to talk his boss into an idea.

M.S. Hershey was not a provincial person; he had lived many years in New York, Chicago, and Philadelphia. He regularly traveled to New York City, generally staying at the Plaza Hotel. He traveled to England, the Continent, and even the Far East. He was familiar with Mexico, and he had a large operation in Cuba, which he visited many times. One of his favorite places was Atlantic City, which in the 1920's was one of America's premier summer-resort towns. Here he saw what forms of entertainment were popular. He often went to the Steel Pier and its ballroom to see what acts and dance bands were popular.

Grandstands were built adjacent to the pool so that people could get a better view of the swimmers. Photograph circa 1925.
(HERSHEY COMMUNITY ARCHIVES)

John Philip Sousa, America's bandmaster, performing in Hershey Park's Convention Hall in 1925.
(HERSHEY COMMUNITY ARCHIVES)

For 1925 the Sherwood Players from New York under the direction of Miss Sherwood played in the theatre. Ticket prices were twenty cents for children, thirty cents for adults, and fifty cents for reserved seating.

The dance pavilion, now called the ballroom, was redone in blue and yellow by Fred Bolts and Frank Edris. Suspended from the ballroom's canopied ceiling were huge lanterns. Wisteria vines were planted around the building.

Under the headline "Americans Crave Action - Sousa Gives it To Them," the *Hershey Press* reported that seventy-year-old John Philip Sousa, America's greatest bandmaster, would bring his band to Hershey's Convention Hall Saturday and Sunday afternoons, July 4 and 5, 1925. "The average American is so filled with nervous energy that it is almost impossible for him to listen for any time to a musical program which does not bristle with action," Sousa told the *Press*. To convey action, Sousa had his bandsmen move about the stage during the performance, and they all advanced to the footlights during the presentation of "The Stars and Stripes Forever." Tickets for his concert were seventy-five cents for both the afternoon and evening concerts.

At least ten thousand people heard Sousa's band in his two concerts in the remodeled Convention Hall. There was standing room only in the hall with more people crowding around the building to try and hear the band or to catch a glimpse of Sousa. The audience insisted upon encore after encore at both concerts, and Sousa graciously responded. The old time favorite, "The Stars and Stripes Forever," brought the audience to its feet, as did "The Liberty Bell," "The Washington Post March," and "Semper Fidelis."

Security and crowd control had become more of a problem, so in 1926 Hershey Park set up its own seven-man police force headed by George Lafferty. The town of Hershey had been chosen as the home for the Pennsylvania State Police School in 1924, and their presence helped to keep troublemakers away.

HERSHEY PARK THEATRE

— THE —
SHERWOOD
— PLAYERS —

MAN=HANDLED

You've Seen the Movie
and Read the Story
Now See the Play

Thursday, Friday and Saturday
[THIS WEEK]

PRICES: General Admission 20c and 30c
Reserved Seats, 50c
Curtain rises   Doors open
7.45 o'clock   7.15 o'clock

Sollenberger, the new park manager, purchased a Skooter car ride from Lusse Bros. of Philadelphia in 1926. He placed the Skooter in a newly constructed forty by fifty-foot building that was located across the bridge from The Wild Cat not far from the Convention Hall.

This bumper car ride ran on electric current which passed through a wire mesh ceiling. There was always the strong smell of grease and electric sparks about the ride. The sixteen metal cars were very heavy and therefore rode on a steel-plated floor. People would bump into one another while driving, and cars were often in need of repair. The park would add new versions of the Skooter ride into the 1990's.

A kiddie Ferris wheel and small aeroplane swing were purchased from W.F. Mangels Company of Coney Island, NY. They were placed on the north side of Spring Creek where the Skyview station was later built. As more kiddie rides were purchased, they were placed in this area, which became a small Kiddieland.

A new Wurlitzer organ for the merry-go-round was purchased in 1926. Forty new band organ rolls were also purchased replacing the ten old rolls that had been used with the old band organ. The *Hershey Press* reported that the new band organ "sounds almost like Phil Fisher's Orchestra." The Dentzel merry-go-round was repainted and looked as good as new.

The ballroom (dance pavilion) was renamed Danceland with Mannix Orchestra of Harrisburg, C. Lloyd Major Orchestra, and Buzz Crawford Orchestra providing the music. Hershey Park had always contracted for local dance bands, usually from Harrisburg, Lebanon, Lancaster, or Reading, but this policy started to change in 1926 when the park booked its first national band. Gordon Kibbler's Orchestra played a one night stand in Hershey's Danceland. The park boasted that Kibbler came directly from an engagement in Miami, Florida. For his dance band, prices were increased to fifty cents for dancing or listening.

Trolley car on the Elizabethtown line of the Hershey Transit System that ran through the countryside. (CHARLES J. JACQUES, JR. COLLECTION)

Bathing beauties were primary attractions at Heshey Park's pool. In the 1920's their suits were made of wool.
(HERSHEY COMMUNITY ARCHIVES)

Summer stock was replaced by vaudeville and moving pictures in 1926. Moving pictures played in the park's theatre on Monday, Tuesday, and Wednesday, while "snappy vaudeville" played Thursday, Friday, and Saturday. The first Kiddie Day was held on August 26, 1926, for children fifteen and under. Rides were free from one to two p.m. Then movies, all comedies, were shown in the theatre followed by another hour of free riding.

M.S. Hershey had definite beliefs on what made a successful operation. He noted regularly the cleanliness and tidiness of the grounds. He believed that patrons appreciated a clean recreation

The miniature railway station at the entrance to Hershey Park.
(RICHARD BOWKER COLLECTION)

area. In inquiring into the day's business, he always asked about the size of the crowd, never the gross income. Apparently he was assured that the size of the crowd would result in adequate spending.

There is a story about M.S. Hershey that he used to walk around the park and if he saw a small piece of litter, he would pick it up and throw it away, unless it was a Hershey's Bar wrapper; then, after making sure that the name HERSHEY'S was right side up, he would leave it.

Through the years, many groups had been given tours of the chocolate plant, but it was not until 1927 that a tour of the factory was formally instituted. M.S. Hershey though that people would enjoy seeing chocolate being made in his plant. He was always fascinated by machinery, and he figured others would be interested in watching machines turning out chocolate bars. Therefore, he converted a corner of the men's lunch room into a lobby and set up a special counter where chocolate drinks could be served. His original tour included bar molding and wrapping, Kiss depositing, box wrapping and label printing (at that time Hershey printed all its own labels).

James T. Smith, one of the first tour guides, recalled "At first, if we had two hundred people all day, it was a big day. Most of our visitors came from nearby communities."

"The location of the Visitors' Lobby was such that company executives had to go through it to get to their offices," Smith continued, "and it was a common sight to see M.S. Hershey himself chatting with the visitors." The tours proved to be so successful that by 1935 as many as two thousand people a day were going through the plant.

Prior to Hershey's financial difficulties in the early 1920's, M.S. Hershey had treated the chocolate company as a private concern. It was his money, and he could do pretty much what he wanted. He was the person who initiated, shaped, and controlled his businesses. He was responsible to no one. After the sugar crisis of 1920 and his borrowing, he was never completely in control again. In 1927, the chocolate company refinanced to liquidate the remaining debt left from the 1920 sugar crisis and to get more money for future expansion. However, the public financing created a problem with Hershey's free spending on improvements for the town and park. To deal with this problem two corporations were created. The Hershey Chocolate Company was reorganized as the Hershey Chocolate Corporation and incorporated in the State of Delaware. Its name was changed to Hershey Foods Corporation in 1968. The park and other non-chocolate assets were put into a new corporation called Hershey Estates, which changed its name in 1976 to HERCO, Inc. After the chocolate company and the non-chocolate company were separated, there developed a more formal relationship between the companies.

Sollenberger arranged to bring Will Rogers, the great cowboy humorist, to the park's Convention Hall in 1927. "The Funniest Man in the World" appeared on the stage of the Convention Hall on Monday, May 30, 1927, at 2:30 p.m. Prices were $2.20 and $1.10, and the Hershey Industrial School boys were permitted to come for free. Rogers' performance included storytelling and rope tricks. M.S. Hershey was so proud of his town that he took the humorist on a guided tour.

Every year the Hershey Industrial School had a day in the park. All the boys and house parents would come to the park in

the morning and have a big picnic lunch. The rides were free to the boys and their house parents. However, they had to be back to their respective farms by four o'clock in the afternoon so they could milk their cows.

In 1929, a new swimming pool complex was created along Spring Creek on the westerly edge of the park. Four pools and a bathhouse were built in the area formerly occupied by the Dentzel carousel pavilion directly across the creek from the park's ballroom. M.S. Hershey spent more than $100,000 on the complex that included a bathhouse made of brick and stucco on a steel frame. It was done in a Spanish Moroccan style, which was very popular at the time, and featured a tile roof and decorative turrets. The men's locker room contained 2,567 lockers. The women's locker room had 2,343 lockers. Both locker rooms had dressing booths and shower rooms.

A new $100,000 swimming pool complex and bathhouse were constructed in 1929. The park's dancing pavilion was located to the right of the pools. (Hershey Community Archives)

The swimming pool at Hershey Park in the 1929. At the far end of the pool were the bathhouse and refreshment stand.
(Hershey Community Archives)

THE FAMOUS
COWBOY HUMORIST
WILL
ROGERS
The Funniest Man in
the World
HERSHEY PARK
CONVENTION HALL
DECORATION DAY
Monday, May 30th
2:30 p. m.
Don't fail to see and
hear the man who has
made millions laugh:
$2.20, $1.65, $1.10
Tax Included
Mail Order: Address Alvin B.
Carmany, Treasurer, Hershey
Trust Building, Hershey, Pa.,
also C. M. Sigler, Inc., 30 N.
3d St., Harrisburg.

The pool complex featured a sand beach. Boys and men still wore two piece bathing suits in the 1920's.
(Hershey Community Archives)

The four pools held a combined total of 1,240,000 gallons of filtered spring water and occupied thirty-five thousand square feet. The main pool was built in two sections: the swimming-diving section being two hundred ten feet by sixty feet, with seventy feet of the length being reserved for diving exclusively and the remaining one hundred forty feet for swimmers. The diving section was six and one-half feet to ten feet in depth, and the swimming section was five and one-half to six and one-half feet in depth. There was also a concrete island in the center separating the two sections, which was approximately thirty feet by thirty feet in size.

The wading pool was semicircular, the depth ranging from two and one-half to four and one-half feet. The smallest pool was the babies' circular pool, which was forty-two feet in diameter and was from six to eighteen inches in depth. A second child's pool was twenty-five feet long by thirty feet wide.

Hershey Park's new swimming complex was officially opened on Saturday, July 13, 1929. The park advertised it as "The Seashore at Your Door!" There were "One and one-half million gallons of water! Filtered! Sterilized! Changed every eight hours!" Admission was fifty cents for adults and thirty-five cents for children. The pools were open from 11:00 a.m. to 10:30 p.m. At night the complex operated under giant flood lights. The park did not rent bathing suits, so people had to bring their own. "At the old pool there was no beach at all. The new pool had a sand beach, which made it very attractive," Monroe Stover recalled. "When kids were too young to get into the ballroom, they would go swimming in the afternoon and stay and listen to the music coming from the open-air ballroom."

John B. Sollenberger entered into another lease with the Philadelphia Toboggan Company to have the company build a Mill Chute for the park. Russell F. Haines, an engineer for PTC, visited Hershey on October 2, 1928, to finalize plans for the new ride. He reported his trip to George P. Smith as follows:

Left [Philadelphia] on 8:36 a.m. train for Hershey and arrived there 11:07 a.m. Went to Mr. Sollenberger's office and he took me to see Mr. Ziegler and from him I got the sketch I had made for the mill. While in Mr. Ziegler's office, he mentions the fact that Mr. Hershey was very well pleased with the idea of putting the mill and carrousel [sic] opposite each other and said to Mr. Ziegler 'Have them paint their tunnel green and we will plant pines and shrubbery along it to give it a better appearance.'

Every winter, beginning in 1925, the Convention Hall was converted into the Ice Palace. (Hershey Community Archives)

The Mill Chute in Hershey Park under construction in 1929. In the background is the old swimming pool's bathhouse that was converted to a fun house in 1930.
(CHARLES J. JACQUES, JR. COLLECTION)

The entrance of the Mill Chute under construction. In the foreground is a section of the park's old swimming pool before it was filled in. In the background is the park's new merry-go-round pavilion under construction. (CHARLES J. JACQUES, JR. COLLECTION)

At the finish of the ride, a boat would plunge down the chute into a pool of water.
(CHARLES J. JACQUES, JR. COLLECTION)

A beautiful windmill on the Mill Chute added a romantic touch.
(CHARLES J. JACQUES, JR. COLLECTION)

The new Mill Chute and carousel pavilion were built along Spring Creek where the park's old swimming pool had been located. Herbert Schmeck, who was now chief engineer for the Philadelphia Toboggan Company, decided to build the channel for the new Mill Chute out of concrete to minimize maintenance costs. The ride included a mill wheel, which moved water through the channel and a covered portion of the channel (old mill section), followed by a lift hill where the boats were pulled up by a chain and then sent down a chute into a pool of water. The old mill portion of the ride had four animated scenes, which were changed every few years. The ride proved to be very popular and easily out earned The Wild Cat. Both rides cost ten cents in 1929.

The Philadelphia Toboggan Company also designed and helped build the new carousel pavilion, which was located in between the Mill Chute and The Wild Cat. M.S. Hershey again wanted a large pavilion so that people could sit and watch the merry-go-round. Because the pavilion was so wide, ninety feet, part of it was built out over Spring Creek. The park's Dentzel carousel, which was purchased in 1912, was moved into its new home in July 1929.

Since the Mill Chute and The Wild Cat were owned by the Philadelphia Toboggan Company and run on a concession basis, PTC hired the managers and employees to operate and maintain them. In 1929, Russell Haines, from PTC's engineering department, was paid sixty-five dollars a week for managing both rides.

M.S. Hershey and a boy, Robert Coleman Sheaffer, from the Hershey Industrial School, circa 1927.
(CHARLES J. JACQUES, JR. COLLECTION)

The following year, William Marquet replaced Haines and was paid sixty dollars a week. Marquet would manage the rides for many years.

George Smith reported to PTC's executive board on an outside offer to purchase the company's interest in The Wild Cat and Mill Chute in 1929, which the board turned down:

The gross receipts for 1928, were $12,717.08, but the net receipts after deducting the percentage to the park were $9,537.83, with an operating profit of $4,602.80, which included repairs and maintenance in the expenses, being an abnormally high repairs charge. In addition not only was Hershey's Coaster afflicted with the usual rainy weather that bothered every other place during the 1928 season, but also it was on a detour—the main road to Hershey was being concreted by the State Highway Department, and a long dusty detour was necessary to get into the park. This took away a great amount of the automobile business which it usually enjoyed. The lease on the Hershey Coaster runs until January 1st, 1938, with a five-year renewal privilege, we to notify October 1st, 1937. In my personal view, we would be warranted, if we have a good season this coming summer, in spending next Fall, $2,000 or $3,000 to liven up the ride and renovate it, and we should greatly increase our receipts, all of course depending on the way Hershey Park is handled this coming summer, under the new management arrangement. They are spending about $100,000 on a new swimming pool and doing a lot of work around the park—installing more zoo, moving the carousel up from the far end of the park to a location between the Coaster and the Mill Chute, grading into the parking section, so that the parking will be greatly improved, and altogether I should judge Mr. Hershey is spending about $200,000 on the place.

Two persons were slightly injured in an accident on The Wild Cat on May 30, 1929. Apparently a piece of the friction rail tore loose underneath a train, which stopped it. This train was then run into by a second train. Fortunately, the first train had come to a standstill on top of a hill. No one was seriously injured, although two girls were kept overnight at the Hershey Hospital. The rest of the riders were treated for minor injuries and sent home. PTC was running three trains at full capacity because of the Decoration Day holiday.

At the September PTC board meeting, Smith again urged renovations be made to The Wild Cat. "The ride is in bad need of a replacement on the back curve. It will have to be done before another operating year and should be done at once. In doing this I think we should change the dip in front of it and make the curve a more modern one—improving the ride considerably. I am asking Mr. Schmeck to work out some details on this so that we will have something more definite to propose to you," Smith wrote. PTC spent more than two thousand dollars in repairs before the 1930 season.

The Hershey Park Ballroom remained the premier summer dance floor in central Pennsylvania. Carsonia Park's Crystal Ballroom, Maple Grove Park and Rocky Springs Park both in Lancaster, and Gretna Gables were competitors, but none played the same class dance bands that Hershey did. In the late 1920's Hershey Park advertised the following orchestras:

Ben Bernie (Himself) and His Famous Hotel Roosevelt
	Dance Orchestra
"Stew" Black and His Band
Ted Brownagle and His Columbia Recording Orchestra.

Eddie Brubaker and His Entertainers
Marlin Burd and His Cadets
Tommy Christian and His Orchestra (just off the Loew Circuit - Only appearance in this section)
Cliquot Club Eskimos, world's most famous radio orchestra
Dan Gregory and His Victor Recording Orchestra
Tal Henry and The Goodrich Silvertown Cord Orchestra, with the Silver Masked Tenor
Whitey Kauffman and His Victor Recording Orchestra
Ken Kehoe and His Windsor Terrace Orchestra
Hal Kemp and His Hotel Manager Orchestra (12 Brunswick Recording Artists)
The Krazy Katz Orchestra
Ferdinand LeJeune and His S.S. Leviathan Orchestra
C. Lloyd Major and His Orchestra
The Mannix Orchestra
Harvey Marburger and His Orchestra
Oliver Naylor's Orchestra of Birmingham, Alabama (A red-hot Dixieland Combination)
Joe Nesbit and His Orchestra Featuring "Saxy" Knight
The Sylvanians (Who have just completed thirteen weeks at the Everglades Club, New York City)

"The Popular Collegiate" L. Roger Wainwright and His Blue Band (10 Master Musical Entertainers)
Art Zellers and His Orchestra

As the 1920's drew to a close, Hershey Park was the leading amusement park in central Pennsylvania. Paxtang Park was fading and would soon close. Competition now came from a new park, Williams Grove, which was located near Mechanicsburg, Pa. The park had started as a picnic grove shortly after the Civil War. Starting in 1874 the Grange held their annual picnic at Williams Grove. It was transformed into an amusement park in 1928 by R.E. Richwine.

With the addition of The Wild Cat, Mill Chute, and new swimming pool, Hershey Park had more to offer than any other park in the area. Just when it seemed that nothing could go wrong, America's economy started having problems. It would be a tough period for America's amusement parks. How M.S. Hershey dealt with the problems created by hard times would determine the park's future.

Hershey Park's ballroom in the late 1920's was redecorated with huge lanterns that were suspended from a canopied ceiling. (HERSHEY COMMUNITY ARCHIVES)

CHAPTER 7

BUILDING PROSPERITY

Manicured lawns and gardens helped make Hershey Park "The Park with a Country Club Atmosphere." Photograph circa 1930.
(HERSHEY COMMUNITY ARCHIVES)

A s Hershey Park entered a new decade, everything seemed in place for continued success. The park opened an 18-hole public golf course on July 15, 1930, and adopted a new advertising slogan to include its course and clubhouse: "The Park With a Country Club Atmosphere." The swimming pool and Mill Chute would operate for a full season. A new fun house was under construction next to the Mill Chute.

To enhance its quality image, John B. Sollenberger, the park's manager, was able to book Rudy Vallee at the very peak of his popularity into the Hershey Park Ballroom. It was an entertainment coup. The park could be forgiven for using a little bit of hyperbole in their advertisement calling Vallee "The Sensation of a Decade."

There was only one trouble with this rosy scenario: America was in a depression that would last almost the whole decade. There were approximately nine hundred amusement parks in America in 1930, but only three hundred survived the decade. The rate of attrition was even worse for parks the size of Hershey Park, where three out of every four closed.

In 1930, *Amusement Park Management*, a trade magazine, noted that Hershey Park was attracting the better, and quieter, classes of people. Sollenberger, the park manager, had done a good job of combining in an average-sized amusement park standard amusements with recreation features. According to the magazine, "Mr. Hershey can often be seen wandering about the park, inspecting this, that and the other thing, and planning improvements with his engineers and estate executives. For this reason there has been no lack of ready capital for the park when it was needed."

The clubhouse for the park's golf course was built in 1930 and was located on a hill above the swimming pool complex.
(HERSHEY COMMUNITY ARCHIVES)

Bathing beauties on the sand at the Hershey Park swimming pool complex, circa 1930's. (HERSHEY COMMUNITY ARCHIVES)

The magazine said that the park's dance pavilion and swimming pool complex were prime examples of the quality operation. In the dance pavilion, a gallery was provided for spectators to view the dancing and listen to the band. Admission to the gallery was twenty-five cents, which brought in enough money to pay the entire payroll needed to operate the ballroom.

At the swimming pool complex, a spacious veranda furnished in wicker extended entirely around the second story of the bathhouse. Here, for twenty-five cents, spectators could sit comfortably and watch the bathers. From the veranda could be seen the clubhouse for the new golf course. This course was operated by the park. "This 18-hole golf course," Sollenberger told *Amusement Park Management,* "is, of course, somewhat of an experiment in connection with an amusement park. But our idea is that there are a large number of men, at least in this territory, who like to play golf. So, while they play golf, the golf widows and children have the park and its attractions with which to amuse themselves."

It was the era of the Big Bands. Many amusement parks survived the depression on the business their ballrooms did during these years. One of the first big bands with a national reputation was Rudy Vallee and his Connecticut Yankees. According to Katherine Gordon, who sold tickets and checked coats at the ballroom, Vallee wanted what was then the astronomical sum of twenty-six hundred dollars for one night at the ballroom.

The miniature railway would pick up and discharge passengers at the bathhouse, circa 1931.
(HERSHEY COMMUNITY ARCHIVES)

*Interior of the Hershey Park
Ballroom in 1932.*
(Hershey Community Archives)

HERSHEY PARK BALL ROOM
HERSHEY, PA.
WEDNESDAY, AUGUST 6, 1930
The Event of the Season
RUDY VALLEE (himself)
AND HIS CONNECTICUT YANKEES
The Sensation of a Decade
Only Appearance Within 60 Miles of Harrisburg
Dancing From 8.00 P. M. Until 1.00 A. M.
Admission $1.50
Spectators $1.00
TICKETS NOW ON SALE

M.S. Hershey was concerned about losing money on the performance, and so he was reluctant to guarantee the money for Vallee's appearance. Sollenberger offered to put up the guarantee, but Hershey said, "No, you're too poor to lose that money, I'll lose it." Rudy packed them in on Wednesday night August 6, 1930, "and they made plenty of money that night," Gordon said. Of course premium prices were charged with admission $1.50 for dancers and $1.00 for spectators, and Sollenberger had Vallee agree that he would not appear again that summer within sixty miles of Harrisburg.

Sollenberger and George Bartels, who became assistant manager in 1931, continued to add rides but not without M.S. Hershey's approval. "Mr. Hershey was always the high consultant in everything," Betty Bartels, George Bartels' daughter, recalled. "In those years he was very active in working with each aspect of his town, and they would not have gone ahead without the blessings of Mr. Hershey. First it [an innovative idea] came from him; maybe with their suggestions, but he was always a big part."

"Mr. Hershey spent a lot of time in the park. I don't think he directed. He looked. He watched, and then if he had suggestions, he would make them," Betty Bartels said. "The candy kitchen was a little different. There, Hershey was more likely to give the workers specific instruction."

Betty Bartels recalled one occasion when M.S. Hershey came into the candy kitchen. He told the girls to keep adding more flavoring to the mint chocolates. But his taste buds were not as sensitive as they had been, and after he left, the candy was so strong that the girls had to throw it out.

Even though Betty Bartels' father was the assistant manager of the park, he never permitted her to ride without a ticket. Some days her father would give her fifty cents and when that was gone, she had to stop riding. However Betty Bartels affectionately recalled the times when Mr. Sollenberger, who did not have any children of his own, would slip her another quarter or fifty cent piece, so she "could do something else delightful in the park."

The park converted the old swimming pool's bathhouse into a fun house, which was located near the Mill Chute. The conversion was done by James A. Fields of Detroit, Michigan,

*A water toboggan slide built next to the ballroom ran
under the Park Boulevard bridge over Spring Creek.*
(Richard Bowker Collection)

who had been in the fun house business for more than twenty years. It was an active fun house that had four wooden slides, a barrel roll, a spinning disk (human roulette wheel), and a ride called the cup and saucer. It also contained a tunnel to walk through. The crazy contraptions were pleasing to both the participants and the onlookers. People simply tried to get through the devices without being too embarrassed. Hardly a day went by that someone was not knocked over, and occasionally a wrist or an arm was broken, but lawsuits were rare for those kinds of accidents in the 1930's.

In 1931, a stock company, The Phoenix Players, returned to the Park Theatre and performed six nights a week. Paid parking was introduced in the lots down by Spring Creek while free parking was offered around the Convention Hall. The park advertised by newspapers, letters, and billboards. The Hershey Park Zoo opened a building containing carnivorous animals and primates. Admission to the zoo was free, and it attracted many people to the park during the depression.

A new, exciting water toboggan slide (shoot-the-chutes) was built and opened in 1931. It was located on the other side of Spring Creek from the swimming pool complex. People who wanted to ride it first had to pay to get into the pool; then they would cross a pedestrian bridge over the creek, and go through an underpass beneath the ballroom to get to the slide. The slide had its own small pool which measured approximately thirty feet by sixty feet. People could rent wooden sleds for fifteen cents for a half hour, and if they moved quickly, they could make four trips down in thirty minutes. Water was pumped to the top of the slide to keep the track wet.

Brad Cassady, who was a swimming champion and who helped around the pool in the 1930's, recalled that the slide was "roughly in the shape of a huge rain gutter with a hump near the end." The fun was "slamming down, belly-whopping all the way and then hydroplaning out over the water," he said.

In 1932, the park developed a new area which it called the Sunken Garden, located on the east side of Park Avenue across from the bathhouse and ballroom. It was in a swampy area down along Spring Creek below the dam which created the lagoon. The garden was exquisitely laid out, and new trees and shrubs were planted. It was used both by swimmers and dancers. This area replaced the pond and gardens that had been located between the park's old swimming pool and Spring Creek.

The park bought a new, spectacular electric fountain, which was installed in the center of the lagoon above the Sunken Garden. The fountain was a thirty-five-projector

The electric fountain at night with the bathouse in the background. The swimming pool complex was lighted and remained open until 10:30 p.m.
(HERSHEY COMMUNITY ARCHIVES)

During the day, bathers would gather in the Sunken Garden, which was opened in 1932.
(HERSHEY COMMUNITY ARCHIVES)

device, which consisted of five small fountains built into one basin, with colored lights coordinated so that the same combination appeared on only two of the jets at one time. It was operated automatically and required thirty minutes to make all the changes. The central nozzle of the fountain could shoot a spray of water sixty-five feet in the air.

To make the effect even more dramatic, the park added two fifty-two-foot long water curtains, which were controlled waterfalls from a tube, along the face of the dam; these were illuminated at night. People could boat down to and around the fountain. The park had problems with people crashing over the dam and damaging the water curtains, so it tried a number of things to warn people, including a wire that was strung from shore to shore.

A Pretzel dark ride was installed in the early 1930's. The

Hershey Park's first fun house was built by James A. Fields of Detroit in 1930 in the structure that was formerly the park's bathhouse. (HERSHEY COMMUNITY ARCHIVES)

ride got its name because the riders were twisted and turned so much during the ride that they felt just like "a pretzel." The little two-seat cars had noisy electric motors and a large pretzel on their sides. The cars would bang in and out of the darkened building. While in the building, cars would pass lighted stunts of snakes, scary faces, and cartoon characters. Bells, whistles, and gongs were also used. The track layout also looked like a pretzel and was meant to confuse riders as they went through the ride. The Pretzel was manufactured by Leon Cassidy from Bridgeton, N.J.

Every ride in the park had its own printed ticket with its name on it. Most rides cost five cents, although larger rides like The Wild Cat and Mill Chute cost ten cents. There were also separate tickets for ice cream, refreshments, and even souvenirs. At the end of the day, tickets were counted by hand and then destroyed.

Map of Hershey Park in 1932. (HERSHEY COMMUNITY ARCHIVES)

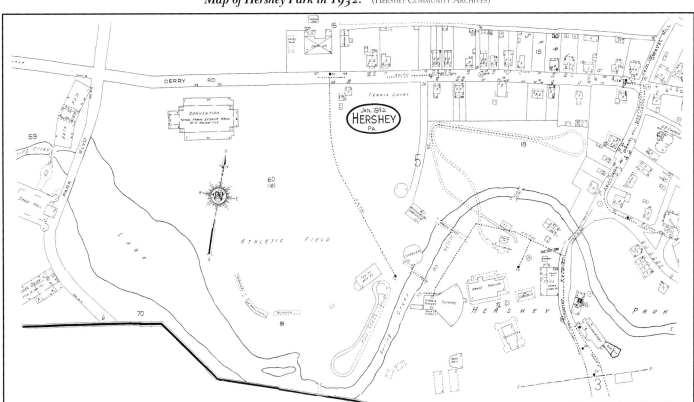

In 1930, the maple bandstand in the Hershey Park Ballroom was moved from above the entrance doors to the middle of the dance floor. The ballroom was redecorated and remodeled every few years to give it a more modern look.

Dance bands that appeared in the ballroom in 1931 included Hal Kemp's orchestra, Joe Haymes and his Missourians, Coon Sanders and the original "Nighthawks," C. Lloyd Major's orchestra, the Original 14 Bricktops with Jen Rankin "America's Greatest Girl Orchestra," Paul Tremaine and his band, and Duke Ellington and his orchestra.

The park's golf course was advertised in 1931 as "fun and entertainment for everyone," and a "Snappy 18-hole course." The clubhouse was open to the public, and dinners were served daily from 5:30 p.m. to 9:00 p.m. Music was furnished by the Hershey Park Club Orchestra.

George P. Smith, general manager of the Philadelphia Toboggan Company, was happy about the improvements Hershey Park made in 1931, and the ones planned for 1932, but he was worried that the park had lost some big picnics to the new Williams Grove Park in Mechanicsburg, Pa. He felt that Hershey Park needed to be more active in soliciting picnics. "The plant is excellent, but the picnic promotion is very negligible at present," he said. "Mr. Hershey is spending a large amount on improvements in the town of Hershey and on the park, a community center, etc. This should bring more visitors and with improved times, more receipts. He has made an excellent Zoo at the end of the park where our rides are located," he concluded.

The depression nearly bankrupted the Philadelphia Toboggan Company. Hershey Park was one of only two park locations that was still making money for the company. In 1932, PTC cut its payroll again, and Smith was let go. Schmeck remained because he could still work on the few small jobs that the

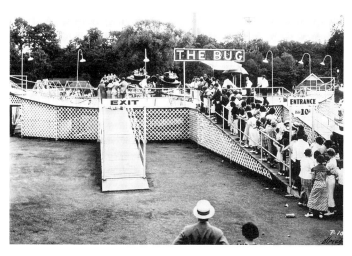

The Bug drew huge crowds when it was purchased by the park in the early 1930's. People enjoyed the thrill of being thrown around during the ride's operation. (HERSHEY COMMUNITY ARCHIVES)

The Bug's seven cars each had strange little caterpillar heads with eyes. (HERSHEY COMMUNITY ARCHIVES)

The Hershey Community Building was constructed in 1933 to provide work during the depression. It was located at the corner of Chocolate and Cocoa Avenues.
(HERSHEY COMMUNITY ARCHIVES)

company was getting. Schmeck, in addition to his engineering duties, became the company's chief salesman, and the main contact with Hershey Park.

Williams Grove Park was Hershey Park's biggest competitor in the Harrisburg area during the Great Depression. The Richwines added a modest roller coaster at Williams Grove Park, which was designed by John A. Miller in 1932. In 1939, Richwine purchased an adjacent farm and he built a half-mile dirt track for auto and harness racing.

Hershey Park added The Bug, manufactured by Traver Engineering Co. of Beaver Falls, Pennsylvania. This new ride was placed near the Mill Chute and carousel, where the old swimming pool had formerly been located. Forty tons of concrete were used to sink the center shaft. It was like a coaster operating on a single track around a center shaft. The cars, which were

circular, were mounted on springs and whirled around the center shaft. Eight people could ride in each "bug-like" car, and they were thrown about, which added to the ride's popularity, as they traveled in a circle around the center shaft. Kids liked to create a ride within a ride, as they would spin in their seats and move around while the ride was operating.

During the depression the Hershey Chocolate Corporation continued to make money. Profits were down a little but not very much. This meant that people in and around the town of Hershey had money to spend in the park. The number of people who toured the plant increased every year except 1931. The tour was free, and during the depression visitors received a Hershey's Bar at the end as a treat.

In 1932, approximately six hundred construction workers were unemployed in and around the town of Hershey, so M.S. Hershey initiated a massive building program. "If I did not provide work for them, then I would have had to feed them," Hershey said. His construction projects provided jobs for about half the town's men between 1932 and 1939.

Old plans that had been shelved at the time of the First World War were brought out and updated. Among these were architect's plans for a community building and theatre. In 1932 work began on the six-story Hershey Community Building at the corner of Cocoa and Chocolate Avenues in the center of Hershey. It was built to serve the recreational and cultural needs of the people of Hershey.

At the same time, M.S. Hershey decided to proceed with his resort hotel on Pat's Hill. The exact site had been selected by Hershey in 1910, and cedar trees were planted near the summit of the hill, leaving a bare spot where the hotel was to be

The Hotel Hershey under construction in 1933. The Spanish-Moroccan-styled hotel, which had two hundred rooms, was located on Pat's Hill. M.S. Hershey had a trolley line extended to serve it.
(HERSHEY COMMUNITY ARCHIVES)

Canoeing along Spring Creek offered a change of pace from The Wild Cat and The Whip. (HERSHEY COMMUNITY ARCHIVES)

built. Hotel Hershey would cost Hershey more than two million dollars, even when the cost of material and labor was extremely low. Hershey was one of the few persons in America willing to undertake such a project during the depression.

As part of the thirtieth anniversary celebration a souvenir booklet was printed which described the park in this way:

> Its thousand acres are delightfully landscaped, its groves of shade trees, shadowy oaks, rustic bridges that span historic Spring Creek, all combine to stimulate a sense of comfort and ease. The park lacks the traditional carnival midway with its bedlam of raucous shouts and insane laughter, supplying instead a beauty spot designed to furnish amusement for the young, diversion for the adult, and relaxation for the elderly.

This publication emphasized the park's quiet side, but the park still had the fun house, games, shooting gallery, penny arcade, The Wild Cat coaster, Mill Chute, The Bug, Pretzel dark ride, bumper cars, the water toboggan slide, and the merry-go-round and band organ.

Certainly, Hershey did not forget the merry-go-round. Elmer Dunkleberger, a former resident of Hershey, recalled, "Mr. Hershey, himself, would sometimes be caught by local children riding the merry-go-round after the park was closed. He would allow them to join him unless they became unruly."

M.S. Hershey was always interested in new ways of developing Hershey. He wanted to make it into a year-round resort. Monroe Stover recalled, "A piece of machinery came in from Link Manufacturing, and nobody knew what it was for or who

ordered it. Finally, it got around to Mr. Hershey. He said, 'Well, I ordered that machine. It's a machine to make ice, and snow. Someday we're gonna build a hotel up there. We're gonna have to have a ski lift, and we'll have to have a snow maker in case the Good Lord doesn't send us enough snow.' But he never built the ski lift, and the ice machine was sent back to the manufacturer."

In 1934 M.S. Hershey hired Alexander Stoddart to do publicity for him. "Milton Hershey, modest though he appeared to be, did enjoy publicity about his factory, his town, and even

Alexander Stoddart became editor of Hotel Hershey High-Lights and publicist for the park in 1934.
(HERSHEY COMMUNITY ARCHIVES)

Hotel Hershey High-Lights

Vol. III   *Open All the Year Around*   Hershey, Pa., May 23, 1936   *"Delightful Living"*   No. 46

Pennsylvania's "Summer Capital" - Hershey Park - Opens Tomorrow With New Attractions

Hershey Park, called "The Summer Capital of Pennsylvania," by reason of the fact that during the summer months sometimes as high as 50,000 people are entertained in one day, will open its season tomorrow.

A new attraction has been added to the amusements, a "Coaster Car Ride" which permits children to drive motor driven autos.

Between 2 and 4 p.m. the Hagerstown Municipal Band led by Peter Buys will give an outdoor concert which will present among other selections excerpts from the famous marches of John Philip Sousa. It will be a tribute to the great march king by Buys' teacher and friend. Buys made many arrangements for the band which were used by Sousa, who considered Buys one of the best band arrangers in the country.

The director of the Hagerstown Municipal Band plans to present Ketelbey's tone picture, "In a Camp of the Ancient Britons"; a descriptive fantasie of "A Hot Time in the Old Town"; selections from themes of "The Three Musketeers," and "Circus Days," a descriptive number from the peanut-eating elephants to "The Man on the Flying Trapeze."

Other numbers include the overture from "Mercedes"; "The Washington Grays" and "The Pilgrim," marches; the fantasie "Faith Eternal" and vocal solos from "The Land of Smiles" and "The Land of the Sky-Blue Waters."

planted; the roads improved and the tables and chairs put into place for picnickers.

The penny arcade has been enlarged. The amusements of Hershey Park now include: a swimming pool and a modern bathhouse with 3,000 steel lockers; a zoo containing a splendid collection of mammals, birds and reptiles from all over the world; 18 hole golf course; a ballroom accommodating 4,000 dancers, water toboggan, fun house, pretzel, giant roller coaster, boating and canoeing, merry-go-round, kiddies' ferris wheel, kiddies' auto ride, kiddies' airplane ride, the bug, children's motor boat ride, mill chute, miniature railway, shooting gallery, skee ball, childrens' playground, tennis courts and baseball diamond.

The Hershey Park golf club has a dining room and the Hershey Park cafeteria has a capacity of 1,000 diners. There are tables and benches for 5,000 picnickers. Sanitary drinking fountains of filtered mountain water are to be found in convenient places and for those who desire to make coffee or tea or keep food hot, there is an outdoor oven where the wood is supplied free of charge.

All that "The Summer Capital of Pennsylvania" needs for a successful day for its opening tomorrow is good weather.

ROW OF HORSE-CHESTNUTS IN BLOOM
The horse...

Picard Plays in National Open at Baltusrol June 4-6

Henry G. Picard, pro of the Hershey Country Club, will play in the National Open golf championship which will be held this year at the Baltusrol Country Club, Short Hills, New Jersey, on June 4, 5, 6.

Last year Picard finished in fifth place with 306 for 72 holes being Gene Sarazen, Horton Smith and A. F. Krueger. These men were led by Sam Parks, Jr. 299; Jimmy Thompson, 301; Walter Hagen, 302; Denny Shute and Ray Mangrum, 303.

Picard made the lowest round of all the 162 entries, 70 for 18 holes. Picard, Krueger and Ted Turner were the only golfers at the National Open, held at the Oakmont Country Club, Pittsburgh, last June, who broke par. 72. Krueger and Turner turned in cards of 71.

The Hershey Country Club pro automatically qualified to enter this year's tournament for his performance in the National last year. The first thirty and ties at Oakmont play in the 1936 National.

Other exemptions include "Torchy" Toda and Seisui Chin, visiting Japanese professionals and Johnny Farrell, Baltusrol professional. Under a recent ruling the professional of the club entertaining is automatically eligible for the tournament proper, providing he has been the club's pro for at least a year.

The exemptions of the first thirty and ties at

Hershey Park Zoo's new bird house was constructed in 1934.
(HERSHEY COMMUNITY ARCHIVES)

Jiggs, an orangutan, entertains a crowd at the Hershey Park Zoo in 1934.
(HERSHEY COMMUNITY ARCHIVES)

The birth of lion cubs was big news at the Hershey Park Zoo in 1936.
(HERSHEY COMMUNITY ARCHIVES)

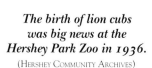

himself," commented Samuel Hinkle, who worked with him at the chocolate company and later became its president. Hiring Stoddart was not a departure for M.S. Hershey, who had worked with public relations firms for years, but having an in-house publicist was new.

For the next seventeen years Stoddart served as public relations director for the park, arena, stadium, chocolate company (in the Hershey area), and the town. He was a master at keeping the name of Hershey (in its diverse forms) in the news. Bob Posey, a local newspaper columnist, once described Stoddart as Hershey Park's "big plug and blurb man, who ran around Hershey all week long without a coat or hat."

Stoddart also edited a small, four-page publication for Hotel Hershey called *Hotel Hershey High-Lights* during his years in Hershey. The paper was a cross between an information sheet for hotel guests of what was happening in the town's attractions, and a weekly paper for the town. It was distributed free of charge to guests of the hotel and to the people in town. The only advertisements in it were for Hershey's companies and activities.

In 1934 Hershey Park Zoo added three new buildings: a bird house, a reptile house, and an entrance building. It also added to its animal collection an Indian elephant, kangaroos from Australia, and two 250-pound turtles from Aldabra Island in the Indian Ocean. The zoo now covered forty acres. The zoo keepers liked to give names to the animals: the orangutans were named Maggie and Jiggs; Hawkshaw was a lion that ran into everything and had a bump on his nose; Julia, a lioness, was named for the wife of Caesar who was associated with lions and

They'll Be SAFE and HAPPY
—at—
HERSHEY PARK
HERSHEY, PA.
JULY FOURTH

Free Open Air Concerts
Dr. Blose's Symphony Band — Lebanon, Pa.
Also, the Berlean Choir of Lebanon in ancient Greek costumes, presenting Native Songs and Folk Dancing.
Afternoon 12.30—2.30—Evening 6.15—8.15
Dancing—Matinee and Night
RAY WELOH and HIS ORCHESTRA
Swim in "THE POOL"—Clean—Safe—Cool

The Allentown Band performed two concerts. In the park's theatre the musical comedy *Spies of 1934* was presented, together with the Baer-Carnera fight pictures, and other short subjects. Fifty-five hundred people entered the swimming pool complex.

Kiddies' Day had been expanded to Kiddies' Week by 1934. Children twelve years old and under were given free rides on the merry-go-round, miniature railway, airplane swing, and miniature Ferris wheel. They were also given free lollipops, and admission to the Zoo was free. Poreli's Society Circus was engaged to give two shows daily at the band shell.

Hershey Park's ballroom underwent a major renovation for the 1935 season. It took workmen nearly three months to complete the job. The interior was painted white with black trim, and the doors were painted silver. Frank H. Edris and Roy W. Deets redecorated the ballroom. They used forty-two hundred yards of cloth in color combinations of blue, green, orange, tan, and red to create artistic hangings from the ceiling. One of the new features was indirect lighting. A border of lumiline tubing was extended around all of the pillars and columns. The lighting fixtures were placed so that with use of a

the early Christians; the black leopards were named Zip and Flash; Malay bears were called Adam and Eve; the black bears were Bud, Scotty, Nancy, and Lancaster (the last of which had come from the Lancaster Zoo); the spotted leopards were Bounder and Betty; the tigers were all Ben (an abbreviation for Bengal); the hyena was Scepter; the rhesus monkeys were named Jack, Sheba, and Baby Mike; and the spider monkey was, of course, Charlotte. Children were encouraged to buy small bottles of milk and feed the baby animals. Stoddart had a field day with the zoo, which was always good for another feature story.

The *Lancaster News* reported in June 1934, "In the summer of '34, Hershey Park's grounds were assuming metropolitan proportions." According to the newspaper "the old park was led out of the soda-pop era by a swell zoo and soul-stirring architecture." The paper was intrigued with the town's new hotel and theatre, as well as the park's newly redecorated ballroom. It complimented the park for preserving some of the old attractions like the bandstand and theatre. It stated that M.S. Hershey had planted saplings, and now they had developed into full-grown trees making it a truly beautiful park.

The Fourth of July in 1934 was the single biggest day in the park's history. *Hotel Hershey High-Lights* reported "sixty thousand people came that day in ten thousand automobiles, which when parked, extended from Park Avenue to beyond the Hershey Park golf course, and as far up as the corn is planted. There were literally acres of automobiles." (Stoddart had a tendency to overestimate the size of crowds.)

In the early 1930's the Mill Chute was more popular than The Wild Cat. (CHARLES J. JACQUES, JR. COLLECTION)

The Hershey Park Ballroom was redecorated in 1935.
(DERRY TOWNSHIP HISTORICAL SOCIETY)

switchboard eight different color combinations could be created. Eight fans were added for cooling. A new microphone and amplifier were installed so the band could be heard in every square foot of the 22,900-square-foot dance floor.

Schmeck, who had replaced George Smith, advised the Philadelphia Toboggan Company's board of directors that "the coaster [The Wild Cat] needs painting badly and Mr. Sollenberger has mentioned it the last three years, but we have always evaded painting." Schmeck finally convinced the directors to redo the contour slightly, so as to speed up the ride, and give it a slightly more thrilling sensation. The coaster was recontoured, and the back curve was more steeply banked. Most importantly the first incline was raised seven feet. After the improvements, Stoddart called The Wild Cat "a rip-snorting ride."

New stunts were installed in the Pretzel Ride and the fun house, and the merry-go-round was repainted. A new kiddie's auto ride with five racing cars and five fire engines was added.

The park adopted a new slogan "Pennsylvania's Summer Capital."

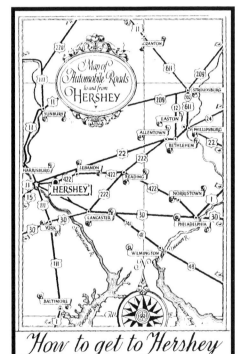

How to get to Hershey

As you will notice by looking at the map, **Hershey Park** is located on U. S. Highway No. 422 and is easily accessible. All passenger trains of the Reading Railroad stop at Hershey. Distances from various cities follow:

City	Miles	City	Miles
Allentown	70	Norristown	77
Altoona	138	Philadelphia	95
Baltimore	88	Pittsburgh	220
Bethlehem	75	Pottstown	66
Carlisle	32	Pottsville	50
Chambersburg	65	Reading	40
Coatesville	55	Scranton	140
Cumberland	150	Shamokin	70
Easton	85	Stroudsburg	110
Frederick	84	Sunbury	72
Gettysburg	50	Tamaqua	65
Hagerstown	90	Washington	130
Harrisburg	13	Waynesboro	75
Hanover	55	West Chester	70
Hazleton	80	Williamsport	105
Lebanon	13	Wilkes-Barre	110
Lancaster	30	Wilmington	70
Lewistown	73	York	40

KETTERLINUS, PHILA.

Variations of this were used for the next forty years. The slogan was a play on the park's close proximity to Harrisburg, Pennsylvania's capital city. The park had grown to more than one thousand acres, and it continued to offer clean and wholesome entertainment. According to Stoddart, "people come from all over Pennsylvania to this community where so much has been done for the worker and his pleasure—a town in the country with metropolitan advantages."

Dance bands that appeared later in the decade included Benny Goodman, Kay Keyser, Wayne King, Freddy Martin, Bob Crosby, Duke Ellington, Hal Kemp, Tommy Dorsey, Les Brown and his Duke Blue Devils, Horace Heidt, Shep Fields, Don Mario, Artie Shaw, Jackie Coogan, Dick Stabile, Ted Lewis, and Guy Lombardo and his Royal Canadians, who drew about 3,500 dancers and spectators in 1936.

Les Brown's band always attracted a sizable crowd to the Hershey Park Ballroom. His parents lived not far away in Lykens, Pennsylvania. Once when Brown was playing, he allegedly told the ballroom staff that "Mom and Pop will be down with a few friends. Pass them in."

The Custer Car Ride was purchased in 1936.

The elder Browns showed up accompanied by twenty-four "friends."

In 1936, the park purchased a Custer Car Ride, which permitted children to drive real gasoline autos on a restricted, quarter mile track. It was manufactured by the Custer Specialty Company of Dayton, Ohio. Kids liked to tear around the track with the feeling that they owned the place. That same year the penny arcade was enlarged. The other buildings received a fresh coat of paint.

Hershey Park held its first Baby Parade on August 28, 1936. It was witnessed by more than two thousand people. One hundred and sixty-six children under five years of age walked across the band shell's stage to the music of the Hershey Community Theatre Orchestra. The first contest was judged by Mary Regan Ross, Jean Dodge, and Rose Gross, society editors respectively of the *Harrisburg Patriot, Evening News,* and the *Morning Telegraph.* Prizes were awarded for the cutest baby, cutest twins, fanciest baby carriage, fanciest doll carriage, best

Couples dressed up to go dancing at the Hershey Park Ballroom in the 1930's.

The Wild Cat's loading station in the 1930's. (Hershey Community Archives)

The Wild Cat was a huge coaster and gave a very exciting ride. The train is in the turnaround. Photograph circa mid-1930's.

(Charles J. Jacques, Jr. Collection)

Under the coaster's superstructure, to the left, was one of the park's automobile parking lots.

(Hershey Community Archives)

Hills leading to and from the coaster's recontoured turnaround near Park Avenue. Photograph circa 1935.

(Charles J. Jacques, Jr. Collection)

fancy costume, most original decorated carriage, fattest baby, and best comic costume.

Spring Creek overflowed its banks in 1936. The fun house, Mill Chute, and the merry-go-round were partially submerged. It took several days to clean up the mess.

By the early 1930's ice hockey was firmly established as an indoor spectator sport in Hershey. Each winter beginning in 1925 the Convention Hall was converted into an ice skating rink and named the Ice Palace. John B. Sollenberger wanted to start a hockey team, and in 1933, with M.S. Hershey's approval, the Hershey Hockey Club was formed. Lloyd Blinco, who later served as general manager of the park, had first come to town as a hockey player with the Brooklyn Hockey Club in 1932 when his team played an exhibition game against the old Swarthmore AC team. Sollenberger got Blinco and his brother, who were born in Canada, to play for the new Hershey B'ars that became a member of the Tri-State Hockey League, and competed against teams from

The Hershey B'ars Hockey Club in 1935. John B. Sollenberger, the team's manager, is on the far right in the second row, and Lloyd Blinco, who was the team's captain, is in the center of the first row. Blinco would later become general manager of the park.

(HERSHEY COMMUNITY ARCHIVES)

Baltimore, Atlantic City, and Philadelphia.

By the 1935-36 season, fans were being turned away from the Ice Palace for both hockey and an ice show that came to town. M.S. Hershey, who became an avid hockey fan and who paid his own way into the games, was once turned away because it was sold out. He supposedly vowed to his driver that he would build a new arena with room for everyone.

The new Sports Arena was designed and constructed by D. Paul Witmer, head of Hershey Lumber Products. Original plans called for a 5,000-seat arena, but when M.S. Hershey found out that it probably could not be expanded later, he ordered the capacity to be increased to 7,500 seats.

The arena was connected to the old Convention Hall. The structure was 232 feet wide and 362 feet long, and 100 feet from the floor of the arena to roof. It was the largest span monolithic concrete structure in America.

Perhaps the most unusual thing about the arena was that it held 7500 when the town's population was less than 2,500. The grand opening festivities held on Decem-

The Hershey Park Arena under construction in 1936.

(HERSHEY COMMUNITY ARCHIVES)

The box office and offices were located in the northeast corner of the new arena. Photograph circa 1937.

(HERSHEY COMMUNITY ARCHIVES)

The Hershey Sports Arena in the 1930's. (Dolly Sitler Collection)

Monroe Stover, who headed the purchasing department of Hershey Estates, in 1935. (Hershey Community Archives)

ber 19, 1936, included a hockey match between the Hershey B'ars and the New York Rovers, and an exhibition of fancy skating and acrobatics.

Monroe Stover, who worked for Hershey Estates in the purchasing department, said that M.S. Hershey once told him, "I've got to get these things done while I'm still living because I don't think the boys that are going to take over when I'm not here any more will have the nerve to spend the money."

Seventy-three picnics came to Hershey Park in July of 1936, which was its best month for picnics. The largest single picnic in 1936 was the Reading Company Boosters' Club, which brought 18,000 people by train and 1,000 by cars. The second largest picnic was the Lancaster Automobile Club which brought 10,000 to the park, and the third largest was the Supplee-Wills-Jones Company of Philadelphia, which carried 5,890 adults and 425 children by train from Philadelphia. The companies and organizations tended to return every year on the same day of the week and month. For example, the Lancaster Automobile Club, which for many years was the park's largest picnic, always came on the third Thursday in August.

George J. Ruth, who lived in Palmyra in the 1930's, recalled attending Palmyra's Annual Community Sunday School Picnics in the park. A colored tag would be placed on each picnic basket and container in Palmyra, and the articles would be taken by truck to the miniature railway station near the park entrance and arranged according to color so that their owner could locate them. Items found in most picnic baskets, according to Ruth, included: ham, homemade bread, butter (in glass jars), red-beet eggs, lettuce, potato salads, layer cakes (one always chocolate), pies, pretzels, chips, assorted cheeses, crackers, and all kinds of fruits. Many families brought a wooden or metal tub along, and somebody from the family would be sent to the park's ice house to bring back a small block of ice, which would be placed in the tub to keep perishable food cool. In the

afternoon children six to twelve would enjoy the rides with free tickets they received in Sunday School on the Sunday before the picnic day. There were games and guessing contests with many prizes for both the children and adults. Families always brought enough in their picnic baskets for lunch and dinner. Here is how Ruth described the evening band concert:

> Between seven and nine the Iroquois Band would render a concert that few bands in the area could match, playing marches, an overture or two, and a few vocal solos and instrumental solos. This would be attended by a large crowd and always was the highlight of the picnic. One year the town policeman came to the concert and was heard to say he made a run throughout the town and saw only about ten people outside, so he came to hear the concert also as that was where everyone else was.

The merry-go-round pavilion was a favorite meeting place because it was located in the very center of the park.
(Hershey Community Archives)

In 1937, Hershey Park purchased a Whip ride from W.F. Mangels Company, Coney Island, New York.
(HERSHEY COMMUNITY ARCHIVES)

After the playing of the National Anthem concluding the concert, the crowd would simply fade into the night and make the return trip to their homes....

Hershey Park's 1936 season closed on September 13. Attendance was up 35 percent from 1935. The zoo, which now charged an admission fee, admitted a quarter of a million people, while an additional 100,000 school children, accompanied by teachers, were admitted without charge.

"America's Most Unusual Park" became the park's slogan for 1937. The park purchased a Whip ride from the William Mangels Company of Coney Island, New York. M.S. Hershey had wanted to purchase this ride in 1920 but had been unable to because of the debt crisis. The park called their Whip the "Whippero." It had cars attached to a wire which threw the cars around each end in a crack-the-whip manner. Riders were thrown together, which added to the excitement.

In 1937 a new maple floor was bought for the Hershey Sports Arena and Tommy Dorsey's band played there. Admission was seventy-five cents for dancers and thirty-five cents for spectators. The park advertised, "Be able to say that 'I danced in the Hershey Sports Arena.'" The Twenty-third Annual May Hop

Boating and canoeing remained popular on Spring Creek in the 1930's. The miniature railway skirted the north side of the creek.
(HERSHEY COMMUNITY ARCHIVES)

Hershey Rose Garden was opened to visitors in 1937. The garden attracted 200,000 visitors in its first season.
(HERSHEY COMMUNITY ARCHIVES)

was held from 8:30 p.m. to midnight in the Hershey Park Ballroom with Les Brown and his Duke Blue Devils providing the music. Special admission price was seventy-five cents with spectators thirty-five cents. Benny Goodman, "The King of Swing," appeared on May 31.

Roller skating was offered nightly in the new sports arena from 8:00 p.m. to 10:30 p.m., and matinees were offered on Saturdays, Sundays, and holidays, 1:30 p.m. to 4:30 p.m. Johnny Davidson, a lifelong ice and roller skater, was the professional instructor and manager.

The Hershey Rose Garden grew out of a conversation Hershey had with Dr. J. Horace McFarland of the Garden Club Federation of Pennsylvania, which held its annual dinner at Hotel Hershey on April 30, 1936. Dr. McFarland asked Hershey to contribute one million dollars to establish a rosarium in the vicinity of Washington, D.C. Hershey thought about it and decided instead to establish a rose garden in Hershey.

Hershey had Harry Erdman, his horticulturist, create the rose garden. Erdman spent the entire summer of 1936 on the project. First, a site was selected, a three and one-half-acre plot just south of the hotel and overlooking the town. Then plans were drawn, and development was started in July 1936. There was a deep erosion gully through the plot, and Erdman used that to form a pond as a feature of the garden.

A gift shop and gazebo were constructed. Necessary grading was done and the beds plotted and soil prepared. Walks were seeded in late August, and the garden was ready for fall planting. The first planting of 12,500 roses in 112 varieties was completed

in late October and early November.

The garden was opened to visitors in late May of 1937, and the first weekend in June the roses were in full bloom and attracted more than 20,000 persons in a single day. In its first season more than 200,000 people visited the Hershey Rose Garden.

In June 1939, the *New York Times* devoted a full page to the garden and Erdman's special garden techniques. The garden of roses had grown to more than two hundred beds of roses. In addition there were two rock gardens, one formal garden, and other gardens on the hotel's spacious lawns.

When asked if the rose garden was among his original plans for the town, M.S. Hershey said, "That was far removed from my mind. I came up there to make chocolate, not to grow roses." However, once growing roses proved popular, he did everything possible to encourage and promote it.

Five different meals - chicken, chicken and waffles, beef, pork, or steak - which cost between one dollar and one dollar and a half, were served at the park's restaurant in the 1930's. M.S. Hershey's favorite dining spot was on the verandah, which overlooked the band shell. Mildred Fisher, a waitress in the restaurant, recalled serving Mr. Hershey. "He always ordered chicken and waffles, and he always got gravy with his." He liked the center of a watermelon, and after the meal was over he would go back to the kitchen complimenting people for the wonderful meal.

M.S. Hershey's eightieth birthday party was held in the Hershey Sports Arena in 1937. William Murrie accompanied M.S. Hershey over to the arena, where John B. Sollenberger met them and escorted them into the building. Immediately upon their entrance the huge crowd, twelve thousand in all, rose from their seats in recognition of him. M.S. Hershey was too surprised for words and stood spellbound for a few minutes. Never before in his eighty years had he ever received such an ovation. His employees presented him with a yellow-gold octagon ring, with eighteen blue-white diamonds set in platinum, enclosing the trade mark of the Hershey Chocolate Corporation - a baby emerging from a cocoa pod. The highlight of the evening was recognition of employees who had served him loyally over the years. They included William Brinker, 47 years of service; followed by William Murrie, 42 years; Ezra F. Hershey, 35 years; Harry N. Herr, James K. Putt, and John F. Snavely, 34 years; Joseph R. Snavely, 30 years; Abraham T. Heilman, 26 years; and many others. The company, the town, and the park were built on the loyalty of these employees, and this was the ultimate recognition of that fact.

The day after the party Hershey suffered a stroke. His doctors did not think he would recover, but he did, although he was never as strong as he had been.

Hershey Park added two new amusements, the Auto Skooter and Death Valley fun house for 1938. One person was so thrilled with the Skooter ride that he took twenty-two consecutive rides. The old fun house was remodeled, new stunts added, and it became "Whoops"; the Philadelphia Toboggan Company did the remodeling work and provided the stunts. A new free playground for younger children was also opened.

The Hershey Sports Stadium, a modern concrete outdoor structure, was the last major component in M.S. Hershey's building campaign. The facility was completed in 1939, just as America came out of the Great Depression. It had a seating capacity of 15,658 and was constructed so that it could be expanded into a horseshoe that would seat 20,000 persons. It covered ten acres.

The park with the "Country Club Atmosphere" was willing to try almost anything to attract people to the park or the arena. One of the decidedly non-country-club-type events offered in the late 1930's was midget auto racing in the Hershey Sports Stadium. Every Thursday and Saturday nights the familiar "Let 'em roll" would echo from the stadium's public address system down into the park. Racing was what the public wanted, and Sollenberger brought it to Hershey.

The back of the park's theatre shortly before it was converted into a fun house, circa 1937.
(Charles J. Jacques, Jr. Collection)

The Death Valley fun house was designed by the Philadelphia Toboggan Company in 1938. It was full of "Laffs and Thrills."
(Charles J. Jacques, Jr. Collection)

The Auto Skooter's building was designed by the Philadelphia Toboggan Company.
(Hershey Community Archives)

In 1938, new Auto Skooter cars were purchased from Lusse Manufacturing Company of Philadelphia.
(Hershey Community Archives)

The biggest of the big bands continued to play in the park's ballroom in 1937 and 1938 with Glenn Miller, Paul Whiteman, Phil Harris, Tommy Dorsey, Artie Shaw, and Phil Napoleon. Improvements were made in the ballroom's amplifying system, and more speakers were added. New walkways were also built around the electric fountain in the Sunken Garden. Dancers could cool off with a slow walk around the fountain.

In 1939, the park built several covered picnic pavilions. No admission was charged for picnicking, and the park supplied free firewood and tables and benches for five thousand. The penny arcade was renamed "Sportland" and a Ferris wheel purchased.

The decade had started with Rudy Vallee in the ballroom, and it ended with Glenn Miller and his orchestra on September 9, 1939. The *Elizabethtown Chronicle* called it "a masterpiece in

booking." It was an appropriate way to close the season and decade. Miller, who was the hottest band director in the country at the time, established a new attendance mark at the ballroom when more than 5,100 people crowded the dance floor and balcony.

Perhaps M.S. Hershey best summed up how and why the park continued to grow and change:

The buildings in the park are of a substantial type. Years ago these were much like those generally seen in other parks, but in recent years we have made quite a number of changes, not only in the buildings, but in the amusements as well. We endeavor to make some improvements each year. That is what makes our park so popular. People like a change, you know.

In 1938, the old fun house was remodeled, new stunts added, and it became Whoops.
(Hershey Community Archives)

The Mangels miniature motor boats featured striped canopies and kid-sized boats that revolved around a lighthouse. Photograph circa 1939. (Hershey Community Archives)

A kiddie ride with racers and fire engines was located in a pavilion in Kiddieland at Hershey Park.
(Hershey Community Archives)

The park's miniature Ferris wheel, sixteen feet high with six enclosed cars, was built by W.F. Mangels Company, Coney Island. Even the ride operators wore neckties in the 1930's.
(Hershey Community Archives)

The miniature airplane ride had a steel tower from which six little two-seat airplanes were suspended.
(Hershey Community Archives)

Chapter 8

Rationing Fun

On August 27, 1942, the Hershey Chocolate Corporation received the Army-Navy "E" production award for creation of Ration "D," an emergency ration for fighting men. William F. R. "Bill" Murrie, president of the company, accepts the banner. M.S. Hershey is third from the left.
(Hershey Community Archives)

Hershey Park's main draw in the 1940's was its ballroom and dance bands (both regional and national). The park advertised one great dance band after another all summer long. Rides, the swimming pool, concert bands, games, and food were secondary attractions. When the United States entered World War II, all that would change. It became a question of whether the ballroom would remain open. There were tire and gasoline rationing and government regulations against pleasure driving. There was also a scarcity of employees to run the park.

The 1940's were the peak of dance bands' popularity. They had played an important part in the early development of radio. Dance bands produced the great majority of the music on the *Billboard* charts. Radio slowly moved from live broadcasts of bands to records of the same bands. In the early 1940's dance music was still played live from ballrooms around the country. Hollywood made hundreds of shorts featuring the top dance bands and brought films into even the smallest towns. Dozens of bands with national reputations crisscrossed the country, and the Hershey Park Ballroom became the leading dance floor in central Pennsylvania. Each band had its own distinctive style. It was no longer a question of whether Hershey Park should play a Rudy Vallee, but how to get the biggest and best national bands. John B. Sollenberger, the park manager, booked the best bands available. The Hershey Park Ballroom became one of the stops on almost every band's tour. They loved the ballroom and the town. It was a short trip from Philadelphia or New York, and the bands enjoyed the country atmosphere.

Harry James, who played one of the hottest trumpets on the swing circuit, and his orchestra opened the 1940 dance season in the ballroom on May 4, 1940. According to the park, it was the twenty-sixth season that Hershey management brought bands of nationwide reputation to the ballroom for the enjoyment of central Pennsylvania swing fans. (In the early years before national bands started touring, the park's ballroom played local bands.) Twenty-eight orchestras played the ballroom in the 1940 season. The most popular band of the early forties, Glenn Miller with his stars Marion Hutton, Ray Eberle, and "Tex" Beneke played the ballroom.

Local dance bands that appeared included bands led by Red McCarthy (who had purchased Ted Brownagle's orchestra), Irving Aaronson, Frankie Hanshaw, Bob Riley, Howard Gale, Phil Napoleon, Bill Marshall, Tiny Hill, Jimmy Livingston, and Henry Busse.

Dancing was sometimes a problem in the ballroom, despite its one hundred ninety foot length and forty foot width. The crowds were frequently so large that it was hard to move, let alone dance. Dances always started at 8:30 p.m. and ran until 12:30 a.m., except when Guy Lombardo played; then, for a reason no one really knew, the time was changed to 9:00 p.m. to 1:00 a.m.

An aerial view of Hershey Park with the park's ballroom to the left and swimming pool complex to the right, circa 1940's. In the foreground is the Sunken Garden. (HERSHEY COMMUNITY ARCHIVES)

Red McCarthy's Orchestra with guest soloists Tommy and Jimmy Dorsey. McCarthy was the closest Hershey Park came to having an in-house band.
(JIM McCARTHY COLLECTION)

There was a thirty-minute intermission when much of the crowd use to go out in front of the ballroom and take the miniature railway around the park. A special boarding platform was constructed near the ballroom for this purpose. Many couples rode the merry-go-round and The Wild Cat during the break.

Because of the number of dance bands booked in the ballroom each year, regular dancers saw the same band only twice a year at the most. During the late summer months, band members liked to play softball on the park's athletic field. Tommy Dorsey would come in ahead of time to play a game before going on at night. Others enjoyed the park's golf course and clubhouse.

Lombardo was rated by the ballroom staff as the best prepared of all the bands who played in the ballroom. He could arrive only fifteen minutes before the starting time, unload the bus, set up the equipment and begin on time looking like he had been there all day.

While the bands played on Wednesday and Saturday nights, the Hershey Sports Stadium continued to offer midget car racing on Monday and Thursday nights. The greatest midget auto drivers in the United States competed for cash prizes. The A.A.A. Blue Circuit ran every Monday night and the Red Circuit every Thursday night. Championship Roller Hockey debuted in the sports arena with a match featuring the Mt. Gretna Tigers, Western Division champs, meeting the Pottstown Bears. Roller hockey was similar to ice hockey, except that it was played on a wood floor with roller skates and a wooden puck.

The tenth annual Kiddie Week of Hershey Park was held August 26 to August 31, 1940. During the week, free shows were given daily in the band shell from Monday to Saturday at 3 and 7:30 p.m. by the Gangler Brothers Circus. The circus performances had a ringmaster and three clowns and an odd assortment of performing animals, including sixteen dogs, five monkeys, two ponies, and a baby leopard, goat, bear, and pig. Free admission to the zoo was given to all children twelve years old and younger. There were tickets given for free rides on the miniature railway, carousel, miniature airplane swings, and kiddie Ferris wheel. On Friday of Kiddie's Week the park held its fifth annual Baby Parade. A gold-plated trophy was presented to the "Cutest Baby." Fifteen other prizes totaling $102.50 were given redeemable in merchandise from the Hershey Department Store.

Many people from central Pennsylvania went to see the New York World's Fair, which was held in Flushing, New York, in 1939 and 1940. After it was over, most of the rides were sold to Luna Park, Coney Island, New York, and were operated under the blanket title of World's Fair of 1941. However, Hershey Park bought one ride, the Aerial Joy Ride, which became an immediate hit in the park.

Kenneth V. Hatt, who worked in the treasurer's office and who later became President of HERCO, recalled that Sollenberger went to New York City after the fair closed and purchased the ride for $25,000. Mr. Hershey was upset with Sollenberger, but when the ride paid for itself the first year, Hershey was grateful for the purchase. The ride was an important addition to the park's attractions, because once America entered the war, no new rides were manufactured.

The Aerial Joy Ride also helped the park get some publicity that summer. The *New Yorker* wrote, "the Aerial Joy Ride has been set up this summer on its [Hershey Park's] grounds in Hershey, Pennsylvania, so that the employees, between chocolate bars, can take spins in its small, earthbound planes."

The Aerial Joy Ride was a thrilling ride. It had a mast eighty feet high which was painted with rings of orange on a deep blue background and four pylons painted in blue and orange squares. Riders would sail through the air in long, graceful glides at dizzying speeds. The ride proved so popular that a great majority of the people remained in the airplane for a second ride.

In 1941 a new Souvenir and Park Administration Building replaced the old wooden structure, which was the park's first pavilion (main pavilion), built in 1905-06 and remodeled many times over the years. The new building, which was two stories high and had a basement, was constructed of reinforced con-

crete faced with light-gray and cream-colored brick. It was one hundred feet long by seventy feet wide. The basement was used for storage. The second floor housed the administrative offices of the park. Neon tubes circled the building, which was located in the very center of the old park.

Hershey Park's offices were in the new Souvenir and Park Administration Building, which was built in 1941.
(Hershey Community Archives)

The Aerial Joy Ride was brought to Hershey Park directly from the New York World's Fair of 1939-40.
(Hershey Community Archives)

Although Hershey was not well and was supposed to have a private nurse with him at all times, he still liked to go to the park. His limousine would pull right up to the park office. There he would get out and almost fly up the stairs of the new administrative offices asking "Where's George [Bartels]? Where's George?" Betty Bartels recalled. He would then go into Bartels' private office, and the two of them would be on their way down the back stairs, and out into the park, before his nurse could catch him. "Mr. Hershey was active till almost his last years," Betty Bartels said.

New roadways were built around the park, some of them forty feet wide. Spring Creek was cleaned of its winter refuse. Three steel bridges with reinforced concrete decks were built. One of them, a high-level bridge, was seventy-five feet long spanning the creek from the top of the hill near The Wild Cat to the hilltop at the Pretzel, eliminating many steps and making the spacious macadam parking lots at the stadium more accessible to the amusement park. The new bridge helped develop the rides (Aerial Joy Ride, Pretzel, shooting gallery, and kiddie rides) located on the hill north of the creek.

The Pretzel was remodeled along more modern lines. An American flag, illuminated with lights that blinked, was installed on the top of the band shell. More park police were added to the force in order to handle increased automobile traffic. There were now twelve highways leading into Hershey, and there were parking spaces for 20,000 automobiles.

M. S. Hershey and his private nurse on the boardwalk in Atlantic City in 1943. (Hershey Community Archives)

In addition to dancing, the penny arcades and games were extremely popular. The park added a number of new games and purchased many new machines and expanded the penny arcade. In the 1930's and early 1940's many new penny arcade machines had been developed. More of them were high tech with electric boards and electric photocells. Some of the games included fortune telling, grip, knockout fighters, punching bag, baseball, coast to coast driving, shoot down the airplane, and pin ball machine.

The park's penny arcade was practically doubled in size, making it one of the largest of its kind in the country. It occupied two complete floors, which totaled 12,000 square feet of space. Two new Skee Ball machines were purchased. A new game was Mow 'Em Down, a machine gun game in which pellet guns were used for fun only.

There were collector card machines in the arcade, which cost just one cent each. The machines dispensed cards of Hollywood movie stars, baseball and football players, and

The Mill Chute remained one of Hershey Park's most popular rides in the 1940's. (Hershey Community Archives)

cowboys. The cards were often outdated with personalities from the twenties rather than the forties. Some of the most popular cowboy cards were of Tom Mix, Buck Jones, Ken Maynard, Hoot Gibson, and Tim McCoy. The penny arcade also sold or gave away as prizes inexpensive novelties such as balls, whistles, rulers, fans, and cheap glass novelties; some had the name Hershey or Hershey Park printed on them.

Richard Hair, who later became general manager of the park, remembered his grandmother and grandfather taking him to the park on Sundays during the war. While they listened to the band concert in the Hershey Park Band Shell, he would go to the penny arcade. It truly was a penny arcade then; he could spend the whole afternoon there and not spend more than ten or fifteen cents.

In 1941, the park installed a new, rather unusual game called Mo-Skeet-O, which was skeet shooting in an enclosed area. It was located in the building at the rear of the candy kitchen and penny arcade, near the roller coaster on the east bank of Spring Creek, and the clay pigeons were hurled across the creek. Walls were erected to keep pellets from straying.

Since the park opened it had continued to add new parking areas. By 1941, the largest parking ground was between the Hershey Sports Arena and Hershey Stadium where there was room for two thousand cars. The second largest parking lot was north of the swimming pool complex where one thousand cars could be accommodated. Within Hershey Park, at the foot of Bowling Alley Hill on both sides of Spring Creek, three hundred cars could park. All of the parking places were free to the public with the exception of the Bowling Alley Hill parking area, where there was a charge of twenty-five cents on Sundays and holidays.

New stunts were added and the fun house's name was changed from Death Valley to Laugh Land. Laffing Sal, a mechanical laughing woman that had been purchased from the Philadelphia Toboggan Company, continued to entertain in the fun house. Similar animated figures were used to ballyhoo the Pretzel. Each figure was five feet ten inches high. A loud speaker was concealed in the base and an amplifier with a continuous-playing record of a laughing voice was used. Whoops, which was the name of the park's first fun house,

Death Valley was rethemed and became Laugh Land in 1940. A fun house had to emphasis laughing, not death, during the war. (Hershey Community Archives)

Laffing Sal was one of the mechanical figures whose head, arms, and body swayed in a shaking motion while a record played a laughing voice.
(Charles J. Jacques, Jr. Collection)

The Whoops front at night was the ballyhoo that helped to attract patrons.
(Hershey Community Archives)

remained, and some new tricks were added. Some of the games included Lucky Kick and Spill the Milk. Lucky Kick was manufactured by PTC; balls were thrown at a wooden horse that would buck if the target was hit.

The swimming pools remained open during the war. Betty Bartels recalled, "In high school we swam Saturday night because you could lie on the beach and listen to the bands. We were too young to get into the ballroom, so it was the next best way to hear the bands."

The swimming pool complex remained open during the war. Swimmers liked to sit on the fence that separated the shallow pool from the deep pool. (Hershey Community Archives)

The zoo set two new attendance records in 1941 when 12,338 people visited it on August 10. Just a few days later, on August 17, 13,289 people visited the zoo, both days topping the previous record of 12,004 set July 4, 1936.

In the summer of 1941, there was fighting in Europe as well as Asia, although America was not yet in the war. However, the country was preparing for one. In 1941, Defense Bonds were sold at the Hershey Post Office and Hershey National Bank. Aluminum was collected for airplanes as part of the National Defense Aluminum Collection. Canadian players began leaving the Hershey Bears Hockey Club to join the Canadian armed forces. The United States Army started training troops in nearby Indiantown Gap, Pa. These soldiers and their families soon became park patrons. America entered the war on December 8, 1941, the day after the Japanese bombed Pearl Harbor.

Earlier in his life M.S. Hershey had traveled widely. Now in his mid-eighties he could no longer travel as he once did. In good weather, he spent a lot of time on the flagstone porch of Hotel Hershey looking out over the Lebanon Valley and the town he had built. He seldom read books, but he was an avid newspaper reader. He followed the war in his favorite newspapers: in the morning *The New York Times*, and the *Philadelphia Inquirer* and in the evening the *New York Sun, New York World-*

Telegram, and the *Philadelphia Evening Bulletin*. For local and state news he read the *Harrisburg Patriot, Harrisburg News*, and *Harrisburg Telegraph*.

The war would temporarily slow the growth of the park, but people were still eating chocolate bars. Sales of the chocolate corporation topped $55 million in 1941. The United States Government started using Hershey's Chocolate Bars as one of the emergency rations for troops.

On May 2, 1942, Vaughn Monroe and his orchestra opened the twenty-eighth season of dancing at the Hershey Park Ballroom. No one knew how the war would affect the ballroom. America had been at war for five months, and John B. Sollenberger did not know if people still wanted to go to dances. Vaughn Monroe was an up-and-coming band leader with a good baritone voice. He had attended Carnegie Tech in Pittsburgh and had just recently organized his band. About 2,000 people were expected, and 4,500 showed up.

For many dancers it was the last chance to come to the park's ballroom before mandatory gas rationing began on May 15. Others, both men and women, would be leaving for the armed forces shortly. Attendance dropped after the first dance. During the war, getting to the park became harder and harder. Automobiles were not manufactured during the war; tires were almost impossible to purchase; gasoline rationing hurt Hershey Park more than the urban parks because many people had to drive to get to the park.

During the war, the Philadelphia and Reading Railroad cut out all reduced-rate train service to the park, but most of the Hershey Transit System was still in operation, bringing workers to the factory and families to the park.

The Ringgold Band of Reading, Robert Mattern directing, played two concerts in Hershey Park's band shell on July 19, 1942. Patriotic numbers dominated the program, and both programs closed with "The Star-Spangled Banner."

The United States Army closed the Hershey Chocolate Corporation's plant to all visitors in July 1942. Through 1941, 668,000 people had visited the plant to see how cocoa and chocolate were made. For many years, the factory's visitors had exceeded those touring the White House, which was also closed during the war.

M.S. Hershey at his home in High Point with his cigar and newspaper in the 1940's.
(Charles J. Jacques, Jr. Collection)

Brad Cassady, who was working part-time at the swimming pool complex, recalled, "At the beginning of the war, the soldiers used to come down from Indiantown Gap to Hershey for the weekend. They did not cause trouble, but they did cause confusion. They would come to the park and rent boats and canoes and they would play around and go over the dam and be soaked."

The Whip was covered and became the Whipperoo.
(Hershey Community Archives)

the other buildings were converted into housing for people, which was badly needed during and immediately following the war. The zoo closed because it lacked experienced personnel to care for the animals and birds.

Sollenberger wrote to Brady McSwigan, president of Kennywood Park in Pittsburgh, on March 26, 1943, "At the present time we haven't made plans for the season. Even though the pleasure driving ban is off, the amount of gasoline available for pleasure driving is very, very small and if we operate at all it will be on a much curtailed basis." Due to the shortage of workers, the park shortened its hours, and it did not open until one in the afternoon.

Hershey Park offered special rates for service men in uniform (except Sundays and holidays). All regular 10 and 15 cent tickets were sold at half price to men in uniform. The United States Department of State took over Hotel Hershey in December of 1942.

The Hershey Park Zoo was closed December 20, 1942, with a public statement by its director, Ward R. Walker, "that the zoo was to be opened after the war, bigger and better than ever." All of the animals and birds were sold, lent, or donated to other zoos in the United States. Some of the empty zoo buildings were used to raise domestic chickens and ducks for the war effort. Some of

Hershey Chocolate Corporation received the Army-Navy "E" production award for creation of Ration "D," an emergency ration for fighting men. The Hershey Chocolate Corporation was given priority to continue to produce chocolate for the armed services and for home consumption during the war.

More women entered the work force and many found wartime jobs at the chocolate factory. Sugar, meat, fruits,

M.S. Hershey petting the baby elephant in the zoo. The zoo was closed in late 1942 for the duration of the war.
(Hershey Community Archives)

Long rows of picnic tables were set up along Spring Creek. People would reserve a spot by leaving their picnic baskets on a table.
(Hershey Community Archives)

vegetables, fats, and cheese were rationed. People even needed ration stamps to buy a pair of shoes. *Hotel Hershey High-Lights* noted, "Rationing means a fair share for all of us."

Sollenberger was shocked when the United States Office of Price Administration announced in early May 1943 that automobiles could no longer be driven to places of amusement. He was forced to close the ballroom. Sollenberger felt that until there was sufficient gasoline to bring people from distances there was no point in trying to keep the ballroom open. It was a tremendous blow to the park. It was the first time in twenty-nine years that the ballroom was "dark" during the season.

Between 1933 and 1942 seventy-three national orchestras played in the ballroom. Leading the list were Mal Hallett and Guy Lombardo who played eight times; Casa Loma, Tommy Dorsey, Gene Krupa, and Ozzie Nelson—seven; Benny Goodman—six; Bob Crosby, Jimmy Dorsey, Felix Ferdinando and Hal Kemp—five; Mitchell Ayres, Charlie Baret, Jan Savitt, George Hall, Artie Shaw, Ted Lewis (wearing his old battered silk hat), and Jack Denny—four. Together 176 different orchestras played in the Hershey Park ballroom in the ten years from 1933 to 1942.

Because of the shortage of employees, the park cut its activities to the lowest level it could and still continue to operate. Starting in June 1943, the park closed on Mondays,

except for people who just wanted to picnic. Edwin P. James of Corning, New York, wrote a letter which appeared in the *Hotel Hershey High-Lights*, "Until the present summer I have come to Hershey many times during the year, usually for some particular entertainment. I hope that gasoline rationing will soon be a thing of the past so that we may drive to Hershey again."

The driving ban for entertainment and recreation was lifted in the fall of 1943. Therefore, Hershey Park Ballroom was able to open for its twenty-ninth year in 1944 with Tony Pastor's orchestra. People were becoming used to rationing and regulations. Many doubled up to save gasoline and wear on their tires when they came to the park or the ballroom.

During the war the electric fountain with its 65 foot high center spray and special lighting effects was illuminated only on Saturday, Sunday, and holiday nights. The Aerial Joy Ride, one of the park's most popular amusements, was repainted in the patriotic colors of red, white, and blue.

Free band concerts continued in Hershey Park. Because of the war the number of people attending dwindled on weekdays, but, according to the *Hotel Hershey High-Lights*, some Sundays more than ten thousand came to the park. Long rows of benches, which could accommodate 3,000 people, were set up under the trees. Others preferred to listen to the music sitting on the grass.

The park purchased Philadelphia Toboggan Carousel #41 in 1944.
(Photograph by Charles J. Jacques, Jr.)

lacked an attendant, so he took his place behind the counter as a mother and several children looked over the selection. He sold them four five-cent candy bars. The family didn't recognize him.

For Hershey Park's fortieth anniversary in 1944 (Sollenberger had shifted the year the park was founded from 1907 back to 1905 for this anniversary) the park purchased a merry-go-round, PTC #41, from the Philadelphia Toboggan Company. The park had not purchased a ride since the war had begun, and buying a used one from PTC was the only way it could get something "new."

The carousel had been manufactured by PTC in 1919. Since it had been built during World War I, the merry-go-round had Miss Liberty and American Flags on the outer rim. It was first placed in Liberty Heights Park, Baltimore, Maryland. Ten years later in 1929, it was moved to Enna Jettick Park, Auburn, New

These band concerts offered a wide variety of music including classical, marches, popular, show tunes, and during the war, more patriotic music.

In June 1944, M.S. Hershey, despite his eighty-six years, helped the manpower effort by selling candy in the park. He noticed that one of the candy counters

The decorative panels were painted by Gustav Weiss. The folk art panels were done in oil on canvas.
(Photographs by Charles J. Jacques, Jr.)

York. During the war Jettick Park closed and PTC, which owned it, needed to find a new place to operate it.

The new merry-go-round was a four-row model with sixty-six horses, considerably larger than the old Dentzel machine, which had only fifty-two animals. The PTC carousel had 1,788 electric lights on it, while the old carousel had 400 bulbs. The park had proudly proclaimed that the old carousel turned at the rate of seven times a minute; the new one made nine revolutions per minute.

PTC #41 had an outside row of stationary horses and three inner rows of jumpers (there were a few small stationary horses on the inside beside the chariots). The horses had many unusual trappings including a prancing hunter, carnival, cavalry,

Several coats of high gloss damar varnish were used to protect the color coat. Unfortunately, this varnish would turn brown on white horses.
(Photograph by Charles J. Jacques, Jr.)

cowboy, rodeo, and circus horse. On the ceiling of the PTC carousel were painted scenes from the outdoors, particularly with butterflies, birds, and flowers.

The outer rim of the new carousel was magnificent. While the Dentzel machine had a few small painted panels on its rim, the new one featured Miss Liberty as seen in two positions with a shield of the USA and the flag draped over her shoulder. Opposite was the eagle, an emblematic symbol of America.

Between the two figures was a mirror. There were a number of patriot eagles on the inner paneling.

There were a dozen folk art paintings on the inside panels of the carousel: a Dutch seaside scene, a mother and child at a brook, a cow and its calf in a meadow, the feeding of ducks, a man riding with his ladylove on a white horse, children and dogs on a seesaw, mother and children leaving home for a walk, a Bavarian home and family with rabbits playing about, a Spanish

The Philadelphia Toboggan Company reconditioned the carousel before delivering it to the park.
(Photograph by Charles J. Jacques, Jr.)

Harry James and his orchestra appeared in the Hershey Park Ballroom Wednesday, July 25, 1945. Admission for dancers was $2.40, spectators $1.20, and service personnel $1.50.
(HERSHEY COMMUNITY ARCHIVES)

Harry James on the trumpet with Kitty Kallen and Buddy DeVito, the band's vocalists.
(HERSHEY COMMUNITY ARCHIVES)

bullfight, and sisters feeding geese.

In the amusement park industry, it was customary for the larger, better known parks to buy the biggest and best carousels. By purchasing a four-row carousel manufactured by the Philadelphia Toboggan Company, Hershey Park was indicating that it was not insignificant, but it was a park with a national reputation, a famous ballroom, beautifully landscaped grounds, and now one of the few four-row carousels in America.

The park's Dentzel carousel was dismantled to make room for the new carousel. It was sold to an amusement park in Ohio. The merry-go-round that had given so much pleasure to thousands of children and adults supposedly later operated at Knott's Berry Farm in California.

Harry James, the king of the trumpet, and his orchestra of thirty-four musicians and entertainers appeared in the Hershey Park Ballroom in 1945. It was the orchestra leader's fifth appearance and he held the record for the largest and second largest crowds in the ballroom. The orchestra requested "twenty double rooms and one suite in the Community Inn, and also the use of the baseball diamond in Hershey Park." James was a baseball fan and perhaps one reason why he carried so many musicians was because he wanted to be sure of fielding two baseball nines.

The Wild Cat roller coaster ran for the last time in September 1945. In its twenty-two years, it had carried millions of passengers and had been the signature ride of the park since 1923. Wood was so hard to find during the war that if the park

had wanted to continue to operate The Wild Cat after the war, it would have had to completely rebuild its structure.

On October 14, 1945, one month after his eighty-eighth birthday, Milton Snavely Hershey died. In one final tribute to its founder, the town of Hershey came to a standstill the day of his funeral. There were hundreds of baskets and sprays from his employees and friends, mostly of red roses, his favorite flowers.

Hershey, who will always be remembered for his philanthropy, commented shortly before his death to Alexander Stoddart about the extent of his giving, "Not bad, eh, a million a year!" He was eighty-seven years old at the time.

Later, Stoddart would write the following tribute to his boss:

Over the years trees grew in and around The Wild Cat.
(HERSHEY COMMUNITY ARCHIVES)

He knew what it meant to be poor, he was more than acquainted with hard work, he experienced failure when starting out in business for himself after he learned his trade as a confectioner, but he also knew the sweetness of success and the great responsibilities that go with great wealth.

Before Hershey went out into the world to earn his living, his mother Fanny Hershey had told him to stick to a job until he mastered it. M.S. Hershey mastered many jobs in his lifetime. One of them was building one of the finest, most distinctive, and most beautiful amusement parks in America.

The Wild Cat remained in operation throughout the war. It carried hundreds of thousands of passengers in the 1940's.
(HERSHEY COMMUNITY ARCHIVES)

Founders Hall, Hershey, Pennsylvania, was dedicated to the memory of M.S. Hershey on September 11, 1970.
(HERSHEY COMMUNITY ARCHIVES)

M.S. Hershey knew the sweetness of success.
(Hershey Community Archives)

CHAPTER 9

HERSHEY'S COMET

During the winter of 1945-46, the sounds of workmen's hammers and electric drills and saws could be heard throughout the Spring Creek Valley as Hershey Park built a new roller coaster, The Comet. The foreman, Frank Hoover of the Philadelphia Toboggan Company, hired local carpenters to construct the new sixty thousand dollar coaster. Hershey Park announced that "The Comet was the biggest coaster in the United States."

This time Herbert P. Schmeck, general manager of PTC, designed a truly great coaster. He was assisted by a young engineer, Thomas S. James, who worked for PTC. Twenty-three years earlier Schmeck designed and built The Wild Cat, but it never lived up to his expectation. He was given a second chance in October 1945 when Sollenberger and the Philadelphia Toboggan Company entered into an agreement to build and jointly own the new coaster.

This time Schmeck's design was built high enough above the creek to prevent damage during floods. The Comet was 3,360 feet long, one thousand feet longer than The Wild Cat, and 248,919 board feet of treated Douglas fir were used in its construction. The Comet was located a little further downstream than The Wild Cat in the western section of the park, and The Comet, like The Wild Cat before it, crossed Spring Creek twice. However, the loading station was located on

Wide-angle shot of The Comet coaster shortly after completion in 1946. The Bug and Auto Skooter are in the foreground.

(CHARLES J. JACQUES, JR. COLLECTION)

the opposite or northern side of the creek. The new coaster then crossed the creek on steel "I" beams and up a hill to the miniature railway tracks and Park Boulevard. This coaster was built so close to town that its riders' screams could be heard on Chocolate Avenue. It then recrossed the creek and traveled around the loading station with a number of dips. The finish was a series of hills or bunny hops that skirted the baseball field with a turn-around and then the home run stretch to the brake curve and loading station.

The Comet's first drop (sometimes called the chocolate drop) was ninety-six feet, and its second drop of seventy-two feet was almost as high as The Wild Cat's first drop. The coaster featured a series of aeroplane curves (curves that dropped while turning) on the third and the fourth runs, which made a more exciting ride. The coaster had three trains made up of four three-seat cars; the ride lasted one minute and forty-five seconds.

The new coaster's structure, like The Wild Cat's, was painted green. The new coaster's pavilion, which had a marquee-rim and wainscoting below the platform and ramps, was painted a pale blue. The ceiling under the marquee was painted light ivory and the handrails and top plate of all fences was done in a permanent blue. A sign for The Comet, which was painted Chinese red, was manufactured by PTC in Philadelphia and shipped to the site.

Park visitors waited in line for their first ride on **The Comet in June 1946. The loading station was still under construction.** (Hershey Community Archives)

The first drop of The Comet was onto a bridge that crossed Spring Creek. (Hershey Community Archives)

The Comet was an immediate success. In its first year of operation approximately 500,000 passengers rode it at twenty-five cents a ride. The Comet was the best coaster in central Pennsylvania, and it enabled the park to compete with other amusement parks in Allentown, Lancaster, and Philadelphia. The PTC carousel and The Comet would remain the heart of the park into the 1990's.

At the same time that The Comet was under construction, renovation began on the Mill Chute, the only major water ride in the central Pennsylvania area. Schmeck's concrete channels made the ride almost indestructible, and it would continue to serve the park for many more years. The Mill Chute and The Comet were owned by the Associated Amusement Company that was owned 51 percent by the Philadelphia Toboggan Company and 49 percent by Hershey Estates. The new company was given a ten-year operating lease by Hershey Park.

A year later the Philadelphia Toboggan Company sold Hershey Park a Cuddle Up ride, which was placed on the site formerly occupied by The Wild Cat's loading station. The Cuddle Up was a large fourteen-car model with each car carrying four people. It zig-zagged in a concentric motion with the cars spinning and looking like they would collide at any second.

Milton Hershey was gone, but Sollenberger and Bartels, who had guided the park since the late 1920's, were still in charge. This was a period during which amusement parks did not change much. Dance pavilions and coasters remained the

The Cuddle Up was built on the site where The Wild Cat's loading station formerly stood. (Hershey Community Archives)

The Hershey Park Rail Road (miniature railway) station was located next to the Whipperoo.
(Hershey Community Archives)

The park had two fun houses in the 1940's. One was Laugh Land, shown above; the other one, built after the war, was placed in the old penny arcade building on the hill.
(Hershey Community Archives)

biggest draws, and Hershey Park was well positioned with its ballroom and The Comet.

The end of the war spelled the finish of Hershey's trolleys. The war had extended the system's life by two or three years, but the final run was made on December 21, 1946. The trolleys were replaced by buses, which were owned by the Reading Street Railway Company. Regular scheduled bus service lasted only a few years before the service closed. However, school buses and chartered buses remained an important way of getting people to the park. Trains continued to decline as a means of transporting passengers to Hershey. The new highways, coupled with inexpensive cars and gasoline, became the principal way of commuting to the park.

In 1946, the Philadelphia Toboggan Company also built a new fun house that replaced the Whoops which had been demolished to make room for The Comet. The new fun house was placed in the old arcade building. The ballyhoo was provided by balconies on the second floor that had "lily pads" with water under them, which people stumbled over, and air valves for blowing dresses up. Inside the building was a dark walk-through section, which was painted a flat black. It had a series of stunts including a luminous spot with spiral threads, vibrating floor, air horn, grotesque heads, and floor air valves. Special fluorescent paint and blacklight lamps were also used on the stunts. The first floor of the fun house had a bowl, roulette wheel, barrel, and ballyhoo stage. Six or eight laughing

mirrors were purchased from National Amusement Devices.

Mary Hubler, a longtime resident of the town of Hershey, recalled The Comet and the fun house in the late-1940's:

The Comet: "Oh, it was just wonderful. We thought we'd never get up to that top hill to fly down. And it really takes your breath when you go down the big hill, then go up and around. When you go around you have to lean over, you know. We had a ball! It was just wonderful! It gave you a thrill. Everybody wants to ride The Comet. There was a line up there all the time."

The fun house: "You go in through mazes and different things pop out at you. And then when you would get out on a big porch, and the women would walk out there, and there goes your skirt up!"

The penny arcade was moved to the main floor of the restaurant building and renamed Sportland. Business in the old restaurant had steadily declined, and the park was no longer making money on waitress-served, sit-down meals. A photo machine and Skee Ball alleys were added to the new arcade.

Aware of the trend toward larger families in the postwar years, Hershey Park tried to increase its school and picnic business. Sollenberger wrote Brady McSwigan of Kennywood

The Aerial Joy Ride was located on the hill near the arena. It remained in the park into the 1960's.
(NEIL FASNACHT COLLECTION)

Park in 1947, "I would like to have our picnic representative, Lloyd Blinco, call on you next week in Pittsburgh. We are very much interested in the method you use to get school outings from around Pittsburgh to your park in the early season."

A new air rifle range was built between Funland and the Lucky Kick game and a new refreshment stand was built below The Comet near the Whippero. The hottest item on the food menu was French fries sold in paper cups from a window in the Souvenir Building. The Skooter was upgraded, and twenty-five new cars replaced the older ones.

The toboggan slide, built by the park in 1931, was dismantled, and the walkway under the ballroom was closed. Sun bathing was permitted on the white sand alongside the swimming pools as well as in the Sunken Garden area.

Hershey Chocolate Corporation resumed its plant tour

after the war. In 1946 more than thirty-seven thousand people visited the factory. In the 1950's the number rose to more than one hundred thousand people annually. The tour became an important part of any trip to Hershey. Many picnic groups would walk over to the factory to go through the plant and get a Hershey's Bar.

John B. Sollenberger, who was very fastidious, insisted on neat dress in the ballroom. Slacks were banned for women, and the men were required to wear coats and neckties. If a man showed up wearing a sport shirt and no tie and still wanted to dance, the management sold him a tie for fifty cents. During the dance intermissions couples would stroll hand-in-hand through the Sunken Garden just across Park Boulevard from the ballroom and view the colorful electric fountain display.

Hershey Park Ballroom had one of its greatest lineups of

Hershey's Air Park was located across Airport Road where park patrons could get a view of the park from the air.
(HERSHEY COMMUNITY ARCHIVES)

nationally famous orchestras in 1947. Between May 3 and September 7, the following orchestras appeared: Tommy Tucker, Jan Garber, Carmen Cavallaro, Harry James, Bob Chester, Sammy Kaye, Buddy Rich, Jimmy Dorsey, Shorty Sherock, Bob Raeburn, Tex Beneke, Vincent Lopez, Charlie Spivak, Louis Prima, Claude Thornhill, Vaughn Monroe, Hal McIntyre, Les Brown, and Guy Lombardo, who closed the season.

Vaughn Monroe's appearance on August 23, 1947, marked the high water mark of the big band era in the Hershey Park Ballroom. That evening 6,945 people paid to see Monroe and his band. It topped the previous high mark of 6,194 set by Harry James on July 8, 1944. It marked the first and only time in the thirty-three year history of the ballroom that the sale of tickets was stopped and people were turned away. Ballroom management felt that it would have been uncomfortable to have any more people on the dance floor.

Several pro and college football games were played in the Hershey Sports Stadium. In 1947 a preseason game between the Baltimore Colts and the Buffalo Bills of the All-American Conference took place. In 1948 The Boston Yanks and Chicago Bears of the National Football League played in the Hershey Stadium, as did the New York Bulldogs and Detroit Lions one year later. For several years the Philadelphia Eagles's first preseason football game was held in the stadium. The Eagles and the Pittsburgh Steelers set the stadium attendance mark in 1951 when they played to a standing room crowd of 18,526 people.

Some of the band leaders complained about having to compete with football games at the stadium. The leaders objected to the games, saying they drew too many people away from the dances, and they requested better scheduling. But the orchestras were still paid a guaranteed minimum of between fifteen hundred dollars and two thousand dollars no matter how few people came to a dance.

In the late-1940's canoeists could paddle under the new concrete bridge across Spring Creek. In the background is The Comet.
(HERSHEY COMMUNITY ARCHIVES)

Stan Kenton's Band Coming to Hershey

Stan Kenton brings his band to Hershey Park ballroom tomorrow night.

During his current dance tour, Kenton is introducing the orchestra's new vocalist, Jerri Winters. Miss Winters, former model and dancing instructor, replaces the popular June Christy, who left Kenton to resume her career as a single.

Free concerts in the park bandshell on Sunday will be played by the New Cumberland American Legion Band. Concerts will be presented at 2 and 7 p. m. In case of rain, concerts will be transferred to the park theater.

In the arena, a baby passing the judges' table in the Baby Parade of 1950. (Hershey Community Archives)

The park's high level bridge, which was built in the 1940's, was used by many people to get to the Hershey Sports Arena. (Hershey Community Archives)

The free outdoor playgrounds remained popular during the late 1940's. (Hershey Community Archives)

In September 1947 Penn State played a regular season home football game in Hershey's stadium. The opponent was Washington State University of the Pacific Coast Conference. Penn State won that year 27 to 6 and went on to tie Doak Walker's Southern Methodist team in the Cotton Bowl. Penn State alumni in the Harrisburg area often held their picnics in Hershey Park with the first one being booked in 1919.

In 1947 and 1948 an amateur jamboree program was broadcast live from the Hershey Park Band Shell on Sunday evenings over radio stations WCMB of Lemoyne and WLBR of Lebanon. George Bartels told *Billboard*, the stations installed an applause meter on the stage, and had two disinterested parties watch the meter as judge. "For prizes we gave items such as bicycles, portable radios, cameras, baseball equipment, and other items of this type," he said.

In 1947 an audience of about three thousand attended the eleventh annual Baby Parade in the Hershey Sports Arena. Up until that year the event had been held outdoors. It took the one hundred seventy contestants approximately one hour to parade before the judges and the audience. Prizes (merchandise from the Hershey Department Store) for the annual parade included $10 and a trophy to the cutest; cutest twins, $10; cutest triplets, $10; best decorated float carrying baby, $10; second best decorated float carrying baby, $7.50; most original float carrying baby, $10; best fancy costume, $7.50; best comic costume, $7.50; and most original costume, $7.50.

Hershey Park's advertising for 1948 returned to an old slogan "The Summer Playground of Pennsylvania." Lloyd Longenecker and his orchestra opened the park on May 16 with a free band concert. Other orchestras that appeared that summer in the band shell included Ed Hall, Red McCarthy, Reg Kehoe, Howard Gale, and Frank Taylor.

Hershey Park provided tables, benches, and pavilions to seat 5,000 people, and there were lawns everywhere for those who preferred to spread the table cloth underneath a tree. For picnickers, the park offered cords of free wood and stoves.

Approximately forty thousand visitors, including eight thousand students, were admitted to the Hershey Museum in 1948. One of the most valuable possessions of the museum was the collection of 146 pieces of Stiegel glass made by Henry William Stiegel, colonial glass maker. The museum also had a collection of stoves and stove plates from 1758 and 1769.

Two new kiddie rides were introduced in 1949: a horse-and-buggy ride and a water ride with eight boats in an oblong channel of water. All of the rides for youngsters were put into

Hershey Park's famous miniature railway with a train load of passengers.
(Hershey Community Archives)

The Pennsylvania Dutch Days promotion started in 1949. In this picture people are making apple butter.
(Hershey Community Archives)

Kiddieland (sometimes called Kiddie Land), which was located near the arena.

Two notable groups that performed at Hershey Park for the first time were the Harrisburg Symphony Orchestra under the direction of George King Raudenbush, and the Syracuse A Cappella Choir, directed by John T. Clough. Programs were given at the Hershey Park Band Shell.

One of the park's most successful promotions, Pennsylvania Dutch Days, got its start when the Hershey Evening School in 1948 offered a class on the Pennsylvania Dutch dialect. The following year it was "shussel off" (leave for) Hershey Park on

August 27, 1949, for the first Pennsylvania Dutch Day. Numerous exhibits of Pennsylvania German arts and crafts were displayed in the Hershey Sports Arena. Included were the seven sweets and the seven sours of food, Pennsylvania Dutch weaving, metal work, pottery, apple butter making, quilting, and Pennsylvania Dutch art. The first event attracted 25,000 people and it was decided to expand and repeat it the next year.

On major holidays the park presented free circus acts in an area between Pennyland and Funland called Hershey Park Plaza. The first act was The Four Fantions, an aerial act, which appeared on July 3, 1949. On Labor Day the park presented Lambertis, motorcycle maniacs, who did their daring act high in the air with a unique motorcycle and trapeze suspension combination.

Hershey Estates purchased a new electronic organ, which was used in the band shell from May through Labor Day and then moved into the arena for the indoor season. The first band shell concert on July 19, 1948, featured Mitchell Grand at the console.

In 1949 Charles F. Ziegler retired as president of Hershey Estates and was succeeded by John B. Sollenberger. In addition to an amusement park, arena, stadium, museum, and rose garden, Hershey Estates owned and operated the Hotel Hershey, Community Inn, and a department store, lumber company, feed mill, farm implement business, abattoir, laundry, dry cleaner, candy kitchen, nursery, green house, dairy, and real estate business. The park was the largest customer for many of these

In the early 1950's the park purchased two Ferris wheels that it operated in tandem. The baby boomers were now coming to the park. (HERSHEY COMMUNITY ARCHIVES)

To build up attendance, Sollenberger and Bartels kept prices low. They did not raise prices for over ten years, until inflation became too strong in the 1950's. Bartels told *Billboard*, "it is important to make visitors feel welcome regardless of how much or how little money they spend." Through the years, Hershey Park had maintained a reputation for a quiet atmosphere. Bartels felt that without any concessionaires there was less high-pressure hawking, which let patrons relax.

In the postwar years, the park had 225 full and part time employees, who were mostly school teachers and students. Twenty-two persons, not counting office help and executives, were employed by the park and arena throughout the year. Bartels was assisted by Lloyd Blinco, whose primary job was handling picnic bookings. The park advertised in an eighty-mile radius. Newspapers and radio stations were the primary methods used.

The Hershey Zoo reopened on May 7, 1950, with Clarence E. Moose as director and Raleigh Hughes as his assistant. The zoo now operated on a much smaller scale than before World War II. Many of the zoo's buildings had been converted to other uses, and no new ones were built. This time the zoo concentrated on a collection of rhesus monkeys placed in a large circular glass cage, which was fitted with a gym bar, trapeze, swings, a circular hoop, and two rings suspended on a chain. Some of the other animals and birds displayed included antelopes, black bear, llamas, bison, a fox wolf (which was donated by the Philadelphia Zoo), raccoons, squirrels, deodorized skunks,

businesses and without the park some of them would not have shown a profit.

George Bartels succeeded Sollenberger as general manager of the park, arena, stadium, ballroom, swimming pools, and golf club. Both Sollenberger and Bartels were thrifty Dutchmen who knew the value of money. George Bartels liked to say he and Sollenberger "built a million dollar industry from nickels and dimes and quarters."

Bartels had begun working for M.S. Hershey in 1916 right out of Hummelstown High School. He held various jobs in the accounting department until he became assistant to Sollenberger in 1931. Bartels was a serious person who made sure he knew what was going on in the park at all times. The park was small enough that the cigar-chomping general manager could still run the whole show. George Bartels' daughter, Betty, recalled "the park was his life, hobby, vocation, and avocation. He spent as many as eighteen hours a day in the park."

George Bartels became general manager of the park in 1949 when John B. Sollenberger became president of Hershey Estates.
(HERSHEY COMMUNITY ARCHIVES)

A long time favorite, Guy Lombardo, appeared in the Hershey Park Ballroom as part of the town of Hershey's fiftieth anniversary celebration.
(HERSHEY COMMUNITY ARCHIVES)

HERSHEY PARK
THE SUMMER PLAYGROUND OF PENNSYLVANIA
(AMUSEMENT FOR THE WHOLE FAMILY)

...HERSHEY PARK BANDSHELL....
Sun., May 28—JOHNNY BARKER & His Orchestra
CONCERTS SUNDAYS and HOLIDAYS
2 to 4 P.M. and 7 to 9 P.M., D.S.T.

DON'T MISS . . . . . THE
AERIAL SENSATIONS
(May 28th thru June 3rd)
PARK ATHLETIC FIELD — Twice Daily
FEATURING
RICARDO AND GRACIE ORTON

MEMORIAL DAY
TUESDAY, MAY 30th
Guy Lombardo & His Orchestra
(The Sweetest Music This Side of Heaven)
IN THE
HERSHEY PARK BALLROOM
Adm. Dancers—$1.50; Spectators $.79, plus tax
Dancing 8:30 P.M. to 12:30 A.M., D.S.T.

HERSHEY PARK BANDSHELL	HERSHEY AIR PARK
Tuesday, May 30th	FLIGHTS DAILY
Specialty Entertainment	See Hershey and Beautiful
BREININGER'S	Lebanon Valley from the Air.
MARIMBA BAND	
Hours	Dine at Hershey
2 to 4 and 7 to 9 P.M., D.S.T.	HOTEL HERSHEY
It's Rose Time	COMMUNITY DINING
During Month of June, at	ROOM & CAFETERIA
Famous	COMMUNITY INN
HERSHEY GARDENS	OYSTER BAR & GRILL
! ! Play Golf ! !	! ! POOL ! !
Hershey Park Golf Club	
NOW OPEN	OPENS SATURDAY, MAY 27th

Lombardo waits for a signal from the radio engineers before starting to play. (HERSHEY COMMUNITY ARCHIVES)

Chinese geese, owls, pheasants, hawks, and a black crow known as "Doc" who could say "Hello."

In the early 1950's the park purchased two Ferris wheels from Eli Bridge of Jacksonville, Illinois. They were large, sixty-six foot-high models and could hold thirty-two adults each in their sixteen cars.

On Memorial Day 1952, Hershey Park offered two band concerts. One was in the afternoon with Reg Kehoe and his Marimba Band, and the other in the evening with the Pottstown Band. Vaughn Monroe and The Camel Caravan played in the ballroom. Dancing cost one dollar fifty cents for dancers and seventy-five cents for spectators.

The town celebrated its fiftieth anniversary in 1953 with the U.S. Navy Band appearing at the Hershey Park Band Shell.

Guy Lombardo performed in the ballroom. Free aerial acts were presented on the park's athletic field at 4:30 and 8:30 p.m. There was another professional football game at Hershey Stadium that summer (August 22, 1953) between the Philadelphia Eagles and the Chicago Bears.

Albertus L. Myers, who had been a member of John Philip Sousa's band and longtime director of the Allentown Band, composed a march which he dedicated to M.S. Hershey. His musical composition called "The Chocolate King March," was introduced by the Allentown Band on August 16, 1953.

Les Elgart played the ballroom in July 1954. The *Hershey News* commented that his band seemed destined "to restore the orchestra business to something of its former glory." Musical tastes were changing in America and the bands were not drawing younger people. By the mid-1950's the park was using the ballroom only one night a week. Rock and roll had replaced big bands on many radio stations. Sollenberger and Bartels and most of the other amusement park owners whose parks had ballrooms did not know how to deal with this new trend.

In the 1950's many young families were coming to Hershey Park. The baby boomers had arrived and the park's kiddie rides were crowded. The Comet and other thrill rides were still

The midway at Hershey Park in the late 1940's with the Mill Chute and The Comet in the foreground and The Bug, Auto Skooter, and Whippero in the background.
(Hershey Community Archives)

popular, but ballroom dancing was no longer attracting teenagers and young adults. For almost forty years Hershey Park had depended on dancing to attract patrons, but now these crowds were dwindling. A change was needed.

In the mid-1950's Hershey Estates added a miniature golf course and driving range northwest of the swimming pool complex.
(Hershey Community Archives)

CHAPTER 10

A NEW STANDARD

The main entrance to the park had changed little in forty years, except that the trees had grown.
(HERSHEY COMMUNITY ARCHIVES)

Through the 1950's into the 1960's the park used the slogan— "The Summer Playground of Pennsylvania"–on billboards in and around Harrisburg. (CHARLES J. JACQUES, JR. COLLECTION)

The opening of Disneyland on July 18, 1955, changed the amusement park industry forever. A national television audience watched as each section of the park was unveiled. The public's perceptions of what an amusement park should look like changed dramatically that day. Many children from Hershey and central Pennsylvania would now dream of someday visiting Disneyland. What was a dream to children proved to be a series of hard lessons for people in the amusement park industry.

Although Disney's television program made the new opening look smooth, Disneyland was far from perfect and needed some refining. Disney experienced a shortage of capital during construction, and some compromises had to be made. Local newspapers complained about long lines and high prices, but the public loved the new park, and things that were not right were soon corrected.

Milton Snavely Hershey and Walter Elias Disney were similar in many ways. Both of them suffered through early failures, but both kept on trying. Both of their names became

As the pools aged, more tar was needed in the cracks to keep the pools from leaking.
(HERSHEY COMMUNITY ARCHIVES)

known worldwide and are still synonymous with the products they developed. Each dominated an American industry: Hershey in producing chocolate and Disney in making animated cartoons. Disney, like Hershey, was willing to risk everything to develop an idea. When Disney announced in 1953 that he was going to build an amusement park in Anaheim, California, some people called him foolish. Why would Disney build an amusement park in an "orange grove"? This was similar to people who thought Hershey was crazy when he built his new chocolate plant in the middle of a "corn field".

Disney and Hershey often fought with their bankers because they wanted total control over their creations. Not only did Hershey and Disney financially control their companies, but they were a dominating presence in their respective companies. Many years after each of them had died, employees would still speak of M.S. Hershey and Walt Disney as if they were still alive and making decisions.

Hershey and Disney were interested in amusement parks, and each built a park. The amusement park industry was in its infancy when M.S. Hershey founded Hershey Park. Over a forty-year period Hershey experimented with his park in an attempt to find what the public wanted. Hershey and his top managers (Heilman, Ziegler, Sollenberger, and Bartels) had continually modified Hershey Park to serve a changing society. Hershey built a unique and lovely amusement park, but his park was always part of a larger plan that included promoting his town and his chocolate company.

Hershey Park was not the only amusement park experiencing trouble in the mid-1950's and trying to decide what direction it should take; the whole industry was uncertain about how to deal with television, rock and roll, drive-in movies, one-parent families, a longer school year, and working mothers.

One of Walt Disney's greatest contributions was to help rejuvenate the flagging amusement park industry. He had the advantage of over half a century of development in the amusement park industry when he decided to build a park. He drew on the industry and used some of the most successful amusement park operators in America as consultants. They helped him develop a workable park, but then Disney added something new. Using his movie background, he themed the park, and employees became performers.

If Disneyland had been built five years earlier, it probably would have failed. Disney used the new medium of television to turn his enterprise into the nation's park. National network television was in its infancy in 1955, and Disney was one of the first persons to use it to create a national desire. The whole country saw Disneyland being built. For months Disney showed on his television program the park's progress from early designs through site selection and construction to its final completion. M.S. Hershey, like Disney, promoted his park on a national scale. He had developed the first national market for chocolate bars in 1909 and capitalized on it. He had even included postcards of the town of Hershey and the park with each bar. If more modern means of communications had existed, Hershey probably would have used them.

Prior to the development of Disneyland, Hershey Park was compared to nearby amusement parks. The best of these, Willow Grove and Woodside in Philadelphia, were larger with more rides, games, and attractions, but by the 1950's they were declining. Hershey was cleaner and greener than its competitors. It had an ambiance that none of the other parks in the area could match.

But after the debut of Disneyland, Hershey Park would no longer be compared just with local parks; it now was being compared to Disney's new park. There was now a new standard by which all amusement parks were measured. Parks that survived would have to change and adapt to a new reality, and parks that were not willing to learn from Disneyland failed.

In 1955, people in the amusement park industry, including Hershey Park's Sollenberger and Bartels were not sure if Disney's park would succeed. They felt that Disney had spent too much money (seventeen million dollars) on the park and could never get it back. The general wisdom among amusement park managers was that Disneyland was similar to a world's fair; after a season or two, attendance would decline, and it would either close or become just another traditional amusement park. No one in the industry, with the exception of Disney, could imagine how profitable the park would become.

Both Hershey Park and Disneyland had one thing in common that most amusement parks at the time did not have. Both of these parks were used by their founders to promote other companies they owned. Hershey used his park to promote

An early Elvis Presley imitator in the 1956 Baby Parade.
(Hershey Community Archives)

Walt Disney's Davy Crockett influenced an entry in the 1955 Baby Parade.
(Hershey Community Archives)

***George Bartels awards a trophy
to the winner of the 1956 Baby Parade.***
(Hershey Community Archives)

The twin Ferris wheels were popular with teenagers and adults.
(Charles J. Jacques, Jr. Collection)

the town and his chocolate company. Disney's new park promoted his television show and movies. Disneyland was a continuing subject for Disney's television show. (This connection of amusement parks to other products owned by the same company is much more prevalent today with park chains now being owned by Busch, Time Warner, and Paramount.)

In 1955, Hershey Park was facing a much more pressing problem than whether Disneyland would succeed or fail. Dance bands, which for many years had been the park's biggest attraction, were no longer drawing the crowds they once did. The park continued to offer Saturday dancing, but the crowds were smaller, and the people who attended were older. Young people wanted rock and roll, and Sollenberger and Bartels were reluctant to change because it might attract the wrong crowd to the park.

The Comet was the park's most famous ride and its biggest attraction in the 1950's and 1960's. (Hershey Community Archives)

Demonstrating flax-breaking and handling at Hershey Park's Pennsylvania Dutch Days in the 1950's.
(HERSHEY COMMUNITY ARCHIVES)

Hershey Park midway in the late 1950's with the Mill Chute, The Bug, and the twin Ferris wheels.
(NEIL FASNACHT COLLECTION)

While birth rates, social patterns, musical tastes, and leisure time activities were changing in the late 1950's and early 1960's, some of Hershey Park's promotions like its Pennsylvania Dutch Days celebration remained a strong attractions with attendance reaching 170,000 in 1955. The event had been expanded to five days, and its activities were spread out in the park, arena, and stadium. Between 1955 and 1964, the Dutch Days celebration usually drew the largest crowds of the season.

In spite of the park's problems and rainy weather during the 1956 season, Hershey Park registered the biggest grosses of its forty-nine-year history (the park had returned to calling 1907 its first year). George Bartels told *Billboard* that "Hundreds of industrial plants, schools, lodges, and church organizations were contacted by Cyril J. Little, of the park's promotion department, who offered special group rates, plus visits to the Hershey Chocolate Corporation's plant, and free admission to the Hershey Museum." The park was leaning more on other activities found in the town to attract visitors.

In May and early June schools made up the majority of the picnic business. As many as seventy busloads of children, some of them from one hundred miles away, would come in a single day. After the schools closed for the summer, Sunday school, industrial, and club picnics kept the park busy. In the mid-

1950's, some excursion trains still brought patrons, including the Leeds and Northrup group from Philadelphia, the Reading picnic, and some church picnics.

The park stopped offering aerial and circus acts in 1956, because it was felt they did not draw people. More money was put into newspaper and radio advertising, and the park produced its first new brochure in sixteen years. Free Sunday and holiday concerts with regional bands, like Lukens Steel Band and Red McCarthy's Orchestra, continued to attract customers.

In hopes of reviving ballroom dancing, Hershey Park remodeled the ballroom in 1957 by removing the center portion of its roof, leaving the dance floor open to the starlit night sky. The remodeled structure was renamed the Starlight Ballroom. The park had borrowed the idea from a ballroom at Coney Island Park near Cincinnati. At the same time the roof was cut out, a concrete and marble terrazzo floor was laid beneath the opened ceiling while the two ends retained the highly polished maple floor. The band shell was carefully moved during the renovation.

The newly remodeled Starlight Ballroom opened on Saturday evening, June 1, 1957, with Claude Thornhill and his orchestra. Sliding doors were installed around the uncovered section to protect dancers from inclement weather. Other

The Hershey Park Ballroom was remodeled and became the Starlight Ballroom in 1957. (Hershey Community Archives)

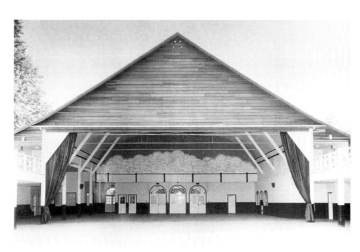

A section of the roof was cut out of the Starlight Ballroom so that people could dance under the stars. (Hershey Community Archives)

changes to the ballroom included a second-floor promenade area on both ends, three refreshment stands (each serving a different level), new draperies, curtains, and an improved sound system to carry the music to all parts of the spacious building. The bandstand was often a subject of conversation among the big band leaders. They liked its size, twenty-five feet deep and forty-five feet wide, and Stan Kenton termed it the best sounding shell he had ever played in. Ray Eberle, Guy Lombardo, Stan Kenton, Buddy Morrow, Sammy Kaye, Maynard Ferguson, Si Zentner, Les Elgart, Ray McKinley and the Glenn Miller Orchestra, and Al Hirt appeared in the remodeled ballroom.

Red McCarthy's Orchestra was the regular opening attraction for the outdoor band shell in the 1950's. A new ride, a kiddie's Ferris wheel, was put into operation in the Kiddieland area. It was the first in a long line of kiddie rides that the park would buy.

Since George Bartels ran both the arena and the park, every May he and his staff would move from the arena to the park office, which was located on the second floor of the Souvenir Building. They would reverse the process after Labor Day and return to the arena's box office. Bartels could tell if the park was having a good day just by

More kiddie rides like the Kiddie Cadillacs were added in the 1950's and 1960's. (Hershey Community Archives)

seeing how many cars were in the parking lots. On Sundays and some Saturdays, Bartels would make his rounds of the park three or four times talking to every ticket cashier and checking with the ride managers. The park was small enough that he knew every employee by name.

In 1959, the National Railway Historical Society celebrated the miniature railway's fiftieth birthday. The Harrisburg chapter of the society held a ceremony marking the occasion by presenting George Bartels a birthday cake. Over the years, the little railway remained one of the best ways of getting around the park and one of the most popular amusement rides.

There were three motormen in the railway's fifty years of operation: Harry "Whitey" Bistline from 1910 to 1925, William "Billy" Brandt from 1925 to 1953, and Clement W. "Clem" Miller from 1953 to 1959. Miller was a veteran of electrified railways who formerly had worked for the Hershey Transit Company's trolley line. Miller estimated that he traveled approximately one hundred miles a day, which meant the line traveled a half-million miles in its fifty-year history.

Hershey Park finally booked a rock and roll group as the 1950's were ending. Bill Haley and his Comets

The park's miniature railway celebrated its fiftieth birthday in 1959. (Hershey Community Archives)

John B. Sollenberger, president of Hershey Estates, at the throttle of the Dry Gulch Steam Rail Road engine in 1961.
(Hershey Community Archives)

The "Little Toot" or "1865" crossing the trestle, which was designed by Terry Faul. (Hershey Community Archives)

appeared at the park band shell for free concerts on Friday and Saturday, July 4 and 5, 1959. The group gave three performances, which attracted many young people.

Disney's influence on Hershey Park can be seen when the park added the Turnpike and Dry Gulch Railroad in the early 1960's. Kids, who had seen Walt Disney at the throttle of his steam train and children driving their own little cars in Fantasyland's Autopia, expected to see similar rides at their neighborhood park.

John B. Sollenberger bought a miniature turnpike ride with gasoline-operated cars for Hershey Park. However, following Disney's lead, the turnpike included theming, a toll gate entrance, and a tunnel along the ride's one-half mile length. The turnpike was designed to cross Spring Creek twice, so special concrete bridges, which could support the cars, were built. Prior to the turnpike ride the park did not theme rides, but generally put some landscape around them so that they would blend into the park. The turnpike was designed and built by the employees of Hershey Lumber Products. The little two-seat cars (Streco Turnpike Cars) were built by Streifthau Manufacturing Company, Middletown, Ohio. Keeping the cars going was never easy, and the ride required continual maintenance.

In 1959, while attending the annual trade show of the National Association of Amusement Parks where manufacturers displayed their latest rides, Sollenberger called Terry Faul and said, "Terry, I bought a [steam] railroad. I want you to build it down through the park, but I don't want you to take any automobile parking spaces," Faul recalled. There was a pay parking lot down along Spring Creek, and Sollenberger did not want to lose any revenue.

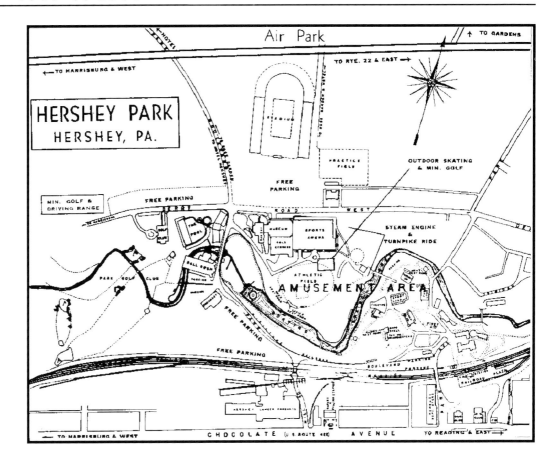

A map of Hershey Park in the 1960's.
(HERSHEY COMMUNITY ARCHIVES)

Faul designed a route, which was one-third of a mile long, so it would run from a spot near the Hershey Park Arena out towards Park Avenue. However, the terrain was hilly and Faul needed to build either a bridge or a trestle, so he secured plans for a trestle from the Baltimore and Ohio Railroad offices in Baltimore. Faul then scaled the plans down, and supervised construction of the two hundred thirty-five-foot trestle, which was built across a forty-foot-deep gorge. The railroad looped on both ends and every trip crossed the trestle twice. When the park was expanded in the 1980's, the railroad was built to make a complete loop and the train crossed the trestle only once. Construction on the Dry Gulch Steam Rail Road (the name later changed to Railroad) began in November 1960 and was completed in time for the park's opening in 1961.

Dave Groy became the Dry Gulch Railroad's first engineer. The railroad's 24-inch gauge, coal-burning, steam engine was called "Little Toot" or "1865". The engine and cars were built by the Crown Metal Products Manufacturers in Wyano, Pennsylvania. The steam engine, which produced approximately sixteen horsepower, had a 4-4-0 wheel base and a Stephenson's link valve gear. Hershey Lumber Products employees built a water tower for the engine.

The Turnpike and the Dry Gulch Railroad were moving Hershey Park in a new direction. Sollenberger enjoyed the new little engine and got his picture taken at the throttle on opening day. The new rides were not cheap, but the railroad carried just over a quarter-million passengers in its first season at twenty-five cents apiece.

In 1961, a new 18-hole miniature golf course was opened. A portable model, it was placed on the Hershey Sports Arena's outdoor skating rink during the summer season and featured a nineteenth hole where golfers could try and win a free round.

The park continued to expand Kiddieland. Two new kiddie rides, a tubs of fun and jet airplane ride, were added in 1961. With the new additions there were now nine kiddie rides that cost only five cents each. The following year (1962) a kiddie outboard motor boat ride was purchased.

Bartels announced a new look for 1962 in the northeast section of the park near the arena. In addition to the new kiddie rides, there was an Aero Jet, which was the park's first European ride and the first to use hydraulics. The new ride, placed near Kiddieland, was similar to a Disneyland ride which had small jets ships that the riders could control when the ships went up and down. The Aero Jet replaced the Aerial Joy Ride, which

Two bridges were built so that the Turnpike cars could cross Spring Creek twice. (HERSHEY COMMUNITY ARCHIVES)

The cars on the Turnpike had double-headlights and tail fins, just like the regular cars on the road. (HERSHEY COMMUNITY ARCHIVES)

was dismantled after twenty-two years of service. It had become impossible to buy replacement parts for the old ride.

After forty-six years with Hershey, George Bartels retired in 1963. He was replaced by Lloyd Blinco, veteran manager of the Hershey hockey team, who also operated the arena and golf courses for Hershey Estates. His assistant was Stanley M. Carpenter, who had been manager of the pool and rink, as well as personnel director for the park and arena. John P. Meszaros was the park's chief horticulturist, and he headed up a crew of eighteen gardeners.

For the park's fifty-sixth season in 1963 the Mill Chute became the "Lost River" ride. The park decided to theme its old Mill Chute to make it a more exciting ride. The old water ride was given a tropical setting. Riders were swallowed into the ride through a huge volcanic cave. They were then transported through the old mill section which had a series of eerie jungle scenes with many weird birds, animals, and foliage. The end of the ride remained the time-proven plunge down the chute into a pool of water. An animated elephant was placed on top of the loading area and was part of the ride's ballyhoo. The theming was done by Bill Tracey of Outdoor Dimensional Display Co., Inc. of North Bergen, New Jersey. Tracey was one of the real characters of the amusement park industry, but also one of the greatest designers of fun houses and dark rides. He built all of the displays for the Lost River.

New attractions like sky diving were booked into the park. Jay North, TV's Dennis the Menace, appeared on the bandstand stage in 1963. The park tried both country music and Dixieland

A second miniature golf course, a portable model, was opened on the outdoor ice skating rink in the summer.
(HERSHEY COMMUNITY ARCHIVES)

The Aero Jet replaced the Aerial Joy Ride.
The ride let riders control their own rocket path.
(HERSHEY COMMUNITY ARCHIVES)

The Hershey Park Zoo featured a monkey island in the 1950's.
(HERSHEY COMMUNITY ARCHIVES)

with varying success. The Harmonica Rascals gave a concert at the band shell. Circus acts, after several years' absence, returned to the athletic field.

Four new rides, two for adults and two for children were added in 1964. They included a Flying Coaster and Bill Tracey's retheming of the old Pretzel dark ride into the Golden Nugget. Tracey again used his skills to create a western-themed ride with a new exterior and new stunts inside the ride. The Flying Coaster was purchased from Aero-Affiliates of Fort Worth, Texas. The ride had at the end of each arm a car that could hold four passengers. As the cars would start to rotate around a center pole, they would go up a jump ramp that would throw them into the air. The cars would then land with a bump and continue until they jumped over the ramp again. Running lights (small lights which create the illusion of motion) were purchased for The Comet coaster and were installed by John Allen of the Philadelphia Toboggan Company. It took 6,640 10-watt lamps to cover the entire 3,360 feet of track.

A kiddie helicopter and a kiddie whip were installed. The helicopter ride was purchased from the Allan Herschell Company of North Tonawanda, New York and had eight little "copters" that could hold two children or adults. The new rides brought the major rides to a total of sixteen and the kiddie amusements to twelve.

The park tried once again to bring back dancing to the ballroom. Sixteen dances, the most in years, were held in the Starlight Ballroom in 1964, which again was redecorated.

John B. Sollenberger and
Lloyd Blinco, park manager,
at an amusement park
outing in 1964.
(HERSHEY COMMUNITY ARCHIVES)

The Mill Chute was themed by Bill Tracey and became the Lost River in 1963.
Ballyhoo was provided by a mechanical elephant. (HERSHEY COMMUNITY ARCHIVES)

Headliners included Guy Lombardo and His Royal Canadians, Sammy Kaye, Mike Pedicin Quintet, the Jimmy Dorsey Band, The Four Coins with Lee Vincent and His Orchestra, Maynard Ferguson, and Chuck Laskin's Orchestra.

Free concerts were given in the bandstand on Sundays and holidays with the United States Air Force Band and Singing Sergeants, Serendipity Singers, Les Paul and Mary Ford with Red McCarthy and his orchestra, Homer and Jethro, the Harrisburg Moose Band, Perseverance Band of Lebanon, and Pottstown Band and Glee Club. The park even tried a four-act variety show at the bandstand.

Hershey Park still attracted more people than all of the other tourist activities in the area combined, but if the park declined the whole tourist area would probably drop off with it. There are hundreds of examples of once prosperous resorts that faded because they did not change with the times. After years of stagnation, the amusement park industry had entered a period of fast growth and development. Hershey Park could only hope to survive and prosper if it made major changes necessary to compete in the decades ahead.

In 1964, the park added the Flying Coaster, an iron ride.
(HERSHEY COMMUNITY ARCHIVES)

The Helicopter could double as either a children's or an adult's ride. (HERSHEY COMMUNITY ARCHIVES)

CHAPTER 11

TROUBLED TIMES

On weekends in the late 1960's, there were long lines for the carousel and Paratrooper ride, but attendance waned on weekdays.
(PHOTOGRAPH BY BARBARA FAHS CHARLES — COPYRIGHT 1996)

Hershey Park had always paid attention to the safety and security of its visitors. It always had a policeman. There had been minor incidents every year, some vandalism, an occasional fight, pickpockets and minor thefts, but nothing that created headlines. As the park got larger so did the size of the security force. By the 1920's the park had a seven-man police force.

Despite sporadic acts of vandalism, theft, and violence, Hershey Park remained relatively trouble free. Most newspaper articles on picnics held at the park ended with "everyone enjoyed themselves and there was no trouble." Hershey Park had an image of a safe family park.

By the 1960's, however, concern over safety, security, and the park's image was mounting. Through the years the primary method Hershey Park used to control persons or gangs who looked like troublemakers was to exclude or evict them from the grounds. The park's police force was able to do this even though no incident had actually occurred. The local police departments and the

minor judiciary tended to back up the park police. However, in the 1960's Hershey Park lost the ability to exclude people at will. There was greater concern for peoples' civil rights, especially in public places like amusement parks. Management could ban people and groups from the park only after some law or park rule was broken. Once trouble occurred, bad media coverage would follow. The park was always afraid that there might be an event that would badly damage the park's reputation.

Just such an incident occurred in 1964 when a group of juveniles, ages fourteen to seventeen, caused damage to Hershey Park. The youths smashed rides and amusements in the park. The Lost River and Golden Nugget were the hardest hit; other rides were also damaged. It was not just a matter of the cost of the actual damage but the damage done to the park's reputation. Some people who heard about the incident stopped coming to the park. Lloyd Blinco and his staff had to deal with all of the adverse publicity the affair caused.

Management immediately increased the security staff and upgraded the park's communications system. Foot police were given walkie-talkies to communicate with the park office. Other units were placed around the park in concession stands so that security could react as quickly as possible to any sign of trouble. The aim was to head off trouble before it started.

However, Hershey Park, like most other parks with an open gate, was very vulnerable. People could enter the park from many different directions. Gangs or groups could congregate or set up a fight with a rival gang in the park. After dark it was very hard to check who was coming and going. An open park also

made it easier for people who caused trouble to leave unobserved. The people in the town of Hershey loved the openness of Hershey Park, but for Blinco and his staff it was increasingly becoming a nightmare. An open gate policy also left Hershey Park vulnerable to vandalism even when the park was not operating. The merry-go-round and other valuable rides were susceptible to night-time misuse and damage.

Dealing with violence in amusement parks in America was not a minor problem but a major problem. Some of the largest and oldest amusement parks in the country closed in the 1960's and early 1970's because they could not cope with violence or overcome the perception that their parks were not safe. Carlin's and Gwynn Oak in Baltimore, Maryland; Glen Echo in Washington, D.C.; Woodside in Philadelphia; Fontaine Ferry in Louisville, Kentucky; Euclid Beach in Cleveland, Ohio; and Steeplechase at Coney Island, New York, were closed because people were afraid of potential violence.

In 1966 the Skyview was built near the Lost River ride.
(Charles J. Jacques, Jr. Collection)

The Tip Top, purchased in 1966, was placed on the south side of Spring Creek across the stream from the carousel and Lost River.
(Hershey Community Archives)

Stories about amusement parks – whether positive or negative – tended to be hyped or exaggerated. An act of violence or vandalism would often make front page headlines or become the lead story on radio and television news programs. Words like riot or rampage were often used to describe a relatively minor incident. Once a story was circulated, irreparable damage was done to a park's reputation.

One solution to youth violence and vandalism would have been to enclose the park with a fence, but Hershey Park was reluctant to restrict its grounds. The main advantage of surrounding a park with a fence was that it gave park security a chance to observe persons and groups entering the park. If persons or a groups looked like they might cause trouble, the park could watch them. A fence also made it much harder for people to flee after causing trouble. A gate with a general admission charge discouraged youths from hanging out at the park. In the 1960's more and more parks adopted an admission charge to enter the park.

During this difficult period Hershey Park's carousel ring machine was removed. For many years a rider had been able to grab for a ring hoping to get the brass one, which entitled the person to a free ride; she or he would then toss the rings back into a receptacle in the shape of a grinning clown face. Unfortunately, by the 1960's the ring had become more of a weapon

than a challenge; too often other riders and bystanders were injured by carelessly or intentionally thrown rings.

A bull pen made out of wire mesh was added to the merry-go-round to hold people while they waited to ride, and a fence was erected around the machine to prevent people from jumping on and off. Riders now had to enter through the bull pen gate and exit by another gate. Hershey Estates considered relocating the carousel from Spring Creek to a site on higher ground to avoid the continual risk of flooding but decided against the move because of the prohibitive cost of building a new carousel pavilion.

For the 1966 season, Hershey Park added the Skyview, which provided a ski lift trip over Spring Creek and the center of the park. The ride, built by Universal Design Ltd. of Wildwood, New Jersey, had twenty cars suspended below the cable. This ride's loading station was located on the hill near The Comet's entrance. It was very popular and was one of the park's first modern, high capacity rides. Another ride, a Tip Top, also was purchased in 1966 and was erected on the site of the former Park Theatre, which had been demolished a year earlier. The Tip Top had a circular platform with four-seat cars and a capacity of approximately forty adults or sixty children. As the platform turned, the ride would bounce up and down. It was manufactured by Frank Hrubetz & Co., Inc. of Salem, Oregon, and cost approximately twenty-five thousand dollars.

A new restaurant, The Chicken House, was built under the Sportland Arcade. A one hundred by sixty foot addition was added to both the arcade and restaurant which afforded a

A children's boat ride was in the park's Kiddieland in the 1960's. (HERSHEY COMMUNITY ARCHIVES)

panoramic view of Spring Creek. The Sportland Arcade now contained one hundred and twenty-five arcade games. A ski machine and six Skee Ball alleys were added.

The old bumper cars were replaced with twenty-four new Auto Skooters from Lusse Skooter of Philadelphia. Four new rides were purchased for Kiddieland. The Dizzy Drums, Granny Bugs, and Bizzy Bees came from Hampton Amusements of Portage Des Sioux, Missouri, and one, a pony ride came from W. F. Mangels Company of Coney Island, New York. Each of these rides had little carts, bees, bugs, or drums which could hold from two to six children.

Cy Little was in charge of Special Group Services. He had come to Hershey in June of 1949, because "Someone had told me that Hershey Park needed a picnic representative," he explained, "So I applied. Soon it was my job actually to tramp through twenty-six Pennsylvania counties in the spring and solicit group picnics for that summer." By 1961 Little was also responsible for booking attractions, buying media, following through with production, and public information for the park and company.

"Hershey's ideas were so far ahead of their time," Little noted, "that most of his buildings are still as functional as they were 30 years or more ago. Take the parking lot outside the Arena and Stadium, for example. We don't have a parking problem today

Cy Little was head of publicity, marketing, and booking attractions and picnics in the 1960's.
(HERSHEY COMMUNITY ARCHIVES)

*John B. Sollenberger was
president of Hershey Estates
from 1949 to 1962.*
(Brad Cassady Collection)

Pennsylvania Dutch Days at the park featured folk and square dancing. (Hershey Community Archives)

because he built it large enough to accommodate the increased number of cars which he was sure the future would bring."

"It is impossible to arrive at an exact figure on the number of visitors here since there is no paid gate," Little said. "But on one day alone, we counted over four hundred bus loads of people. And from May to August there are over four hundred group picnics in the park." Most of the bus groups were from urban areas, and Little was trying to build the local market back up. "You know," Little reflected, "we who live in the Hershey area sometimes forget what advantages are available to us or else take them for granted."

In the mid-1960's, Little and his staff were searching for the right blend of entertainment. They tried a wide variety in hopes of finding what the public wanted. Appearing on Sundays and holidays on the band shell stage were the Musical Butchers, Fran Daniels and the Moonlighters, Walter Procanyn's Polka Dancers, Winged Victory Chorus, Smiley Burnette and the Broadway Buckaroos, Flatt & Scruggs, the Noveleers, American Indian Drum Beats, Expressions and Impalas, Shangri-Las with Red McCarthy and His Orchestra, Buck Benson and His Country Neighbors, Sonny James and the Southern Gentlemen, Pee Wee Kings and the Collins Sisters, the Carter Family, Burger's Animal Circus, Johnny and the Holidays, Neapolitan Sextette, Herman's Hermits with Caravan of Stars, and the Ginny Tai Show.

In 1967, Hershey Park added a Paratrooper ride and a shooting waters concession. The Paratrooper was a ride in

which people would hang under a canopy in a two-seat car. The ride would then turn and slowly and hydraulically lift to a height of forty-two feet. The ride was purchased from Frank Hrubetz & Co., Inc. and cost about thirty thousand dollars. In 1968, a Hrubetz Round-Up was purchased. The ride rotated faster and faster until the speed raised the oval-shaped cages and its thirty-one riders to an angle of thirty degrees. The centrifugal force held the riders against the ride's metal frame. Although these were good rides, they were attractions that even carnivals carried.

Two new picnic pavilions were built in 1967 to provide sheltered picnic facilities for an additional six hundred persons. The picnic pavilions could now accommodate up to six thousand, and the park was doing more catering. For the kiddies, the Traffic Jam, a Hampton umbrella ride, was added. It had four motorcycles, two limousines, two sport cars, and one fire engine.

The Lost River (the Mill Chute) was starting to show its age. The ride remained popular, but it was a hard ride to load and unload. It therefore had a very low ride capacity per hour and on holidays and Sundays the wait in line could be more than an hour.

The Turnpike ride was vulnerable because it had been built without a steel center rail to control the direction of the cars. Instead, each car was controlled by an accelerator and brake pedal, and ran freely between the two sides of the track. When the park was crowded on weekends and employees were too busy to properly supervise, drivers would sometimes crash into the side rails of the track, badly damaging both the cars and the rails. To prevent line jumping, the fence around the Turnpike's queue line was doubled from four feet to eight feet.

Although Hershey Park continued its policy of not selling beer or alcohol, more people brought alcohol to the park. Arrests for intoxication increased. At times crowds became unruly, and it became harder to attract women employees to work in the park because of the difficulty with crowd control.

John B. Sollenberger died in 1967. He had led Hershey Park and later Hershey Estates for nearly forty years. Sollenberger always brought a sense of enthusiasm to the job. Whether it was Rudy Vallee, the hockey team, the Aerial Joy Ride, or the Dry Gulch Railroad, Sollenberger loved every minute.

Harold Sitler, who was a 1941 graduate of the Hershey Industrial School (the name was changed to Milton Hershey School in 1951), was hired by the Hershey Lumber Company immediately following World War II. In 1968 Sitler transferred to the park from the lumber company. One job that he especially disliked was having to remove the neon Pretzel sign from the back of the ride after Labor Day. The park was afraid that the sign would be stolen or broken if it was left in the park during the winter. Since the Pretzel sign was more than thirty feet in the air, Sitler had to climb a very tall ladder, which swayed back and forth, to remove it. In the winter the sign and other signs and parts of rides were stored all over town because the park did not have a warehouse.

In 1939, Sitler met his future wife, Dolly, on one of the park swings, near the bandstand. The Sitlers had five children and, like many families in Hershey, four of them worked in the park during the summers to help pay their way through college.

The Hershey Zoo underwent some drastic changes in the late 1950's and 1960's. The work force of the zoo was cut, and some of the animals were sold. The zoo was open on and off and finally officially closed about 1969 (although some animals seemed to remain on the premises). The doors were closed because of fear of vandalism and the high cost of properly protecting the animals.

By the mid-1960's Hershey Park's pool complex was no longer the money maker or the attraction it had once been. Over the years, more public and private pools had been built, and there was a fear of polio as well as violence in and around

A Paratrooper ride was purchased in 1967. It replaced the Tip Top, which was moved to the northeast section of the park.
(Hershey Community Archives)

the pool. The park did not have the money to properly maintain or refurbish the pools.

As time passed, the joints in Hershey Park's swimming pools started to leak. "Every year, without fail, we had to get blowtorches and melt out the asphalt in the joints and pour new asphalt, and that's a terrible job," recalled Terry Faul, who was head of maintenance for the park during the 1960's. "That was the lumber company that had to do that. It cost a fortune. Finally it got to the point where it cost too much to run." The pools and bathhouses were closed after the 1967 season. The bathhouses were demolished and the pools filled in during the winter of 1972. The lighthouse, which was part of the complex, was left standing as the only reminder of the once great swimming complex.

Although the ring machine had been removed from the merry-go-round, the clown with his gaping mouth remained and it often was filled with refuse left by park patrons. The two-roll band organ, a product of the Rudolph W. Wurlitzer Mfg. Company of Tonawanda, New York, was badly in need of repairs, so a tape player was used.

Hershey Park was drifting. Management did not know how to cope with the changes in the amusement park industry or society. Disneyland had been joined by a number of new theme parks like Six Flags Over Texas, Astroworld, and Six Flags Over Georgia, with many more on the drawing boards. Some of the old parks like Cedar Point in Sandusky, Ohio, had been upgraded and a theme area added. Another old park, Coney Island, Cincinnati, moved its rides from the Ohio River to another location twenty-five miles away, and became Kings

Fun Land (sometimes called Funland) in the early 1970's.
(Photograph by Harold Sitler)

Island. Other theme parks were in the planning stages like Walt Disney World (Florida), Kings Dominion (Virginia), Magic Mountain (California), Opryland, U.S.A. (Nashville, Tennessee), and Carowinds (Charlotte, North Carolina).

Hershey Park continued to make minor additions. In the spring of 1969, two large cranes loaded Reading caboose No. 9238 onto a heavy duty trailer and the twenty-ton railroad car was hauled up Park Boulevard to an area east of the sports arena. The Reading Railroad caboose, which was built in 1942, was moved to the Kiddieland area of the park and became the Little Red Caboose, a place to have family picnics and birthday parties. Twenty-seven years of grime were removed, and after scrubbing and painting the new attraction was dedicated by Stanley M. Carpenter, the park's manager, and officials of the railroad.

In 1969, Hershey Park took a major step forward with the addition of the Monorail. The 5,380 foot ride, which traveled in a counterclockwise direction, was built inside and outside the park. The entire system was computerized (a first for the park) for maximum safety. There were two stations: one at the northeastern end of the Arena, and a second station in the town of Hershey between the post office and the Hershey Drug Store. The Monorail crossed Spring Creek twice and the height of the track varied from twelve to twenty-five feet, depending on the contour of the ground. The Monorail cost $258,000 to build. The ride gave its passengers an excellent view of Hershey Park, Chocolate Avenue, and the factory.

The Monorail's three trains were purchased from Universal Mobility of Utah, although they were designed in Switzerland. Each train was seventy-three feet long, had five fiberglass cars, and

The chute on the Lost River attracted
riders and spectators who stood along the fence.
(Hershey Community Archives)

could hold fifty-four people. Each car had its own electrical motor.

The new ride was not owned by the park, but by a new corporation, the Monorail Amusement Co. that was jointly owned by the Hershey Chocolate Corporation and Hershey Estates. The chocolate company wanted to do something about the heavy traffic in downtown Hershey and around its factory and so it helped finance the system to make it easier for visitors who wanted to tour the chocolate plant. Hershey Park wanted the Monorail because it added a major new ride to the park and helped show off its grounds.

The Magic Carpet Slide, a giant slide, was constructed in 1969 on the slope next to the Chicken House where the Park Theatre once stood. It was a fifteen-lane thriller that was thirty-five feet high and one hundred sixty-five feet long. It was an adaptation of the old slide-on-a-bag wooden indoor slides which were found in many fun houses. The new slide was constructed of heavy reinforced fiberglass and had a polished slick surface which was treated to remain slippery even after a rain.

A number of skill games including The Dart-A-Card, Ring-A-Coke, Balloon Burst, Dart-An-Apple, Bowl 'O Fish, Tic-Tac-Toe, and a Fish Pond were installed in the carousel annex, which was formerly a refreshment area. The following year two more games were introduced, a Cat Game and Money Race.

In 1969, Hershey Estates decided not to move its office into the park during the summer. Instead, the arena became the permanent home of the park's offices. The old office space

Harold Sitler points out carvings on one of the carousel horses.
(Hershey Community Archives)

located above the Souvenir Building was converted into a hospitality lounge. The new room was used for people making personal appearances at the bandstand and by picnic committees who visited the park while negotiating picnic dates and arrangements.

Hershey Park was at a crossroads. Important new rides like the Monorail and Skyview helped attract new visitors, but they were not enough. Much of the park was showing its age and something major had to be done. It was no longer the clean and green park that it had once been. Park officials were reluctant to place hanging baskets in the park because so many had been stolen. People who went to Disneyland and the other new theme parks expected a clean park, but Hershey Park was thoroughly cleaned only once a week. Some trash was picked up every day but the midway, walkways, and parking lots were often littered. This standard was no longer acceptable.

Major rides had to be added and the infrastructure had to be rebuilt if Hershey Park was to remain one of the leading parks in America. Hershey Park also had to retain control of its grounds at all times to keep its reputation as a safe family park.

In the early 1960's, J.O. Hershey, superintendent of the Milton Hershey School, joined the board of directors of Hershey Estates and was named vice president in 1968. He was given the job of cleaning up the park. Hershey said that "I probably succeeded because I did not have any preconceptions of what the park should be. I really did not know anything about the amusement park business and therefore I was open to any and all suggestions." The first thing he did was to visit some of

Both the Turnpike and Monorail were built across Spring Creek.
(Hershey Community Archives)

The new Monorail, which was opened in 1969, curved past the deer and main entrance.
(Hershey Community Archives)

the most successful amusement parks in America: Knotts Berry Farm, California; Cedar Point, Sandusky, Ohio; and Disneyland again in Anaheim, California. "I didn't just visit the parks, but I talked to the management and asked their advice on what we [Hershey Park] should do," Hershey said. "I also visited Walt Disney World, Kings Island, and Magic Mountain [California], which were all under construction."

When J.O. Hershey traveled to Disneyland in 1969 he was amazed at how many people (10,000,000) were visiting the park each year. Hershey put the facts together into a coherent plan for the park. "I presented the facts about the amusement park business to the [Hershey Estates] board of directors and let them make the decision. The facts spoke for themselves," he said.

J.O. Hershey was then put in charge of contacting experts in the amusement park industry who could help restructure and redirect the park. He had the courage to make tough decisions and convince the board of directors to spend substantial sums in seeking outside guidance and direction.

As the 1969 season came to a close, the

J.O. Hershey speaking at the Tudor Square dedication.
(Hershey Community Archives)

Hershey Estates board of directors took the first steps toward a new park when they retained Randall Duell and Associates of Santa Monica, California, to develop a five-to-ten-year master plan for the future development of Hershey Park. It was to include plans for reorganization of the existing park, proposals of new rides, creation of a new main entrance, and development of the parking areas.

A Rotor from Chance Manufacturing Co. of Wichita, Kansas, was purchased in 1969 and placed adjacent to The Comet on the flat land along Spring Creek. The Rotor had a small circular room that spun, sticking its riders to the wall. Then the floor was dropped out. Finally, the floor rose and the spinning stopped.

For the 1970 season, Stanley Carpenter, manager of Hershey Park, announced that the park was reviving old-fashioned ballroom dancing in the Starlight Ballroom every Saturday evening during the season. The ballroom, which in the late 1960's had been used mainly for teenage dances, was repainted. The dance bands for the 1970 season were Tom Darlington (Philadelphia's "regal dance master") and his orchestra, and Hal Schiff and his Multiphonic Orchestra. Ballroom dancing in Hershey Park's Starlight Ballroom might bring back fond memories of the great bands, but its time had passed. The era of evening gowns, white suits, Guy Lombardo and "The Sweetest Music This Side of Heaven" was gone forever.

Some people in the town of Hershey thought that the park should go back to an earlier simpler time, but that was not possible – society had changed forever. A few people who worked at the park argued that the risks in making major changes were just too great. These employees felt the park should not act precipitously but should continue on the same course. But this was no longer a viable option. Something dramatic had to be done to renew the park.

The Saturday night dances in the Starlight Ballroom in 1970 were really the last echoes of a time past. Labor Day arrived and the final dance was held. As the closing strains of the orchestra died away, it was a sad time, because it was truly the last dance of summer, – the end of an era.

Underneath layers of paint, the carvings on this horse could still be seen. (PHOTOGRAPH BY BARBARA FAHS CHARLES— COPYRIGHT 1996)

Philadelphia Toboggan Carousel #41 was in need of a complete restoration in 1969.
(PHOTOGRAPH BY BARBARA FAHS CHARLES— COPYRIGHT 1996)

The carousel pavilion and merry-go-round along Spring Creek in 1969.
(PHOTOGRAPH BY BARBARA FAHS CHARLES— COPYRIGHT 1996)

CHAPTER 12

HERSHEYPARK

J.O. Hershey at a press conference announcing the redevelopment of Hersheypark in 1971.
(Hershey Community Archives)

The pinwheel design was adopted by Hersheypark in 1971.
(Hersheypark)

The new name, Hersheypark, was a stroke of genius. If the old name had been retained, it would have taken years to tell people that there was a new and exciting Hersheypark out there. The park had to reestablish itself rapidly as a clean family-fun activity. The new name helped, and it instantly indicated that the park was changing.

In 1970, Hershey Estates approved a master plan, a five-year, six-phase development program, which was designed to turn the park into a major cultural, entertainment, and leisure-time complex. This multimillion dollar plan was to change the park in many ways, but it also preserved the park's history and tradition. Hersheypark was on the move; however, this move did not involve a change of location, but a change in the concept, size, and design of the park.

In addition to the substantial physical changes, Hershey Estates decided to bring in a new management team of John T. Hart and J. Bruce McKinney to run the park. Hart was named the manager, and he immediately reorganized the park's staff to serve a larger facility. Before coming to Hershey Park, Hart, a graduate of the Milton Hershey School, had been the chief operating officer of the Harrisburg Chamber of Commerce.

J. Bruce McKinney was working for Hershey Foods (the new name of the Hershey Chocolate Corporation) when he was tapped for the job of assistant manager of Hersheypark. John O.

Hershey knew McKinney from his days as a student at the Milton Hershey School and wanted him for one of the executive positions.

J.O. Hershey convinced McKinney that Hershey Estates needed young, dynamic leadership. McKinney described the move, "like divorcing your wife to marry her sister."

McKinney's first association with Hershey Estates had occurred in the 1960's when he replaced Cy Little as announcer at the Hershey Bears hockey games. McKinney recalled that the first time he reported to the arena box office before a hockey game "the place was a mad house." He thought to himself, "Thank God, I don't work for this company [Hershey Estates]." When he accepted the job as assistant manager of the park, McKinney found himself working full-time for that company.

Hersheypark was the core business of Hershey Estates – its very heart. The park drove the whole corporation. If the community was to retain its uniqueness, the park had to be renewed. The town was a blend of the chocolate factory,

Hersheypark, the chocolate plant tour, gardens, golf courses, the Museum, the Hotel Hershey, the Hershey Motor Lodge, schools, and other tourist-related businesses.

The most important changes for the 1971 season were fencing the park's grounds and moving the main gate from Park Avenue across Spring Creek to a spot near the northeast end of the arena and monorail station. During this period a few people insisted on climbing over the fence rather than coming through the main gate. The park's policemen usually caught them, charged them an admission, and then evicted them from the park. The park continued to operate the miniature railway, even though the station on Park Avenue near the Hershey Department Store was now outside the fence. The train entered through an electrical gate, which was located down along Spring Creek.

The slogan "Summer Playground of Pennsylvania," was finally retired. In its place were new slogans like "Make like a kid again at Hersheypark!" and "Come On Out And Play!" In

A map of the park in 1972. (CHARLES J. JACQUES, JR. COLLECTION)

1 Monster Ride	7 Crafts Barn	14 Whipperoo	21 Giant Slide	28 Aero Jet	35 Dry Gulch Railroad
2 Milk Bar	8 Comet	15 Toboggan Ride	22 Electric Substation	29 Round Up	36 Plaza
3 Childrens Rides	9 Sky Ride	16 Twin Ferris Wheel	23 Chicken Restaurant	30 Tip Top	37 Aquatheater
4 Scrambler	10 Lost River	17 Auto Scooter	24 Games Arcade & Food	31 Picnic Shelters A-B	38 Restrooms
5 Restrooms	11 The Bug	18 Paratrooper Ride	25 Turnpike	32 Attractions Tent	39 Cuddle-up Ride
6 Souvenir Shops	12 Rotor Ride	19 Picnic Shelters C-O	26 Golden Nugget	33 Monorail Station	40 Flying Coaster
6a Penna. Dutch Restaurant	13 Food	20 Bandshell	27 Childrens Rides	34 R.R. Station	41 Games
					42 Funland
					43 Souvenirs...Food
					44 Monorail
					45 Offices & First Aid
					46 Monorail Snack Shop
					47 Restrooms

John T. Hart, general manager of the park, presents the cutest baby trophy for 1971 to Triss Alyne Bishop, who is held by her mother, Mrs. Robert A. Bishop.
(HERSHEY COMMUNITY ARCHIVES)

most respects 1971 was a transitional year. The park was open seven days a week from May 31 through Labor Day. Most of the rides (twenty-one adult and eleven kiddie), games, and food stands remained the same. Besides the gate the biggest change was daily live entertainment throughout the park. Hershey Park introduced a one price admission plan. Adults were charged $3.50, juniors age five to eleven $1.75, and children under four free. There was an optional plan with a small general admission charge and ride tickets.

In January 1972, James Bobb, president of Hershey Estates, held a press conference where he laid out future plans for the park. The *Harrisburg Patriot* reported that Bobb would not estimate costs, but it was to be a "multimillion dollar development." It would be done in six phases over five years rather than all at one time. "Hershey Estates has given its stamp of approval to go ahead with the first two stages," he said.

Hershey Estates did not do it all at once because it did not have the funds to build a totally new park. Many of the old rides and buildings had to be retained, some for a year or two and others indefinitely. Hershey Estates was not sure that building a new larger theme park was the right move, so it wanted to keep its options open to modify or terminate the plan at any time. The company was forced to borrow heavily, more than it had ever borrowed before, to fund the new plan. Recalling the

change, J. Bruce McKinney believed "it was the only way the park could survive. It had to have a new image."

Headlines in the *Harrisburg Evening News* for December 13, 1971, stated "Hershey plans a 'Theme Park' - Second Only to Disneyland." Although the changes were dramatic, startling, and substantial for Hersheypark, there were a number of other parks that were larger, and more money had been spent in developing them. Hershey Estates wanted to make the town of Hershey into a destination point rather than just a place to stop during the day.

R. Duell & Associates, which had done the feasibility studies and preliminary recommendations, was hired as the architect for the project. The firm, with a staff of fifty-four including nineteen registered architects and engineers, was a pioneer in the planning, design, and development of theme and amusement parks. The California-based firm was founded by Randall Duell, who had been an art director at the MGM Studios in Hollywood for twenty-three years. He was an expert in set creation and decoration and had used this skill in such well known parks as Six Flags Over Texas, Six Flags Over Georgia, Houston's Astroworld, Cedar Point in Sandusky, Ohio, and California's Magic Mountain.

Economic Research Association, a California-based consulting firm, was hired by Hershey Estates to analyze and review the long-range plans for the park site. The park had approximately 780,000 attendance in 1971 and it hoped to raise that to 850,000 and ultimately over one million. The staff, which had been three hundred in 1971, was increased to four hundred for 1972 with the plan to eventually employ twelve hundred persons.

At the same time the park was being redeveloped, Hershey Foods Corporation decided to build a simulated chocolate tour facility called Chocolate World across Park Boulevard from the museum. The chocolate company decided to retain the same firm, R. Duell & Associates to develop the attraction. With new safety regulations, insurance regulations, and product control, permitting hundreds of thousands of people into the plant was no longer feasible. In 1970 a total of 899,465 visitors, including some 16,000 daily during the peak summer periods, toured the plant. This figure was up from 231,196 who took the tour in 1960 and 522,190 in 1965. Prudy Meily, who worked at the plant said, "What I recall most about the plant tours were those incredibly long lines." So many people toured the plant during the summer months that the company had trouble controlling the temperature in certain areas in the factory. In addition, tourist traffic around the facility during the summer had become almost impossible.

Chocolate World's Visitors Center's primary attraction would be a World's-Fair-type simulated 12-minute tour that explained the process of making chocolate from harvesting the cocoa bean to packaging the finished product. The tour was made in fifty-four cars on a continuous moving system that took up to seven passengers each. The attraction would be opened in 1973.

Phase I of Duell's master plan, which was to be completed for the 1972 season, included Carrousel Circle (the park spelled carrousel with two r's), a Pennsylvania Dutch area, an animal petting zoo, and an aqua-show arena. The second phase, to be completed for the 1973 season, included a new English-styled entrance and a section featuring the region's German heritage.

Other attractions planned from 1974 to 1977 in Phases III to VI included a contemporary area with a 300-foot observation tower, an Indian village, a frontier town, a New England fishing village and wharf, and a Pennsylvania coal mining village. Hershey Estates also considered expanding the Monorail and building a full-sized theatre outside the park on the site of the Starlight Ballroom.

The park redevelopment called for rerouting Park Boule-

vard after it passed the site of the Starlight Ballroom to connect with Route 39 instead of continuing north past the museum and stadium. On the opposite side (west side) of the park all of the homes along Derry Road west of Park Avenue were to be demolished. Most of these homes were owned by Hershey Estates and the rest would be purchased by the company.

Expansion plans for Phases I and II were presented in 1971 to the Derry Township Board of Supervisors who gave their approval. Some local residents objected to closing a portion of

Exterior of Hershey's Chocolate World, free visitor complex of Hershey Foods Corporation. The facility replaced the company's former chocolate plant tour.
(CHARLES J. JACQUES, JR. COLLECTION)

Visitors to Chocolate World ride through a simulated world of chocolate.
(CHARLES J. JACQUES, JR. COLLECTION)

A bird's-eye view of Hersheypark of the future as designed by R. Duell & Associates in 1971.
This was the master drawing for turning the park into a theme park.
(Hershey Community Archives)

A drawing by R. Duell & Associates showing how the
Giant Wheel would look adjacent to Der Deitsch Platz.
In the background is Rhineland and the arena.
(Hershey Community Archives)

Duell's preliminary drawing of the new Tudor Square theme area.
(Hershey Community Archives)

The carousel pavilion with the addition for games that had been added in the 1960's. (Photograph by Harold Sitler)

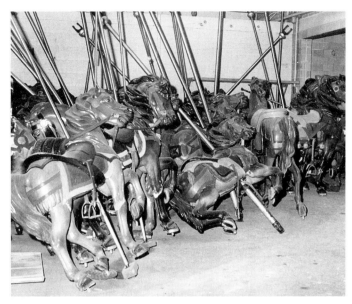

The carousel horses still on their poles in storage during the winter of 1971-72. (Harold Sitler Collection)

Derry Road and rerouting Park Boulevard. Other townspeople simply did not like the idea of the park expanding and changing. One person was so upset he said, "Why must we suffer to accommodate people from all over the country?" Actually, the park's new entrance and Chocolate World would cut traffic dramatically in the town of Hershey. For many years cars had parked in the residential areas surrounding the park. Once the new entrance was built, people started to park in the parking lots around the arena and stadium, and traffic was shifted from Chocolate Avenue to Airport Road (later renamed Hersheypark Drive).

During the winter of 1971-72, Phase I was completed. The park's carousel, PTC #41, was completely dismantled, partially

renovated, and moved from its location along Spring Creek to the new Carrousel Circle section of the park. The carousel in a new red, white, and blue pavilion was the center or the hub of the new area. The Wurlitzer band organ was put back into working order and moved with the carousel. Once the merry-go-round had been removed, the old carousel pavilion and its annex were torn down.

Carrousel Circle was officially dedicated at a ribbon cutting ceremony held May 7, 1972. Arthur O. Whiteman, chairman of the board of Hershey Estates, and James E. Bobb, president of the company, presided. Visitors were then given a ride on PTC #41 and a tour of the park's other new sections and attractions.

In March 1972, the first steel for the roof of the new carousel pavilion was lifted into place. (Harold Sitler Collection)

The new carousel pavilion and merry-go-round in the Carrousel Circle theme area. (Charles J. Jacques, Jr. Collection)

Mrs. J.O. (Lucille) Hershey and Dolly Sitler share the first ride on the park's rededicated carousel. (PHOTOGRAPH BY HAROLD SITLER)

Arthur R. Whiteman, chairman of the board, (on the right) and James E. Bobb, president, of Hershey Estates, cut the ribbon which opened Carrousel Circle. (PHOTOGRAPH BY HAROLD SITLER)

On the perimeter of the Carrousel Circle were three adult rides: the Monster by Eyerly Aircraft Company of Salem, Oregon; the Scrambler by Eli Bridge Company, Jacksonville, Illinois; and a twin Toboggan ride by Chance Manufacturing Company, Wichita, Kansas. A fast food restaurant and a milk bar were also constructed. There were also covered queue lines, which was a first for the park.

The Toboggan was actually two rides that were operated at the same time to try to improve the capacity. Riders would board a small two-passenger car on a track and be pulled vertically through a large cylindrical tunnel until ejected at the top; then the car would spiral down seven different levels to the bottom of the shaft. Although the twin Toboggan was popular, people often got stuck in the main tube and maintenance men had a hard time getting them out. The ride was removed after only a few seasons.

Hoping to capitalize on its successful Pennsylvania Dutch Days promotion, which was in its twenty-third year, Hersheypark created Der Deitsch Platz (the Pennsylvania Dutch Place), located between the Carrousel Circle and The Comet roller coaster. The main structure in the area was a full-sized Bank Barn, a unique Pennsylvania Dutch structure built from limestone and wood. It was used as a craft barn where local craftspeople including a blacksmith, glassblower, weaver,

Original rides in the Carrousel Circle included the twin Toboggans, the Monster, a children's umbrella ride, and a kiddie Helicopter. (HERSHEY COMMUNITY ARCHIVES)

Der Deitsch Platz under construction on March 1, 1972. Work had just started on the barn, which had to be completed in two months. (Harold Sitler Collection)

spinner, and leather worker demonstrated their art and made crafts for sale. Employees in Der Deitsch Platz wore Pennsylvania Dutch style costumes.

Construction of the barn was delayed by bad weather, and extra construction workers had to be hired to work nights to finish the barn in time for the park's May opening. Perhaps the barn was too authentic because it cost hundreds of thousands of dollars over estimates. This was the beginning of the cost overruns which plagued the early redevelopment of the park.

The park reported that the zoo was to be phased out (although the zoo records indicate that it was not being operated) and its few remaining animals sold and replaced with an animal contact area called the Animal Garden, where children could play with barnyard and more exotic animals (small llamas, deer, and a baby elephant). A trained animal show was given for about five seasons. And finally, to complete the animal area an aqua theatre-in-the-round with a seating capacity of 1,000 was built. Six dolphin shows were presented daily and became an important part of the park's free entertainment policy.

R. Duell & Associates was careful to protect the park's natural setting. "Our main concern was to save as many trees as possible," said Henry Navarete, one of Duell's architects. During the first phase of construction, signs were posted on the trees that read, "Save This Tree," to protect them from the busy construction activity. Duell's landscape architect, Larry Shafkind, felt that "The physical setting itself was the finest in

Extra carpenters were hired to help complete the roof on the craft barn. (Harold Sitler Collection)

the country. The best means of building and blending everything together was because of the trees." He added that "One tree saved is worth ten new trees."

People soon discovered the best way to see the redevelopment in progress was to ride the Monorail. It zigzagged through the park and gave a wonderful view of the new attractions under construction. However, once the park opened for the 1972 season, many people would rather pay thirty cents to ride the Monorail than to pay an admission charge to enter the park. John T. Hart, the park's manager, hired a barker to stand near

The Aquatheatre's pool under constuction.
(PHOTOGRAPH BY HAROLD SITLER)

the Monorail's entrance across from the arena trying to get people to come into the park.

Allan Alberts, the former lead singer and originator of the Four Aces, produced a television show called *Al Alberts' Showcase* from the park in 1972 and 1973. It was taped in the park and aired by Harrisburg, Johnstown, Philadelphia, and Washington D.C. television stations. This television exposure helped the park gain the recognition it needed during this time of change. Other live entertainment included two shows, held four times daily at the old band shell and Scollon's Marionettes, which had appeared at the White House.

Most of the old rides remained including The Comet,

Skyview, Lost River, The Bug, Whipperoo, Twin Ferris Wheels, Auto Skooter, Paratrooper, Giant Slide, Turnpike, Golden Nugget, Aero Jet, Round Up, Cuddle Up, Flying Coaster, Tip Top, and Dry Gulch Railroad. These rides still provided most of the park's ride capacity.

Although attendance and revenues were up for the 1972 season, they did not reach the economic projections. Hershey Estates had spent millions of dollars in redesigning the park and building the first two phases. This up-front money would not all be returned the first year but would be slowly paid back over the next ten to twenty years. Another factor that the park had not anticipated was that so many people from Hershey did not seem to like the new park. It was hoped that the new theme areas and rides would help overcome their dislike of the fence and a pay-one-price admission policy. Many people who visited the park in the past had paid for the rides, games, and food, but the thought of paying just to get into the park irrated many people. The park redevelopment plan's full benefits would not be realized until more of it was completed.

The most notable event in the 1972 season was when Tropical Storm Agnes hit Hersheypark in June. Torrential rains caused Spring Creek to overflow and flood the low lying areas of the park. Gary Chubb, who worked in the maintenance department at that time and who later would become assistant manager of the park, remembered maintenance personnel moving what they could to higher ground. Since Chubb was in charge of the Turnpike ride, he drove the little cars to the

The park was flooded by Tropical Storm Agnes in 1972.
This photograph is looking from The Comet coaster towards
The Bug, Skyview, and Giant Slide. (PHOTOGRAPH BY HAROLD SITLER)

Flood water covers the bottom of the Whipperoo and Rotor.
(PHOTOGRAPH BY HAROLD SITLER)

highest point on the track, thinking that "there was no way on this man's earth that the water would ever rise that high." He was wrong and the water kept rising and finally some of the cars were carried away by the flood. Chubb said "when the water reached ten feet above flood stage, lots of things floated away."

"Muddy water, the color of chocolate, from Spring Creek inundated nearly two-thirds of the park," Chubb said. The flood poured through and around the Lost River Ride taking most of the ride's scenes, decorations, and boats with it. The Lost River ride never reopened, and the few boats that were retrieved after the flood were sold to Dorney Park. The Giant Slide, which was located next to the creek, was so badly damaged by floating debris that it never reopened.

Hersheypark was fortunate that the winter before Tropical Storm Agnes the park had removed PTC #41 from its pavilion which extended over Spring Creek and moved it to its new home on higher ground. If the merry-go-round had not been moved some of the horses

One of the Turnpike cars floats down Spring Creek.
(PHOTOGRAPH BY HAROLD SITLER)

probably would have been lost.

Heavy damage was sustained by the Animal Garden and Aquatheatre. The dolphins, Skipper and Dolly, had to be evacuated from their pool. The only access to the dolphins, which weighed between two hundred and two hundred fifty pounds, was down a steep bank behind the Cuddle Up ride. Because muddy water covered the pool, the rescuers could not see the dolphins, and the trainers could not get the dolphins' attention because they reacted to sight and sound and neither was effective. Hersheypark's maintenance crew used nets to drag the animals to the side of the pool and then took the dolphins from the water. They were then taken on stretchers to a fresh water pool at the Cocoa Plaza in Hershey (salt had to be added to protect the animals' skin). Once the flood waters subsided, it took another two days to pump the muddy water out of the dolphins' pool.

Most of the animals from the Animal Garden and zoo were saved by park employees. The baby

131

elephant was led to safety and taken to the arena box office. People from Hershey heard about the elephant's rescue and many came to see her and brought her food following the flood.

Attendance for 1972 was 854,787, a 9.7 percent increase over the previous year but short of the projected attendance of 910,000. Most of the shortfall was caused by the park being closed by Tropical Storm Agnes for nine days in the month of June. With attendance down, revenues too fell short of anticipated levels.

For 1973, the park moved its main entrance from the northern Monorail station near the arena box office to a spot close to the museum. It was themed to resemble a Seventeenth Century English village and named Tudor Square. The new section was the most elaborate and costly theme area that the park would build. Tudor Square was located outside the park's fence, so it could remain open all year round. Hersheypark now had one of the most unique entrances of any theme park in America. It featured two man-made lakes, a moat, a stone bridge, and an English-styled tower. The entrance gate to the park proper was through a ten-position admission gate named Tudor Castle.

Cut stone and brick along with slate floors and genuine lead glass windows were used to lend authenticity to Tudor Square. Several century-old oaks shaded the area and provided a timeless touch to the setting. Each structure within the area reflected seventeenth century English architecture.

R. Duell & Associates felt that the Tudor Square entrance should be a work of art. It was done with quality construction and materials. The architects, as they had done with the Pennsylvania Dutch barn, designed something truly beautiful but very costly. While most theme parks used false fronts on their entrances, Hersheypark's Tudor Square was built with complete four-sided buildings which cost much more. But in the end, the quality of the theming would endure and set the right tone for the rest of the park. It proved to be worth the higher initial cost.

Tudor Square's first employees were dressed in costumes reminis-

The Lost River was so badly damaged by the flood that it was never reopened.
(Photograph by Harold Sitler)

The park used the town's old fire truck to pump the muddy water out of the dolphins' pool.
(Photograph by Harold Sitler)

cent of Seventeenth Century England, but management soon found out that costumes in all the new theme areas were not very practical. Employees could not dish ice cream with ruffled sleeves, and the costumes were too hot for the summer months. Within a year or two the costumes were replaced with more general park outfits.

The second major theme area built in 1973, was Rhineland, (at first called Rhine Land). This German theme area started at the Tudor Castle admission gate and ran to the Carrousel Circle. Wood, plaster, and brick were used in Rhineland in contrast to the brick and cut stone of Tudor Square. The buildings in Rhineland had steeply-pitched wood shingle roofs. There were a variety of shops and three refreshment areas. Young employees (now called hosts and hostesses by the park) were dressed in bright period costumes to further enhance the rural

German atmosphere. Plans originally called for Hersheypark to move its old bandstand, which was located on the otherside of Spring Creek, to Rhineland, but engineering and height problems made such a move impossible. The area by the admission gate was called Lower Rhineland and the area up the hill near Carrousel Circle was called Upper Rhineland.

Tudor Square under construction with the Hershey Museum in the background. (Charles J. Jacques, Jr. Collection)

shooting gallery for one or two seasons, were torn down. Many of the games located in the penny arcade were moved to the former souvenir shop nearby. All the pavilions and picnic tables were removed from the park, and no picnic lunches were permitted. Picnic tables were available in the grove adjacent to one of Hersheypark's parking lots on a first-come basis.

Several rides were planned for the Rhineland section, but only a sky ride station was built. The park had hoped to build a Rhine River Boat ride on Spring Creek, but the stream was too small and shallow. (M.S. Hershey had found the same thing with his Mayflower in the early years.) There were also plans to convert the miniature railway into the Rhine Land Express, but the idea was abandoned because of the train's poor shape, the lack of parts, and the difficulty in trying to lay out a route in a crowded section of the park.

In 1973, the Sunken Garden, electrical fountain, and electric miniature railway were all removed. The Giant Slide and Golden Nugget dark ride, which had been converted to a

Hersheypark's first spectacular European ride, the Giant Wheel (Swizzling Wheel) was purchased in 1973 from Intamin AG of Zurich, Switzerland, and placed on the edge of the Carrousel Circle area. The custom-built, 135-ton ride required a special foundation with more than two hundred cubic yards of concrete in a slab twenty-five feet square and ten feet thick. It had two rotary wheels mounted on a 116-foot crossbar. Each wheel had twelve cabins that held eight persons. The two wheels would alternately rise to a height of one hundred thirty feet above the ground. The ride was designed to carry two thousand people per hour.

During the fall of 1972 the Lost River ride was demolished. It had never reopened after the flood, and the park now needed

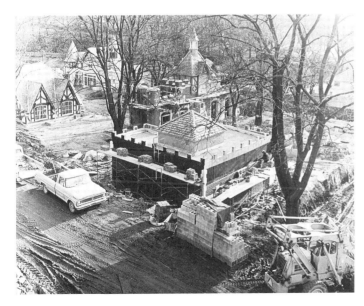

In the winter of 1972-73, Tudor Square in the foreground and Rhineland in the background under construction.

(Hershey Community Archives)

In Tudor Square were the Tudor House Restaurant in the foreground and the Tudor Apothecary in the background.

(Hershey Community Archives)

The entrance to the park and Tudor Square featured a moat and stone bridge.
(Hersheypark)

The new entrance sign for Hersheypark was located just outside Tudor Square.
(Charles J. Jacques, Jr. Collection)

a water ride. It was decided to tear down the band shell and build a new style flume ride, which was named the Coal Cracker. The ride and the area immediately around the flume were themed as a Pennsylvania mining town. The hydroflume was built by Arrow Development Company of Mountain View, California, and was the first of its kind in the world. It was a new type of flume, which used two 45-foot chutes and a small hump at the bottom which sent the little coal-car boats into the air for a second splash down.

The Coal Cracker trip lasted about three and one half minutes. The ride was approximately two thousand feet long. All of the water for the ride was stored in a fourteen thousand square foot man-made lake that had a capacity of 100,000 gallons. Water was pumped through the system by two pumping stations. According to the general manager, the pumps used more electricity than all of the other rides in the park combined.

At the top of the first of two lift hills, the boats carried passengers to a height of fifty-five feet. After traveling through a zigzag course the boats climbed to the top of a second lift and then hydroplaned down one of two twin 45-foot spillways at an angle of 45 degrees. The boats reached a speed of thirty-five miles an hour just before they hit the water.

The hydroflume with its unfinished rough wood and metal exterior resembled a nineteenth century Pennsylvania mine complex. It had an air-conditioned rotating forty-two foot circular loading station. (The air-conditioning was removed from the ride the following year as part of the park's energy saving campaign. The architects, who had designed parks primarily in the sun belt states, were not acquainted with central Pennsylvania's summers.)

With the bandstand demolition, Hersheypark opened a new open-air theatre, the Amphitheatre, in 1973 on the same spot as the park's first amphitheatre (later occupied by the Giant Slide). The new Amphitheatre would later be covered with a roof. *Al Alberts' TV Showcase* and *Hersheypark Revue* were staged in the new Amphitheatre.

Mark Wilson, a magician, brought his "Magic Spectacular" to Hersheypark in 1973 and performed in a tent adjacent to the Monorail station. Wilson and McKinney had picked the spot, which was eventually developed into the Dry Gulch Theatre (later renamed the Music Box Theatre). An outdoor stage replaced Wilson's tent.

During the redevelopment years, Hersheypark did not forget the environment and landscaping. Thousands of seasonal flowers and new trees were planted. The park was much cleaner because it was cleaned thoroughly every morning and there were fifty sweeperettes on duty during the peak summer months. The U.S. Department of Agriculture presented the park with an ecological award signifying the park's anti-pollution work in 1973.

The Giant Wheel under construction during the winter of 1972-73. (Photograph by Harold Sitler)

Just prior to the opening of the 1973 season, J. Bruce McKinney was named the manager of the park replacing John T. Hart. The energy crunch hit Hersheypark that summer and although gasoline was rationed for only a short time, the fear of a shortage of gasoline and oil played an important role in the later reluctance of Hersheypark's parent corporation, Hershey Estates, to continue to develop the park. J. Bruce McKinney appointed a four member energy team to work on energy-saving alternatives for the Hersheypark complex. Serving on the team were Paul Serff, Ernie Bretz, Harold Sitler, and Bob Sternberger. The team, which worked with the Hershey Electric Company, recommended cutbacks wherever possible, and the first thing to go was most of the outdoor air conditioning. "We want to make certain that we are doing our part," McKinney told the *Harrisburg Patriot News.* McKinney felt optimistic about the park's future, telling the *Patriot* that "54 percent of the nation's population is within a four hundred to five hundred mile radius of Hershey."

Hersheypark's expansion plans for 1974 were dramatically curtailed. The energy crisis was one of the factors leading to the changes. "Our major concerns for 1974 will be increased ride capacity and better visitor comfort," McKinney told the *Patriot.* Two new major rides, the Trailblazer and Sky Ride, were still scheduled to open in 1974, but the modern contemporary area and revolving tower were put on hold.

The Trailblazer, a modern high-speed steel roller coaster, was built by the Arrow Development Company of Mountain

Blacksmithing was one of the crafts demonstrated in the Der Deitsch Platz area.
(Charles J. Jacques, Jr. Collection)

The barn in Der Deitsch Platz with the Giant Wheel in the background. (In 1976 the name would be changed to two words Der Deitschplatz.)
(Charles J. Jacques, Jr. Collection)

View, California. It was the first major coaster to be added to the park in eighteen years. It was built near Spring Creek using the hillside across from the Animal Garden. Again designed by Duell, the ride blended into its surroundings. Because of construction delays it opened the second week of June 1974. The coaster was 1,874 feet long and featured a series of tight curves that turned riders completely sideways. The ride had three trains with five cars each that could carry up to twelve hundred passengers per hour.

Mid-way through the 1974 season, Cy Little, the park's publicity director, booked a country and western band. There was no place for them to play, so Little and McKinney picked a spot near the Trailblazer coaster and had some tan bark thrown down for the band and audience. The park's maintenance crew then constructed in less than a week a stage with a western motif, and the Trailblazer Theatre (sometimes called Trail Blazer Theatre) came into being. The Trailblazer area along with the Dry Gulch Railroad was the beginning of the park's frontier theme area.

The Sky Ride was a cable car ride strung high above the park, and it traversed the park in such a manner as to function both as a ride and as a means of transportation. It had two stations, one in Rhineland and the other near the Coal Cracker flume ride, which enabled people to more easily cross the park. The ride had thirty enclosed gondolas, which traveled 1,268 feet between the two stations. The Sky Ride was manufactured in Europe and purchased from Intamin AG of Switzerland. The

Along Spring Creek were the Dancing Waters, similar to the old electric fountain and The Comet. (HERSHEY COMMUNITY ARCHIVES)

The Carrousel Circle area from the Giant Wheel in 1973.
(CHARLES J. JACQUES, JR. COLLECTION)

highest point of the ride was one hundred fourteen feet above the park, which gave a wonderful scenic view of the Carrousel Circle area and The Comet.

Although the Sky Ride was a smooth ride, many people did not like to ride it because of its height. One of those was the park's merchandise manager Robert B. Payne. Occasionally Payne would have to ride it if he was back near the Coal Cracker and he was called to the front gate. However, when he rode it, his gondola would often get to the highest point and mysteriously stop. A minute or so later (although it always seemed much longer to him) the ride would start again. When he would ask an employee what happened, the answer would invariably be "I don't know; it must have been something at the other end."

Hersheypark's timetable called for the completion of its three hundred foot observation tower in 1974, but construction was delayed. McKinney told the *Harrisburg Patriot News* that the construction of the tower would have involved major renovation to several existing buildings in the area and as a result, the Hershey Estate board of directors had decided to postpone opening the tower until 1975 or 1976.

In 1973, Hersheypark started using corporate sponsors. The most important was Hershey Estate's sister corporation Hershey Foods. Hershey's chocolate products came to life at the park. Strolling characters such as Hershey's Bar, Reese's Peanut Butter Cup, Krackel Bar, and the Hershey's Kiss were featured. In addition, the park added its own costumed characters, the Furry Tales, consisting of a skunk, bear, and chipmunk in 1974. Other early sponsors included Coca-Cola, Hershey's ice cream, Finnaren & Haley (paint), and Red Rose animal feeds.

As disappointing as the 1971 and 1972 seasons had been, the 1973 season was the opposite. It was a huge success and was the first indication that the park was on the right path. In 1973 the park drew over one million (1,086,258) for the first time in its history. The new name, theme areas, new rides, and the focus on entertainment were finally working. The park was attracting more people from the Philadelphia and Baltimore regions.

For the 1974 season McKinney announced personnel changes for the park. Bob B. Payne was named operations manager, and Al Rimby took over Payne's old position of merchandise manager. Cy Little had his title changed from publicity director to promotion and entertainment director and Paul L. Serff was named McKinney's assistant.

Another change that would have important consequences to the park was the elevation of Edward "Ned" Book to the presidency of Hershey Estates. Book's background was in the hotel and resort business. He felt that Hershey Estates should diversify geographically. Book also wanted to streamline Hershey Estates by closing unprofitable companies.

The 1974 season was Hersheypark's best ever. The park pulled in 1,272,000 visitors, which was an increase of 17 percent over 1973. The large attendance jump led to a corresponding 34 percent increase in gross revenues. The top attendance day was a Saturday – August 24 – when 23,115 visited Hersheypark. In

Splashing down at speeds up to 35 miles per hour, the Coal Cracker's boats literally skimmed over the water. (Charles J. Jacques, Jr. Collection)

The electric sign in the shape of a flag was carefully removed from the bandstand by the demolition workers. (Photograph by Harold Sitler)

The bandstand was razed on October 23, 1972, by the Melvin Cassel Co. of Grantville, Pa. (Photograph by Harold Sitler)

Mark Wilson, a famous magician, performed on an outdoor stage, which later became the Music Box Theatre.

The Trail Blazer Theatre started as a small open air theatre.

A tower for the Sky Ride being lifted into place in 1974.

The Sky Ride ran from Rhineland to the hill near the Coal Cracker flume ride.

The park built a mine ride, the Trailblazer (sometimes called the Trail Blazer) in 1974. (CHARLES J. JACQUES, JR. COLLECTION)

all, the amusement facility experienced thirty days where daily attendance exceeded 15,000. The Coal Cracker flume ride was the most popular, followed by the Trailblazer and The Comet.

Transforming the park had not been easy, but revenues were up and the park could now afford to continue its expansion and modernization strategy. Future development should have been determined by the park's attendance and revenues, but instead other concerns (diversification and the need of capital elsewhere in the company) would govern the park's future.

The Sky Ride's loading station in Rhineland.
(CHARLES J. JACQUES, JR. COLLECTION)

The Sky Ride traveled over most of the park and gave a spectacular view of its attractions.
(CHARLES J. JACQUES, JR. COLLECTION)

CHAPTER 13

GETTING LOOPED -
THE SOOPERDOOPERLOOPER

The sooperdooperLooper's fifty-seven foot high loop offers its rider a truly exciting experience.
(HERSHEYPARK)

The Monster in the foreground and twin Toboggans in the background. Circa 1975.
(PHOTOGRAPH BY CHARLES J. JACQUES, JR.)

The park's admission gate is located between Tudor Square and Rhineland. (PHOTOGRAPH BY CHARLES J. JACQUES, JR.)

By 1975 Hersheypark had modified its future development plan to include saving more of the existing park. The message was, "We've been here awhile, but we're new." More old rides and buildings would be kept longer. However, some of the rides were too old and hard to maintain because of the difficulty in getting spare parts; others could carry so few passengers per hour that they had to go. Some of the buildings were impossible to bring up to current safety standards.

Hersheypark was a park with a history and tradition to lean on and learn from. In nearly seventy years of operation, it had been owned only by M.S. Hershey and his corporation, Hershey Estates. It was not like some theme parks that were bought and sold every few years and given a new corporate name. The park did not need to follow the latest fad in the outdoor amusement industry that might be forgotten in a year or two.

In 1975 Paul L. Serff was named general manager, while J. Bruce McKinney was promoted to a vice president and group director of the park's parent company, Hershey Estates. Plans were increasingly made on what worked for guests and employees. Traffic flow was analyzed and decisions based on the best use of the money available. Decisions were made as a group and then presented to the board of directors.

For 1975 the Hershey Estates board of directors approved the development of a four-acre site immediately behind the Coal Cracker flume ride that included a 330-foot high tower, and a new double-track Turnpike ride. The name Kissing Tower was suggested by J.O. Hershey. Hershey also thought that the tower should be distinctive and liked the idea of windows in the shape of Hershey's Kisses. At first the manufacturer balked at the idea, but when the Kiss-shaped windows idea was presented as "either do it or lose the order," it was done. McKinney told the *Harrisburg Patriot News*,

*The Crown Manufacturing
steam train on the Dry Gulch
Railroad in 1975.*
(Photograph by Charles J. Jacques, Jr.)

*A skeleton and Indian
tepee were located along
the train's route.*
(Photograph by Charles J. Jacques, Jr.)

*Entrance to the
Animal Garden, an
animal contact area.*
(Hershey Community Archives)

Goats, sheep, and other small animals could be fed by hand.
(Photograph by Charles J. Jacques, Jr.)

*One problem with the animal contact area was
when the animals would push or bite a small child.*
(Photograph by Charles J. Jacques, Jr.)

A section of the Kissing Tower being lifted into place by a huge crane. (Photography by Harold Sitler)

The 330-foot high Kissing Tower was built on the hill behind the Coal Cracker flume ride in 1985. (Hershey Community Archives)

"Both the tower and the turnpike rides will be family rides that can handle high capacities. Our emphasis this year will be on rides and ride capacity. We want to cut down on the time people have to wait in line for rides whenever possible."

The spot chosen to erect the tower was the highest point in the park and occupied the area that was formerly the southeast entrance to old Hershey Park. This section of the park had many mature trees and as many of them as possible were saved during the construction. More than 3,138,759 pounds of concrete were poured into the base of the Kissing Tower and some 50 gallons of silver and brown paint were used. Tower Plaza, located at the foot of the tower, featured a brick terrace and bubbling reflection pool that was designed for sitting and relaxing.

Because of its height, the Kissing Tower was clearly visible from all of the park and the town. The tower was equipped with a blinking red light at the top in order to meet Federal Aviation Administration regulations and was grounded to serve as a lightning arrester for the surrounding area. The structure was designed and manufactured by Intamin AG, the same firm that supplied Hersheypark with its Giant Wheel and Sky Ride. The

At the dedication of the Kissing Tower from right to left: Ivan Keener, a Derry Township supervisor; J. Bruce McKinney, vice president of Hershey Estates; Paul L. Serff, general manager; Edward R. Book, a Hershey Estates vice president; Arthur R. Whiteman, chairman of the board of Hershey Estates; and James E. Bobb, president of Hershey Estates.

(Paul L. Serff Collection)

tower was a one-of-a-kind, custom-designed ride with a brown and silver cabin and bubbled observation windows that simulated Hershey's Chocolate Kisses. It had a capacity of twelve hundred passengers per hour.

The Kissing Tower's doughnut-shaped cabin was raised to the height of two hundred fifty feet. During the ride the cabin made three complete revolutions: one as passengers ascended the tower, one at the top, and one as the riders descended. The trip lasted approximately three and one-half minutes and could carry a maximum load of fifty-five adult passengers. It was one of the tallest structures in central Pennsylvania and provided a panoramic view of Hershey and the Lebanon Valley. On top of the tower the park placed a flag pole and every day of the year, weather permitting, maintenance men would climb the tower and unfurl a 20-foot by 30-foot American flag. It quickly became a focal point for people in the town of Hershey. J. Bruce

McKinney recalled, "when the flag was not flying, I would receive calls from the town asking me what was wrong in the park."

The new Turnpike ride was built next to Tower Plaza and featured gasoline-powered cars driven along a double track. The riders had to choose between riding in a sports or an antique car. Like the park's old Turnpike, the ride featured drive-it-yourself cars, but the new ones ran on a track and were equipped with safety bumpers and speed governors. One track had seventeen two-seater sports cars (only thirteen operating at a time on the track) manufactured by Gould Limited, Winnipeg, Canada, and the other had seventeen four-seater antique autos (again with only thirteen operating at a time) manufactured by Arrow Development Company of Mountain View, California.

The twin Ferris wheels were removed and replaced with a 1975 Reverchon Himalaya. The ride went in circles while climbing up and down hills. The Himalaya went forward and backward. It was made in France and had a capacity of fifteen hundred riders per hour. The Ferris wheels had always been popular, but they were able to handle a small number of riders per hour. In addition, the park now offered four other high rides: the Kissing Tower, Giant Wheel, Skyview, and Sky Ride.

Mark Wilson continued to appear at the Dry Gulch Theatre with his magic act. For 1975 the park showcased forty-six shows a day. The dolphins shared the Aquatheatre with a comedy diving team. Benches were added to the Trailblazer Theatre, which presented country and western music. The Furry Tales, which had been created by Scollon Productions of *Banana Split* fame, were given their own ten-minute show. Dutch, the blue bear; Chip, the chipmunk; and Violet, the skunk sang, acted, and danced. In the Animal Garden, baby pigs were permitted to run free. When they got hungry, they seemed to be able to distinguish between the petting zoo workers and guests, and they would head for the nearest worker to get their milk.

The antique cars could hold four passengers.

(Charles J. Jacques, Jr. Collection)

The new Turnpike ride in Tower Plaza featured gasoline-powered cars. It was a double ride with a double track, and one side had sports cars.

(Photograph by Charles J. Jacques, Jr.)

The Furry Tales frolic in the snow outside the park entrance.
(Charles J. Jacques, Jr. Collection)

There was a shop called Furry Tales, which featured stuffed animals. (Photograph by Charles J. Jacques, Jr.)

The Furry Tales were transported around the park in a specially outfitted electric-powered cart.
(Photograph by Charles J. Jacques, Jr.)

Holiday magazine in 1975 named Hersheypark the cleanest and greenest theme park in America. Its landscaping featured mature trees. In 1975, Bill Bowman, general manager of the Hershey Nursery, was chosen for the dual role of director of Hershey Gardens. He spent the next four years expanding the Gardens by adding six thematic garden areas.

The year ended with a torrential downpour from another tropical storm, Eloise. This time the park was prepared. Paul L. Serff, Robert B. Payne, Elmer "Zeke" Zartman and Harold Sitler directed the effort. The Skooter cars were moved to higher ground, motors were taken out of the Himalaya and Rotor, food trailers were relocated, and all of the animals were safely removed from the Animal Garden. There was some minor flooding, but the only real casualty of the heavy rains was the park's long Labor Day weekend. The whole summer was the rainiest season that anyone could remember with forty-seven rain days. To better handle rainy days, a roof was put over the park's Amphitheatre during the winter of 1975-76. Attendance for 1975 fell slightly to 1,206,000. The poor weather contributed to the drop, as well as a more competitive market. There were three new theme parks (Great Adventure, Jackson, New Jersey; Kings Dominion, Doswell, Virginia; and the Old Country, Williamsburg, Virginia) competing in Hersheypark's markets.

A small Allan Herschell coaster introduced children to the fun of roller coaster riding.
(Photograph by Charles J. Jacques, Jr.)

In 1976, a new two-story U-shaped maintenance and service center was constructed across from the stadium, off Airport Road. This new 130,000-square-foot building was needed by the park to house its wardrobe department for the more than thirteen hundred summer employees, along with a maintenance department, machine shop, and offices. Rides were stored inside and worked on in the winter months. The park's maintenance department previously had been located in town adjacent to the Hershey Lumber Company. All maintenance calls were made over CB radios, and service was slow and cumbersome from town. The other major construction project that spring was the addition of a dressing room and two hundred additional seats to the Aquatheatre.

For the first time since the park's redevelopment had started in 1972, the park did not add a spectacular ride or attraction. This was probably caused, at least in part, by the energy crisis of 1973. Ride purchases and plans had to be made years in advance. After 1973, Hershey Estates slowed down the park's development.

Almost every year, the park added one or two new rides to its Kiddieland. In 1976 the park purchased a used Tiny Tanks ride which had been built by Allan Herschell Co., Tonawanda, New York. In 1981 this ride was rebuilt by the park and became Earthmovers.

On June 23, 1976, Hershey Estates, founded by M.S. Hershey in 1927, changed its name to HERCO, Inc. so that people would not think it was a land company of Milton Hershey's estate. The name would be changed again on April 1, 1980, to Hershey Entertainment & Resort Company.

The weather for 1976 was dry and warm, a welcome change from 1975, which had been wet and cool. The good weather helped the park register a 22 percent gain in attendance over

Children really enjoyed the kid's motor boat ride.
(Photograph by Charles J. Jacques, Jr.)

A kiddie Mangels whip had been in the park for many years.
(Photograph by Charles J. Jacques, Jr.)

146

1975 to a record 1,472,000. Paul L. Serff said, "it was good traveling weather," and "it was also a good economic year." A preseason football game in Hershey's Stadium between the Baltimore Colts and the Washington Redskins on July 24 and a successful Dutch Days promotion in August helped boost attendance.

Although Hersheypark set an all-time attendance record in a year when nothing major was added, it was more of a catch up year when the public continued to find out about the new Hersheypark and how it had changed and grown. The outstanding changes and the money spent on buildings and rides were finally paying off. People realized that Hersheypark had some of the finest entertainment of any amusement park in the country. However, the park had to keep growing and changing if it wanted to increase attendance every year.

In 1975 only the stage section of the Amphitheatre was covered.
(PHOTOGRAPH BY CHARLES J. JACQUES, JR.)

Inside the Arcade was a mix of old penny arcade machines and the newer electronic machines.
(PHOTOGRAPH BY CHARLES J. JACQUES, JR.)

Each prize bear had a tag that reminded the winner, "I was won at Hersheypark."
(PHOTOGRAPH BY CHARLES J. JACQUES, JR.)

A ball game that cost 50 cents offered a giant dog as one of the prizes.
(PHOTOGRAPH BY CHARLES J. JACQUES, JR.)

Parts of the soooperdooperLooper being lifted into place by a large crane. The coaster was designed by Anton Schwarzkopf of West Germany.
(PHOTOGRAPH BY HAROLD SITLER)

Hersheypark announced on July 16, 1976, that it would build a new steel looping roller coaster for 1977. This new coaster was the first looping coaster built in the east. The only other looping coaster in America had been built early in 1976 at Magic Mountain, California. The concept was actually an old one. At the turn of the century a looping coaster had been developed, but it had a low ride capacity with its small four-seat car and produced such a neck-jarring ride that it proved unpopular with operators and riders and soon disappeared.

The new coaster would be the park's most expensive ride costing more than three million dollars. A sign was erected on the site where the new coaster would be built and ground was broken in September for the new ride which was being manufactured in Germany. The Himalaya ride and several game booths were removed to make room for the coaster.

McKinney had the honor of naming the new coaster. He finally narrowed it down to two names, and then around the kitchen table one evening, presented his choices to his wife, Sally, and two daughters, Kelly and Katie. The names were Super Duper Looper and Merry Derry Dips. McKinney liked the Merry Derry name since the coaster was located in Derry Township, but he was outvoted three to one, and so the coaster got its new name. The spelling was later changed to soooperdooperLooper.

Hersheypark's new coaster could carry twenty-four passengers and was 2,614 feet long. It was built under the supervision of Edward Houser, the park's construction manager and assistant general manager. Each of the looping coaster's three trains (only two were used at a time) had six cars.

The soooperdooperLooper's orange coaster trains were distinctive.
(HERSHEYPARK)

148

The sooperdooperLooper's trains were lifted up an incline to a height of seventy feet above the station. After going over the top, the train plunged down the track at a speed of sixty-six feet per second into a fifty-seven-foot-high loop that turned the passengers upside down. Since the Amphitheatre abutted the new coaster, there were plans to have a tunnel to muffle the noise, but it was not built because the coaster ran so quietly. The loudest sounds were the screams from the passengers. After traveling through the loop, the train circled back and passed through the center of the loop, then took a few dips and banks at angles of up to sixty degrees before returning to the loading station. It was the most complex ride the park had ever built.

Traveling upside down in a coaster was new for the public, and people had to be reassured that the new coaster was safe. Lap bars were used, but early publicity indicated that the passengers would be strapped in. However, as in all coasters that go upside down, centrifugal force holds riders in their seats. Edward Houser further reassured the public by saying that the ride would be inspected daily before the park opened and twice during the day. Also two or three maintenance men were specifically assigned to take the first ride of the day. Prior to the opening, Hersheypark stressed the coaster's safety features as follows: ratchet-type lap bars would fit snugly regardless of the rider's size, rotary wheels could slow the train in bad weather, electronic relays (a fail safe system) would prevent a second or third train from being released, air brakes at various points on the track would operate even during a complete power failure, catwalks would be used if riders had to leave the train, and the entire duration of the ride would be monitored electronically by a computerized control panel. In addition, gravity made it almost impossible to become stuck in the loop.

The sooperdooperLooper was introduced to the public at the park's Media Day in May 1977. Hersheypark adopted the slogan, "I survived the sooperdooperLooper," and tens of thousands of T-shirts were sold with

The Furry Tales characters were used as height markers in the 1970's.
(Photograph by Charles J. Jacques, Jr.)

the new slogan. J. Bruce McKinney, along with other company executives and special guests, were to take the first ride on press day. McKinney had talked his wife, Sally, who did not like to ride coasters, into riding, saying that it was the duty of the vice president in charge of the park to take the first ride. With cameras from the local media outlets covering the event, McKinney and twenty-three other riders left the loading station, climbed to the top of the first hill and stopped. After what seemed like an eternity, Harold Sitler, assistant maintenance manager, had to climb the new coaster's structure to tell McKinney and his guests that they could not get the train started again and they would have to climb down.

In front of almost every newspaper, television, and radio reporter within one hundred miles of the park, J. Bruce and Sally McKinney, the latter with her eyes closed, slowly hand-over-hand descended from the coaster. McKinney told the reporters that it was only a minor glitch that would soon be corrected. At the end of the day he felt that he really had "survived the sooperdooperLooper." Harold Sitler remembered the experience as the worst day in almost forty years of working at the park. It proved to be an embarrassing moment, but the sooperdooperLooper became one of the greatest rides in the history of the park.

For the first time in its history, Hersheypark was forced to close its gates Saturday, July 23, 1977, when more than 25,000 people jammed into the park. Many of the park's all time daily attendance records were broken that summer. Attendance passed the million mark on July 31, the earliest date in park history that that milestone had been reached.

The new $3 million plus coaster, moved Hersheypark into the major league of amusement parks in America. The publicity department produced eighty different campaigns themed around the new coaster. By the time the coaster opened, almost everyone in the eastern United States seemed to know about it. The coaster was designed by Anton Schwartzkopf of West Germany and purchased through

Aerial view of the park in the late 1970's. The sooperdooperLooper is in the lower right hand corner.
(Hershey Community Archives)

The interior of the Starlight Ballroom during the demolition.
(Hershey Community Archives)

A giant crane rips into the roof of the old ballroom.
(Hershey Community Archives)

Intamin AG of Switzerland. The structural engineer was R. Duell & Associates. They designed the coaster's loading station in the same style as Tower Plaza.

The ride was a fantastic addition with a great location. "So many things were right about it, but that first season it did not run well," Paul L. Serff explained. "It drained resources and the amount of time it was down was frustrating." The ride broke down so often that finally the park's maintenance department had to rebuild the lift system to the top of the first hill.

As a dazzling new attraction was added, an old one that had served the park well for many years, the Starlight Ballroom, was being demolished. Melvin E. Cassel, Inc. brought in the bulldozer and wrecking crane to demolish the building in March 1977. Small explosive charges weakened the pillars, and then the wrecking crane knocked down one of the walls and the three-story wooden structure collapsed. One enterprising person set up a souvenir stand near the demolition site, selling pieces of lumber from the building with Starlight Ballroom pictures attached. He sold them for four dollars each.

The ballroom had been closed since 1969, and primarily for safety reasons Hersheypark decided to remove it. The structure did not fit into the park's future plans. It would have cost more to remodel the building and bring it into code compliance than to build a completely new building. It also was located in an area that was no longer easily accessible, and there was no parking in the area. In the future the park would grow to the northeast, where the park owned some undeveloped land.

Beer was served by the park for the first time in 1977. There were some protests from various church and civic groups, but beer was merely offered as an addition to a food, and not as an activity in itself. Security personnel were given the responsibility of making sure people consumed beer only in the two locations where it was sold, and that it was not sold or given to minors. Competitive pressure from Hersheypark's new park rivals, Anheuser-Busch's Old Country, Great Adventure, and Kings Dominion, all of which sold beer, forced the park to make the move.

In the mid-1970's, Hersheypark started booking big name entertainers including Dick Clark's Rock and Roll Revue, Ricky Nelson, Ray Stevens, The Shirelles, the Golddiggers, Bobby Goldsboro, and the Starland Vocal Band.

All attendance records were smashed in 1977 when more than 1,700,000 people visited the park. However, all of the support services were taxed to their limits. As large as the food operation had grown (eight sit-down restaurants and numerous fast foods stands), it was not large enough to handle the crowds that jammed the park on weekends and holidays that season. All of the park's rest rooms, souvenir shops, and entertainment facilities were crowded during the summer months. Even the park's high capacity rides like the Coal Cracker, Kissing Tower, Trailblazer, Sky Ride, Giant Wheel, Monorail, The Comet, and sooperdooperLooper were packed, and some of the old rides were unable to handle the crowds.

Hersheypark's attendance in 1977 had grown 17 percent over the preceding record year. Thomas Cantone, the park's marketing director, told the *Harrisburg Evening News* that the increase "makes us the number two park in the U.S. in terms of percentage increase." From 1973 to 1977, the park attendance increased from one million to 1.7 million, a 58 percent increase, Cantone said.

In 1976, John Strawbridge III, the director of the Hershey Museum, had proposed rebuilding the zoo and renaming it ZooAmerica. By the mid-1970's the old zoo buildings sat empty and even the fences were not maintained. McKinney helped get Strawbridge's project approved in 1977. Construction started immediately, and Strawbridge and the creative team of Troy Stump (who later became the director of ZooAmerica), Mike Patton (draftsperson), Renna Grimmer (graphics consultant), and Priscilla Rothermel (artistic coordinator who dealt primarily with the interior exhibit designs), designed the attraction. This small team brought the fantastic new addition to Hersheypark on schedule and on budget.

It was the park's first expansion outside its gates in five years, and it reused 10 acres of the former zoo site. A covered walkway built over Park Avenue connected Hersheypark to ZooAmerica. The day of the sneak preview, it snowed and the

ZOOAMERICA ®
North American Wildlife Park

The Comet's two trains can carry almost one thousand people per hour. (Charles J. Jacques, Jr. Collection)

The Comet's trains have been given different names over the years. In the late-1970's one of the trains was called Mork's Comet. (Photograph by Chuck Woldarczyk)

park searched for hot drinks for everyone. The official opening took place May 7, 1978. Visitors first entered an orientation building that properly guided them through the exhibits. The zoo contained sixty to sixty-five animals found in North America. McKinney noted that the zoo featured authentic North American animals and the environment was perfectly matched for these animals. The site incorporated two existing buildings from the old Hershey Park Zoo and two new buildings. Modern zoological techniques were used with exhibits more open but protected by plexiglass. ZooAmerica offered people the opportunity to explore and walk through five different areas: Grassy Waters, North Woods, Gentle Woodlands, Cactus Community, and Big Sky Country. The Monorail provided another way of viewing the exhibits. ZooAmerica was included as part of the park's one price admission plan during the season, but it remained open after the park closed with a separate admission charge. After ZooAmerica opened, the park spent between $20,000-$25,000 annually on capital improvements for the facility.

Although ZooAmerica was not a multimillion dollar attraction, it served the park well over the years. It added an important educational element to the park and created an attraction that would be open year round, which was good for tourism in the Hershey area.

One of the casualties of this hugely successful season was the Toboggan ride; it was sold at the end of the season and was replaced with a Flying Bobs purchased from Chance Manufacturing of Wichita, Kansas. This ride was similar to the Himalaya ride with suspended cars. Two other new rides were also added for the 1978 season: one was a Trabant from Chance and the other was the return of a refurbished Cuddle Up (Coal Shaker), manufactured by the Philadelphia Toboggan Company. It was hoped that these three attractions, although not spectacular rides, would help keep the attendance at the 1977 level. They also gave the park some much needed increased ride capacity.

The park remained clean and green. For 1978 there were 1,664 hanging baskets, fifteen thousand flowers in one hundred ten flower beds, and more than two hundred plants at ZooAmerica. Over three hundred fifty tons of tanbark were also used during the season. The park had a crew of eleven people who were responsible for planting, watering, mowing, and weeding the sixty-nine acre park. To discourage people from stepping on the plants, small signs were designed and painted by Paul Boyer, the park's resident sign painter, and placed around the park. The signs included: "These Flowers Like Sunshine, Not Footprints," "It's Tough Growing Up, Everyone's Always Stepping On Me," and "Around the Bend is Better in the End."

John Strawbridge III, ZooAmerica's Development Director (left) and J. Bruce McKinney, Vice President of HERCO, discuss progress of the new theme area in the spring of 1978.
(CHARLES J. JACQUES, JR. COLLECTION)

In addition, a few kiddie rides were added in 1978, but there were no major new attractions. Attendance was down slightly in 1978 to 1.6 million, a decrease of about 8 percent from the 1977 record. At the end of the 1978 season the Golden Nugget dark ride, which had been turned into a shooting gallery, was demolished and replaced with the Fender Bender, an Auto Skooter. This was part of a trend in the amusement park industry to get rid of dark rides and walk-throughs. They were usually low volume attractions that created many security problems for the park. The maintenance department wanted to move the Skooter cars from the low lying area near Spring Creek to higher ground, and so the ride was moved to the former Golden Nugget site. The Auto Skooter was expanded to forty-five cars which were purchased from Lusse Brothers of Philadelphia. In the bottom of the new Skooter building the park added a mini Skooter for 1978. The Comet was also remodeled in 1978 and a new sign with the name was added.

The Furry Tales were given their own mini-theatre located in the Rhineland section of the park. Six times a day they sang, acted, and danced in a ten-minute variety show. They also served as representatives for the park with guest appearances all over the area. They appeared for one Philadelphia Phillies ballgame in Veterans Stadium.

The Furry Tales appeared at a Philadelphia Phillies baseball game.
(CHARLES J. JACQUES, JR. COLLECTION)

Some of the old zoo buildings were renovated and used in ZooAmerica.
(CHARLES J. JACQUES, JR. COLLECTION)

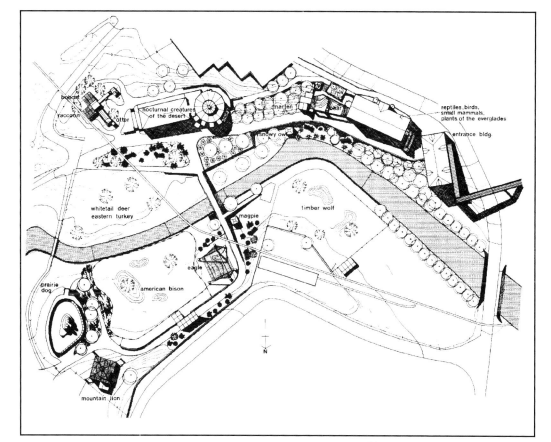

A drawing of the redesigned ZooAmerica.
(CHARLES J. JACQUES, JR. COLLECTION)

The maintenance department, now located in the new service building, had grown to one hundred and five full-time employees with an additional one hundred thirty part-time positions added in the summer.

Bob Lorenz was the food and beverage manager. Under his supervision the food operation expanded to twelve sit-down restaurants and thirty-eight refreshment stands. The park had four picnic groves that it used for catering group outings. One grove could seat one thousand and the arena could be used on rainy days. By 1978, employment had grown to more than fifteen hundred workers during the summer. The security force consisted of eight full-time people and one hundred part-time employees.

Perhaps 1979 would be best remembered for the Three Mile Island incident and the fear of a nuclear meltdown. In the 1950's Civil Defense had designated the Hershey Arena as safe in case of nuclear fallout. When trouble developed on March 28 at the power plant which was located about twenty miles southwest of Hershey, the park and arena staff were mobilized to help handle the emergency. Hersheypark's experience in handling crowds helped them cope with the situation.

Paul L. Serff, general manager, recalled, "It seemed like a lifetime in seven days. They [Civil Defense] called us on a Friday morning and said that they might have to evacuate between 18,000 and 20,000 persons to our arena. The hockey season was not over yet, so the first thing we had to do was to put the wooden floor on over the ice." Before provision was made for regular meals, the Hersheypark Arena opened its three concession stands and immediately served hot dogs, milk, and

Coca-Cola free of charge to early arrivals. During the emergency one stand remained open for late night snacks. In all, Hersheypark, through its commissary, provided 1,275 meals with the help of the Red Cross.

Serff ordered his staff to pass out balloons, coloring books, and other toys to all the evacuated children who wanted them. Richard Hair, assistant general manager, ran back and forth between Hershey and Harrisburg picking up movies that the park rented for the children. Serff even donned the costume of Coco the Bear, the mascot of the hockey team, to entertain the children during the evacuation. (It was not the first time that

(R to L) Paul L. Serff, general manager of the park, Pennsylvania Governor Richard Thornburgh and his wife, Ginny Thornburgh in the cabin of the Kissing Tower, shortly after the Three Mile Island incident. (PAUL L. SERFF COLLECTION)

A tram unloads passengers at the entrance to the park.
(CHARLES J. JACQUES, JR. COLLECTION)

Dutch the blue bear mixes with park visitors.
(CHARLES J. JACQUES, JR. COLLECTION)

The first performers to be honored with name and handprints in the Starlight Arcade were the Osmond family. J. Bruce McKinney, vice president (on the far right), and Paul L. Serff, general manager (second from the right), present a plaque to the Osmonds.
(PAUL L. SERFF COLLECTION)

This youngster is following in the handprints of one of her favorite celebrities at the Starlight Arcade. (CHARLES J. JACQUES, JR. COLLECTION)

Serff had donned a bear costume. Serff had wanted his employees that were costume characters to be more energetic, but they objected saying that the costumes were hot and not very maneuverable. So one day, Serff dressed as Dutch, the park's blue bear, and with a handler went out into the park. While the usual costume character was out for only twenty minutes, Serff decided to stay out for an hour to test his theories. He waved, high-fived, and even rolled on the ground. As he left the park proper, he almost collapsed. He lost about ten pounds and it took wardrobe almost two days to dry out the costume. He later admitted that "running around in a costume was harder than I ever imagined.")

In the end, only about one hundred fifty people – most of them pregnant women and children – used the arena as an evacuation site. At times, the press and media outnumbered the evacuees. "I've never spoken to so many reporters in my life," Serff said. The Governor of Pennsylvania, Richard Thornburgh, and his wife toured the park and took a ride up the Kissing Tower.

Three Mile Island was not the only negative factor that the park experienced during the summer of 1979. There were also gasoline shortages and reports of a polio outbreak in Lancaster County. It was also one of the worst seasons for weather in the park's history.

In 1979 two antique kiddie rides were purchased. Both were manufactured by W. F. Mangels of Coney Island in the 1930's. The rides were a kiddie carousel and a pony cart ride. The carousel weighed 4,700 pounds and had sixteen galloping horses, eight stationary horses, and two decorated chariots. The rounding boards were decorated with ornamental shields and circles of lights. The kiddie carousel was added on the sixtieth birthday of the park's 1919 PTC carousel. The rides were from Steeplechase Park, Coney Island, New York, which closed in 1965.

A 150-foot tunnel of rough textured lumber featuring sound and light effects was added to the sooperdooperLooper in 1979. During the winter of 1978-79, the park's merry-go-round, PTC #41, was completely refurbished under the watchful eye of Harold Sitler. A new wooden floor was installed. To help protect the antique horses, stationary stirrups replaced the old moveable leather and brass stirrups. Sitler noted, "The carousel had a maximum speed of six miles per hour, but it seemed more like forty miles per hour as riders watch people whirl by."

Handprints of the stars in cement, similar to those at Hollywood's Grauman's Chinese Theatre, were first displayed in 1979 at the Starlight Arcade in Carousel Circle. These were for celebrities who performed or visited Hersheypark or the arena.

The Osmonds were the first Hersheypark guest performers to provide their name and handprints. The name for the area was taken from the old Starlight Ballroom. A large bronze star accompanied handprints, signatures, and dates of performance.

The Music Box Theatre was totally enclosed in 1979 to make a better setting for the audience and performers. An acoustical ceiling, new sound system, and stage floor were also added. It was the park's first enclosed theater since the old Park Theatre had been torn down in the 1960's. A regular musical stage show was now presented in the Music Box Theatre.

Changing times and the fencing of Hersheypark brought Pennsylvania Dutch Days to an end. In 1949 the Dutch celebration was the whole show, the only major folk arts and crafts celebration in the area, but over the years many others had sprung up. Attendance had been declining, especially when the park went to a pay-one-price admission. At first, the event had been held in the arena with outdoor activities held in the park. In 1975, the celebration was held in a field adjacent to the stadium and then from 1976 to 1979 Dutch Days celebrations were held at the park's service center.

Even with Three Mile Island and the other negative events, Hersheypark's 1979 season attendance was off only 5 percent. Thomas Cantone, director of public relations, commented in the *Harrisburg Patriot News* about the gas crunch, "Central Pennsylvania cannot support the park by itself. We have to attract people who are traveling and stop at the park and those who journey here from further distances to give us the kind of attendance figures we want." He said that the drop at the gate was most noticeable on weekdays, traditionally days that the park attracts the so-called "tourist market." Local residents generally visited the park on weekends when they were off work, and attendance figures on weekends remained stable.

The decrease in attendance put a serious dent in HERCO's operating budget. J. Bruce McKinney told the *Lebanon Daily News* in August 1979, before the final attendance figures were in that, "Such a decrease would not put us [Hersheypark] in the red for the year, but it would adversely affect the overall corporate picture." The parent corporation was leaning heavily on the park to generate needed capital.

Hersheypark paused in its development. It had been ten years since the first bold steps had been taken to transform the park into a major amusement park and destination point. It was time to evaluate the effort, but HERCO's attention was about to be diverted from the park and the town of Hershey to problems it was having with its new resort properties. Future development would be more dependent on HERCO's financial capabilities than on what the park needed to compete and grow.

The sooperdooperLooper's running lights add to a nighttime ride.
(PHOTOGRAPH BY CHARLES J. JACQUES, JR.)

CHAPTER 14

A SHORTAGE OF CAPITAL

The Cyclops was purchased by the park in 1980.
(CHARLES J. JACQUES, JR. COLLECTION)

The Pirat symbol and ride.
(CHARLES J. JACQUES, JR. COLLECTION)

"The day we stop adding is the first day of a down trend," Tom Cantone, director of public relations, said the year after the sooperdooperLooper was opened. HERCO, Hersheypark's parent, was strapped for cash, so capital spending on the park was cut drastically. Companies drift through cycles. Now the park entered a period where it had to use what was given to it by HERCO and wait for times to change. Fortunately, the park had built a reputation as one of the best amusement parks in America, and this would help the park weather a slow down in its development.

Not only was there a shortage of capital, but at times even the marketing budget was cut. The days of eighty separate marketing campaigns in one year were over for a while. However, ZooAmerica had taught management that a lot could be done without spending much money.

Pinball machines were popular in the arcade in the early 1980's.
(PHOTOGRAPH BY CHARLES J. JACQUES, JR.)

Shoot Out The Star was placed next to The Comet.
Later more games were added in this area.
(PHOTOGRAPH BY CHARLES J. JACQUES, JR.)

After the recession of the early 1980's, Hersheypark faced increased competition from Six Flags Great Adventure, Kings Dominion, Busch Gardens' Old Country and even venerable old Dorney Park. All of these parks were expanding and adding new rides and attractions. Highways, which traditionally had brought people from Philadelphia, Baltimore, and New York could also permit people from central Pennsylvania to travel to those parks, and Hersheypark had to continue to grow and change.

In 1980 Hersheypark expanded its boundaries for the first time (excepting ZooAmerica, which was almost a separate attraction) since it had fenced the park in 1971. A new theme area was planned northeast of the existing park, and in 1980, 1.7 acres opened. Two new high capacity rides (the Cyclops and Pirat) were added in the newly developed area, which was adjacent to the Dry Gulch Railroad. The railroad was rerouted to make room for the new rides, and a walkway was extended into the new section.

The Cyclops was a high-speed vertical wheel ride that lifted its cars hydraulically, while the Pirat was a swinging boat ride. Both rides were purchased from Huss & Company of West Germany. In the Pirat the riders found themselves on a swiftly moving pendulum-motion boat ride that hurled them high above the sea, then swooped down again, only to have them repeatedly tossed above the stormy waves. The ride was well liked because of its moments of weightlessness at the top of each swing. The Pirat's boat reached a height of

Benny the computerized piano player from the Dry Gulch Railroad in storage during the winter.
(PHOTOGRAPH BY CHARLES J. JACQUES, JR.)

sixty-six feet at full swing. The actual boat, which weighed twenty-eight tons, was forty-three feet wide and eighty-six feet long.

The Cyclops was a spinning wheel that began slowly at first then increased to about 35 mph as it spun rapidly in circles until it was lifted perpendicular to the ground. There were twenty two-passenger gondolas; the diameter of the wheel was fifty-six feet. The height of the thirty-five ton wheel when fully extended was sixty-five feet. The ride traveled in a clockwise direction. The generic name for the ride was Enterprise. A food stand was built in the new area, but no theming was done. Theming cost money and the park did not have the extra money to theme the area, but it was landscaped.

The Pirat and Cyclops were extremely popular, and both rides had a much higher capacity than most of the existing rides in the park. Both easily loaded and unloaded passengers. These were significant rides and helped increase the park's ride capacity per hour. At the same time some of the older rides like the Paratrooper and Tip Top were retired.

In its marketing plan the park emphasized that it had expanded and now contained seventy-six acres. Again the park was trying to tell the public that if you came in 1977 and had to wait in long lines now the park was growing and adding more rides and food facilities.

A 228-seat, cafeteria-style restaurant called the Pennsylvania Fest Haus was opened in 1980. It was located in the former Fascination

The handprints of the Harlem Globetrotters were added to the Starlight Arcade in 1980.
(Charles J. Jacques, Jr. Collection)

To handle the increased attendance, the park added more food and drink carts.
(Charles J. Jacques, Jr. Collection)

games building near Tower Plaza. The restaurant-theatre, which was done in a Bavarian style, had a fourteen-by-twenty-foot center stage where the audience participated with costumed entertainers. This was the park's second enclosed dining area with the other one located in Tudor Square.

In 1980 a survey was done which showed that people identified the park with Hershey's chocolate. Marketing decided to emphasize chocolate and the brown and silver of the Hershey's Chocolate Bar wrapper in the park logo. Several new advertising slogans were initiated including "Go For the Chocolate - Stay For the Fun!" The park's familiar "Hersheypark happy" was replaced with "Only the name is tame." The pinwheel design was retained for park entertainment and some promotions.

The Music Box Theatre, which had been totally enclosed in the late 1970's, was air-conditioned in 1980 and given an all new show, *Window On the World*. Strolling clowns, oompah

The Cyclops spins its riders upside down on each turn of the wheel.
(Charles J. Jacques, Jr. Collection)

After the Music Box Theatre was enclosed, it became the home for the park's second biggest show. (Hersheypark)

Erecting the Pirat ride in 1980.
(Hershey Community Archives)

The Pirat offered a moment of weightlessness as the ride reached its highest point.
(Charles J. Jacques, Jr. Collection)

The Sky Ride traveled almost directly over the third hill of The Comet and gave this view of the coaster.
(PHOTOGRAPH BY EUGENE KRALL.)

Hershey Resort and Entertainment Company's offices were moved to the former clubhouse of the Hershey Parkview Golf Club.
(PHOTOGRAPH BY CHARLES J. JACQUES, JR.)

bands, and puppeteers were used around the queue lines.

In 1980, HERCO moved its corporate headquarters from downtown Hershey to the clubhouse of Hershey Parkview Golf Club, which it renovated into offices. The headquarters were located across Park Boulevard from the park and provided easier access to the park. In 1981 HERCO added the Cocoa Suite Complex to the Hershey Lodge making it more attractive to convention groups.

Officials of HERCO had projected a 9 percent increase in revenues for the 1980 season, but receipts fell quite short of the goal. Attendance was up in 1980 1 percent from the 1,497,000 for 1979. The weather for the summer of 1980 was near-perfect and the park did not have to deal with gas shortages or Three Mile Island, but the country was in its worst recession since the 1930's. Group sales accounted for almost a quarter of the attendance. Season pass holders, which came mainly from the Harrisburg, Hershey, Lebanon, Lancaster, and York areas, had increased each year from 3,000 in 1977 to 10,117 in 1980. "This past summer was not what we looked for," Paul L. Serff told the *Lebanon Daily News.* "In light of what the economy did–a significant number of theme parks were below last year–we didn't reach our projections

but we weren't down." He said that there were no record-breaking weekends in 1980.

For its seventy-fifth anniversary season in 1981, the park placed heavy emphasis on its entertainment lineup and youngsters were given a new area of their own called Kid Stuff, which replaced the Animal Garden. The Furry Tales—Chip, Dutch, and Violet —in their shaggy costumes were located within the area and continued to entertain children and pose for pictures. Attractions included a strolling clown, a puppet booth where "Grandpa Hershey" told fairy tales, and a mini barn-theater that showcased a computer-controlled *Hound Dog Jamboree.* Activities included face painting, ball crawl, rope climb, a tubular sliding board, and teeter-totter horses.

The season's shows ranged from upbeat choreography in *Dance, Dance, Dance '81* at the Amphitheatre, western comedy in *Shoot- out at the Trailblazer Saloon,* amazing aquatic maneuvers in the *Dolphin & Sea Lion Show* at the Aquatheatre, a world tour in a hot air balloon that took visitors *Up & Away* from the Fest Haus, and a 1940's song and dance review which promptly put every guest *In the Mood* at the Music Box Theatre. The two major shows *Dance, Dance, Dance '81*

The Bug was removed from the park at the end of the 1981 season.
(PHOTOGRAPH BY CHARLES J. JACQUES, JR.)

and *In the Mood* jointly cost approximately $250,000 to produce. Allan Alberts wrote, directed, and produced the shows for the park.

At the *Hound Dog Jamboree*, three computer-controlled dogs in hillbilly costumes entertained with country music and Broadway hits. The three hounds played a banjo, a washtub bass, and a harmonica. Some of their music included "When the Dogs Go Waggin' By" and "Anything Kids Can Do, Dogs Can Do Better," some holiday tunes, a *Star Wars* takeoff ("CP3 Bow-Wow"), and "Talk To The Animals."

J. Bruce McKinney's official title was now Vice President of Sports and Entertainment for the park, arena, stadium, hockey club, rose gardens, museum, drug store, and vending. Even he had to laugh when someone used his full title when introducing him to a group visiting the park. Paul L. Serff was Assistant Vice President of Hersheypark, Hershey Arena and Stadium, and ZooAmerica; Robert B. Payne was Director of Operations and Arena Manager. In 1982, Serff also served as president of the International Association of Amusement Parks and Attractions (IAAPA), the primary trade organization to which parks belonged.

A "Creatures of the Night" promotion was introduced in October 1981. It started as a one night flashlight tour of ZooAmerica. The first year free refreshments were served and a film presented. The zoo was accredited by the American Association of Zoological Parks & Aquariums in 1982.

A production number from Dance, Dance, Dance '81 in the Amphitheatre. (HERSHEYPARK)

Robert B. Payne, Director of Operations, was married August 27, 1981, on the park's antique carousel by the Reverend Jame E. Stough. Payne married the former Maxine Cassel. Payne's three best men were his sons John (next to Maxine), Tracy (middle), and Kim (left). Payne's granddaughter (John's daughter), Kelley, was flower girl, and Maxine's daughters, Lisa and Jody, served as bridesmaids. (HERSHEYPARK)

A ball crawl was one of the activities in Kid Stuff.
(CHARLES J. JACQUES, JR. COLLECTION)

Snow covers Der Deitschplatz.
(PHOTOGRAPH BY HAROLD SITLER)

Lights on the bridge leading to the sooperdooperLooper's loading station. (PHOTOGRAPH BY HAROLD SITLER)

In 1982 two rides, a Wave Swinger and a Balloon Flite, and a Cinema Vision were added to the park. The area where The Comet and the sooperdooperLooper were located was completely revamped and renamed Spring Creek Hollow. A nautically themed cafe was placed in the building which formerly held the Skooters. Paddle boats were added on Spring Creek. The boats, suggested by Bob Payne, were a big success and more boats were purchased the following year. The paddle boats cost two dollars for a half hour.

The new Wave Swinger replaced The Bug, which was extremely noisy and hard to maintain. It took workmen nearly a week to dismantle the old ride and jackhammer the concrete foundation to make way for the new ride. The Wave Swinger, purchased from the Josef Zierer Company of West Germany, was a swing-type ride with an oscillating wave-like motion. It whirled its passengers through the air around a central tower in separate seats that were suspended by chains from the ride's ceiling. All of the art work on the ride was hand painted. The ride had thousands of electrical lights that looked spectacular at night.

The Balloon Flite, purchased from Bradley and Kaye, Long Beach, California, simulated a hot-air balloon ride and could handle approximately six hundred forty persons per hour. It was located at the top of the hill near Rhineland replacing the Flying Bobs, which was removed from the park. Although it was a kiddie attraction, adults were also permitted to ride it.

Cinema Vision, purchased from Fred Hollingsworth and Omnivision, Inc. of Sarasota, Florida, continuously showed action-packed panoramic films on a 180-degree, floor-to-ceiling screen. The geodesic-domed theatre was placed at the edge of the park in the new northeast section. Hamilton Watch

The Bug was dismantled to make room for the new Wave Swinger.
(PHOTOGRAPH BY HAROLD SITLER)

A jackhammer was used to remove the concrete center foundation of The Bug.
(PHOTOGRAPH BY HAROLD SITLER)

The Wave Swinger provided a swing-type action and an oscillating wave-like motion. (CHARLES J. JACQUES, JR. COLLECTION)

Company donated a big clock that was used as the official time.

In 1983 the park purchased a Tilt-A-Whirl from Sellner Manufacturing Company of Faribault, Minnesota. Its gondolas tilted and dipped causing riders to be flung around its circular track. It replaced the Monster ride in Carrousel Circle. The two trains on The Comet coaster were named Halley's Comet and Mork's Comet. A restaurant in Tudor Square was renamed the Tudor Rose Tavern.

Also in 1983, HERCO spent six million dollars building seventy-five additional rooms and public space for its Pocono Resort Hotel, which it purchased in 1976. This was probably the park employees' favorite hotel, because they were given discounts, which they could use in the off season to go skiing.

Edward R. Book, CEO of HERCO said, "We do 60 percent of our business in four months—Memorial Day to Labor Day. If we hit a streak of bad weather, our sales and profits can plummet." This was one of the reasons he wanted to diversify into resorts in different parts of the country. It made sense, but only

as long as the hotels made money. In the 1980's there was a glut of hotel rooms around the country, and most of HERCO's hotels outside of Hershey lost money. HERCO now found itself competing head-to-head with the likes of Hilton, Marriott, Sheraton, Four Seasons, and Hyatt. All of the major hotel chains suffered, but for HERCO, which had limited resources, the challenge proved to be insurmountable. Hersheypark remained HERCO's most profitable business, but it was not receiving the capital that it needed to grow and compete.

Without new multimillion-dollar thrill rides to capitalize on, the park had to depend more on advertising. "Hersheyeeeeeeypark - What Screams Are Made Of" was the park's new slogan for 1983. The advertising campaign was aimed at the 18-25 year old, thrill-seeking age group, rather than families. The slogan "What Screams Are Made Of" was altered slightly to "What Screams and Dreams Are Made Of" for 1984. While most theme parks were adding new roller coasters and thrill rides, Hersheypark continued to advertise its total entertainment package. Ride

Cinema Vision showed panoramic films on a 180-degree, floor-to-ceiling screen. (Charles J. Jacques, Jr. Collection)

Aerial view of the park with the park's new service building next to the stadium; to the right is the Cinema Vision geodesic dome and Pirat in the right center.
(Charles J. Jacques, Jr. Collection)

Paddle boats on Spring Creek gave a wonderful view of the sooperdooperLooper. (Charles J. Jacques, Jr. Collection)

Before the descent on The Comet. (Hersheypark)

A wide-angle view of The Comet taken from the Sky Ride.

(Charles J. Jacques, Jr. Collection)

Tracks of The Comet and the sooperdooperLooper cross Spring Creek beside one another.

(Photograph by Charles J. Jacques, Jr.)

The first drop on The Comet.

(Hersheypark)

capacity had been increased to 22,700 per hour, but more capacity was needed if the park hoped to attract larger crowds.

In 1983 Paul L. Serff turned over day-to-day operation of the park to Jack Silar, who became general manager, and Serff began to concentrate on developing new ventures for HERCO. Silar had worked for Hersheypark from 1972 until 1976, when he left to go to Mariner's Landing in Wildwood, New Jersey. Hersheypark finished the 1983 season with its first substantial increase in attendance since 1977. A total of 1,605,000 persons visited the park, which was an eight percent increase over 1982. The weather was generally good, although hot, with more people coming in the afternoon and staying through the evening. Silar felt that when the weather was hot, the main competition came from the beaches of New Jersey, rather than other parks.

For the holiday season in 1983 Hersheypark erected a 65-foot lighted Christmas tree atop the Kissing Tower and introduced its first annual Christmas celebration, Candylane. The new event included everything from choral concerts and chamber music to a Shari Lewis Christmas Show. Tudor Square was transformed into a Christmas Village sparkling with holiday delights. Three kiddie rides were opened around the carousel, which was called Candy Cane Circle. The celebration also featured carolers, ice carving, tree-decorating contests, wassail bowls, and visits from the

HERSHEYPARK CHRISTMAS CANDYLANE

Candy canes were used for decoration in Rhineland.
(CHARLES J. JACQUES, JR. COLLECTION)

Santa waves at riders on the park's antique carousel.
(CHARLES J. JACQUES, JR. COLLECTION)

Hersheypark's famous train sign announces Christmas Candylane.
(CHARLES J. JACQUES, JR. COLLECTION)

Gingerbread man at Christmas Candylane gives a sweet hug to a little visitor.
(CHARLES J. JACQUES, JR. COLLECTION)

Sesame Street characters in the twinkling glow of 25,000 Christmas lights.

The idea of a Christmas celebration in the park originated with Kenneth V. Hatt, president of HERCO. In the early 1980's Hatt had been given the books of a small amusement park that HERCO was thinking about purchasing. This park made about one-third of its profit from a December Christmas promotion. Hatt suggested that Hersheypark try a Christmas celebration. The maintenance crew was given the job of decorating the park. At about the same time the maintenance department was replacing the piping that helped make the ice surface in the arena. Someone in maintenance got the smart idea of cutting the pipes and painting them so they resembled candy canes. The department made dozens of them and this is one of the reasons the name Christmas Candylane was chosen. For the first few years, the park barely broke even with its Christmas promotion but kept it

Kenneth V. Hatt, president of HERCO, 1980-86.
(Hersheypark)

going because it increased occupancy in the Hotel Hershey and the Hershey Lodge during a traditionally slow period.

In 1984, Hersheypark expanded five acres beyond its existing boundaries as part of a $1.8 million capital investment program. "The plan now is to get into that five acres," Jack Silar told *Amusement Business.* "We've moved the perimeter out by refencing the area for development over the next five years in an attempt to alleviate the dead ends in the park." The development included nearly three hundred thousand dollars spent to run plumbing and electrical lines into a new western theme area called Pioneer Frontier.

More than half of the nearly two million dollars was spent on two new European rides for the area. One was a Rainbow, which was custom-themed and renamed by the park the Conestoga ride, and the other an Apollo, which was renamed the Timber Rattler by the park. Both rides were purchased

The Timber Rattler featured a rattlesnake and cactus in the center of the ride.
(Charles J. Jacques, Jr. Collection)

The Conestoga ride and Kissing Tower.
(Charles J. Jacques, Jr. Collection)

through the Huss Trading Corporation of America, Corfu, New York.

The Timber Rattler had thirty gondola cars which were mounted on six arms that lifted and rotated as the ride went around a central axis. It spun its riders around at dizzying speeds. The ride was manufactured by Carrousel Holland B.V. in Apeldoorn, Holland, and imported by Huss. After the Timber Rattler ride had been open for several weeks, three minor accidents occurred, so the park added some more restraints especially for shorter riders. The ride tended to jar its riders and was not for the faint of heart.

The Conestoga ride weighed approximately forty-one tons and was counterbalanced by a large pendulum. The ride rocked its passengers to a height of seventy-nine feet and then made several full-circle rotations forward and backward.

Hersheypark's newest theme area, Pioneer Frontier, was situated on the hilltop overlooking the main area of the park. It was accessible by a midway extending beyond the Cyclops and Pirat rides and through a new walkway which linked Pioneer Frontier with the Trailblazer area. This new walkway, blasted out of the limestone and named Canyon Pass gave the new area a second access and helped the flow of traffic around the park.

Pioneer Frontier was a western town, which was more child and family oriented. It featured a blacksmith, Spring Creek General Store, a food stand, and two antique kiddie rides, which had been moved from other locations in the park. Entertainment was provided by the computerized hound dogs from Kid Stuff. Daniel and Dixie Diggers, hound dogs, and their canine friends performed from a gazebo located in the town square. The kiddie rides were the Mangels whip and the small Mangels merry-go-round, which were placed under cover in buildings in the western town. A new costume character, Sheriff Bob, was added to the western area.

The Dry Gulch Railroad's tracks were rerouted from the previous figure-eight configuration into an oval layout. A second engine and train from Crown Metal were added. Two new computer figures and a tunnel were also added to the train ride. The engine chugged through outdoor sets including a wild west ghost town, an Indian village and burial ground, and a gold mine. During the ride an animated snake sprayed a fine stream of water on passengers. The train ride also had two actors who held up the train in the ghost town.

Daniel and Dixie Diggers, hound dogs, were located in a gazebo in Pioneer Frontier. (Charles J. Jacques, Jr. Collection)

Sheriff Bob, Pioneer Frontier's new costume character in front of the Spring Creek General Store. (Hersheypark)

Two visitors receive a sweet greeting from one of the park's product characters, the Krackel Bar.
(Hersheypark)

Richard Hair, assistant general manager, greets a group of visitors to the park.
(Charles J. Jacques, Jr. Collection)

Santa Claus adds his handprints to the Starlight Arcade area in 1985.
(Charles J. Jacques, Jr. Collection)

Santa Claus' handprints were added to the Starlight Arcade area in 1984. There were now impressions of hands of twenty-seven stars like Bob Hope, Barry Manilow, and Liberace in the park's version of the Walk of Fame.

By 1984 workers' payroll for the park-arena-stadium complex had grown to $7.5 million annually with 1,800 summer employees. Full-time employment was approximately 160. Seasonal workers were mostly high school and college students, but some were as old as their mid-seventies. During the recession of the early 1980's, some employees commuted from as far as Bethlehem, Pennsylvania, after they were laid off from the steel plant there.

In August the park often experienced an employment crunch when college and high school students resigned to head back to school. Over the years earlier school starts had increased the problem. Rides were not shut down, but people were pulled from nonessential areas like sales and games and used elsewhere in the park.

For 1984 Richard A. Hair, assistant general manager, reported that more than 1.6 million people visited the park, falling just short of 1983's 1,605,000. Two new one-day records were set in August as the season finished strongly. Still it was another year that did not match 1977's attendance record of 1.7 million. Hair told the *Patriot* in October, "things like that [the Timber Rattler and the Conestoga ride] don't draw unless you add a blockbuster ride."

In February 1985 Jack Silar, general manager, told the *Lebanon Daily News* that the park was preparing to develop thirty-five acres in the northeast corner of the park. He also promised a spectacular new addition perhaps in 1986. Silar said, "Much depends on the 1985 season, the size of the crowds and the visitors' favorite attractions, but I foresee either a water-oriented ride or a major theatre."

In 1985 approximately fifty weather-sheltered television monitors were placed around the park in queue lines and high traffic areas. A 60-minute program mixed park information with special events. During the 1985 season the park experimented with a combination ticket for big name stadium acts like the Beach Boys and admission to the park. Other entertainers like Larry Gatlin & The Gatlin Brothers were merely included in the general admission price. The park had wanted to replace the 375-seat Music Box Theatre with a new one-thousand seat theatre, but the capital was not available.

In the early 1980's, HERCO also looked at diversifying into other amusement parks. In 1980 the company had looked at Rye Playland, Rye, New York, which was seeking a partner with experience.

The Cyclops and Kissing Tower at night.
(Photograph by Harold Sitler)

Marriott was finally awarded a management contract by Rye Playland, but pulled out after only two years of operation. In 1985 HERCO became the general partner for a traditional amusement park in Bristol, Connecticut. Turning this operation around would have been a long-term proposition, and when attendance did not meet projections, HERCO disposed of its interest in May of 1988.

In 1985 Hersheypark concluded its third consecutive season where attendance exceeded 1.6 million. Park attendance had plateaued. To increase the number of park visitors and therefore park revenues, major new investments would have to be made.

The Comet and sooperdooperLooper at sunset.
(Photograph by Harold Sitler)

CHAPTER 15

TURNING THINGS AROUND

J. Bruce McKinney, chairman of the board of HERCO.
(HERSHEYPARK)

he announcement was brief. J. Bruce McKinney, HERCO's executive vice president, had been elected by the company's board of directors to succeed Kenneth V. Hatt as president and chief operating officer, effective March 1, 1986. Hatt had served HERCO in many capacities for 45 years and would remain on the board of directors until 1993. At the same time, J.O. Hershey, who had been essential to the redevelopment of the park and who had been instrumental in hiring McKinney, retired from the board after nineteen years of service, and McKinney was elected to fill his seat on HERCO's board.

McKinney had received a bachelor's degree from Dickinson College, Carlisle, Pennsylvania, in 1959 and had attended Dickinson Law School. He had grown up in the town of Hershey and was a graduate of Milton Hershey School. He remembers returning to Hershey Park with a date during his college days to attend a Four Freshmen concert in the Starlight Ballroom. He did not have the money – he was 25 cents short and was reluctant to admit it – and although he loved the Four Freshmen, he made a hard decision and took his date to a movie instead.

When McKinney took over control of HERCO, he had some more hard decisions to make. The company was composed

The Pirat.
(CHARLES J. JACQUES, JR. COLLECTION)

The sooperdooperLooper.
(MARK WYATT/INSIDE TRACK)

The Wave Swinger.
(CHARLES J. JACQUES, JR. COLLECTION)

The Conestoga ride.
(CHARLES J. JACQUES, JR. COLLECTION)

Four of the most popular rides in the 1980's were located in different sections of the park.

170

HERSHEYPARK

1. **HERSHEY'S CHOCOLATE WORLD®**

2. **TUDOR SQUARE**
   Restaurant, restrooms and shops.

3. **RHINELAND**
   Restaurant, shops and the Sky Ride entrance.

4. **CREEKSIDE CATERING**

5. **HERSHEY MUSEUM OF AMERICAN LIFE**

6. **HERSHEYPARK ARENA**
   Top name entertainment.

7. **CARROUSEL CIRCLE**
   Kiddie Rides and our famous Carrousel.

8. **DER DEITSCHPLATZ**
   Crafts, gifts, food and first aid.

9. **LOST CHILDREN CABOOSE**
   Lost parents and children.

10. **PIRAT**

11. **CYCLOPS**

12. **MUSIC BOX THEATRE**

13. **KIDDIE RIDES**

14. **WAVE SWINGER**

15. **PADDLEBOAT CAFE**

16. **PADDLEBOATS**

17. **SOOPERDOOPERLOOPER**

18. **COMET ROLLERCOASTER**

19. **TRAILBLAZER THEATRE**

20. **TRAILBLAZER ROLLERCOASTER**

21. **AQUATHEATRE**

22. **KAPTAIN KID'S KOVE**

23. **AMPHITHEATRE**

24. **COAL CRACKER FLUME**

25. **TOWER PLAZA**
    The Kissing Tower, Sky Ride entrance, Twin Turnpike.

26. **ZOOAMERICA ENTRANCE**
    A 10-acre environmental walk thru zoo.

27. **PENNSYLVANIA FEST HAUS**

28. **ARCADE**

29. **DRY GULCH GALLEY CATERING**

30. **CINEMAVISION**

31. **CONESTOGA**

32. **TIMBER RATTLER**

Map of Hersheypark for 1986. (CHARLES J. JACQUES, JR. COLLECTION)

of three divisions: the hotel and resort group, which accounted for approximately 50 percent of the company's sales; sports and entertainment, which brought in 30 percent; and the commercial group, which brought in the remaining 20 percent. However, the only businesses that were earning any money were those located in Hershey – primarily Hotel Hershey, the Hershey Lodge, and Hersheypark. The rest of the businesses that had absorbed most of the company's capital for the preceding ten years were losing money. McKinney knew it was time to face the reality of the situation and stop saying "if this or that happens, then we will be all right." As soon as he took control, McKinney wanted to buy a major ride for the park but he had to put this off until HERCO's finances were in better shape.

Instead, 1986 was another year of making do for the park as the existing Cinema Vision dome was converted into a Magic Room called the Frontier Meeting House. The work was done in-house by the park's own maintenance staff. The ride mechanism was built by the Arrow Huss Company, Clearview, Utah. The entire project cost about $650,000. A second project was the renovation of the interior of the Music Box Theatre to include raked seating and new stage, light, and sound equipment. Again Hersheypark's maintenance department acted as the general contractor to save money. The total cost was $56,000.

The Frontier Meeting House was a false sense of motion ride that included light, sound, and motion illusions. The ride,

Kid Stuff was made over in 1986 and became Kaptain Kid's Kove.
(CHARLES J. JACQUES, JR. COLLECTION)

Face and arm painting was one of the activities offered in Kaptain Kid's Kove.
(HERSHEYPARK)

Artist's sketch of the Magic Room from Huss Arrow shows how the scenery revolves, creating an illusion of swinging, while guests are securely seated.
(CHARLES J. JACQUES, JR. COLLECTION)

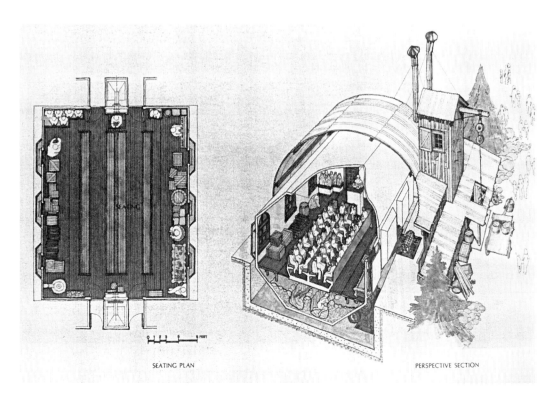

SEATING PLAN

PERSPECTIVE SECTION

although slated to open sometime in 1986, did not officially open until 1987. The attraction was similar to a revolving room or house illusion that was quite popular in amusement parks at the turn of the century. Hersheypark's attraction was done to resemble a late 1800's western meeting house. Patrons filed in and sat on benches in a dimly lit church-like hall occupied by a boy's choir, a piano player, and an elderly pot-bellied-stove sitter. A revival-style speaker ranted and raved about the evils of gold mining as the building revolved around them. An explosion rocked the hall, and the ceiling started oscillating back and forth, finally completely turning over and revealing an underground mine in which the demons of greed turn on the miners.

The Frontier Meeting House was never very popular and was soon removed and sold to an amusement park in China. Jeffrey W. Budgeon, director of planning, recalled, "the ride replaced Cinema Vision, which some people did not like, and therefore they avoided the new attraction thinking it was the same thing." The whole concept by Arrow never was very successful and only a few Magic Rooms were ever built.

For the children, Kid Stuff was made over in 1986 and became Kaptain Kid's Kove. Here from a pirate ship Mimi the Mermaid was featured in an animated show. It also had a multicolored ball crawl and a forty-foot sail with a rope climb. The section was the home of Salty Crackers, a puppet character with tales of real sea adventures.

For the eightieth summer season, 1987, the park installed

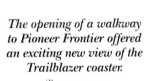

Trailblazer Theatre was expanded in the 1980's. The general store was named after Elmer "Zeke" Zartman. (CHARLES J. JACQUES, JR. COLLECTION)

The opening of a walkway to Pioneer Frontier offered an exciting new view of the Trailblazer coaster. (PHOTOGRAPH BY MARK WYATT\INSIDE TRACK)

A performer in the Trailblazer Theatre. (HERSHEYPARK)

Young singers and dancers performed country and western hits in the Trailblazer Theatre. (HERSHEYPARK)

***Sign at the entrance of the
Canyon River Rapids.***
(Photograph by Charles J. Jacques, Jr.)

***A raft in a curve on the
Canyon River Rapids.***
(Charles J. Jacques, Jr. Collection)

its biggest and most expensive ride in ten years. Canyon River Rapids, a white water rapids ride, was located at the northeast perimeter of the park in the Pioneer Frontier theme area. The new ride expanded Hersheypark by five acres to eighty-seven acres.

"The ride will give riders the exhilarating sensation of white-water rafting," Gary Chubb, director of operations, told the *Harrisburg Patriot.* "These rides always have high ridership. It's the type of ride the whole family can ride together."

According to Richard A. Hair, assistant general manager, "One of the nice things about this ride was that we brought the ride in ahead of schedule and under budget." The $4 million raft ride was built by Intamin A.G. of Switzerland, which also had supplied the sooperdooperLooper. Elmer "Zeke" Zartman was the planning engineer in charge of the project for the park. The

A series of waterfalls makes Canyon River Rapids a wet ride.
(Charles J. Jacques, Jr. Collection)

trip, which was made in six-passenger fiberglass and inner-tube rafts, lasted four to five minutes, and Jack Silar, vice president and general manager, said, "It's our promise you will get wet." Research suggested that people did not return to other rapids rides unless they got wet, so the park packed a wave maker, five waterfalls, and three geysers into the ride.

Drenched passengers found that no two rides were alike because of the narrow channel and wavemakers installed along the waterway. Each trip down the canyon was a slightly different experience, and part of the fun of the ride seemed to be who got wettest. If the raft remained in the center of the canyon, the ride was swift and relatively dry, but more often the rafts banged into the sides of the canyon, which sent them spinning wildly, first in one direction and then another. The rafts circled from the left to the right bank, turned backward, forward, sideways, and rocked up and down naturally. Passengers dripping in water-filled rafts were proof that "You will get wet on this ride." People who wanted to stay dry had the option of purchasing plastic cover-ups.

The water that coursed through the 1,700-foot long concrete channel was generated by four large pumps (three active and one backup) that could pump 36,000 gallons per minute from the ride's one million-gallon reservoir. The whole ride operated in only two feet of water. Eighteen rafts, which could operate simultaneously, gave the ride a design capacity of 1,500 riders per hour. The park provided an observation area for the new ride near the Timber Rattler that provided an excellent spot for taking pictures.

In addition to the park's eightieth birthday, the Hersheypark

Arena celebrated its fiftieth anniversary with a special show April 11, 1987, that featured George Burns as the headliner. Also on the bill were Patti Page and *Entertainment Tonight* co-host Mary Hart. Inside Hersheypark Arena was the Bears' Den, a unique history showcase of celebrities who had performed over the years at Hersheypark Arena and Hersheypark. More than 200 autographed pictures from favorites like Billy Joel, David Bowie, Bob Hope, Barry Manilow, Alabama, Liberace, and Kenny Rogers were displayed. Some of the old pictures were from the Sollenberger era and included band leaders Kay Kyser, Benny Goodman, and Sammy Kaye.

For the kids in 1987, a miniature Himalaya was added to the

Jack Silar, Vice President of HERCO, presents a giant Hershey's Chocolate Bar to George Burns at the fiftieth anniversary celebration at the arena. Mary Hart is on Burns' left and Patti Page on his right. (Charles J. Jacques, Jr. Collection)

The second largest show was presented in the Music Box Theatre.
(Hersheypark)

Young singers and dancers perform in the Amphitheatre.
(Hersheypark)

Audition and tryouts are held in the early spring for positions in the park's shows.
(Hersheypark)

Carrousel Circle section of the park. It was called the Snowball Express, and it fit in well with the annual Candylane celebration.

The Hershey Gardens were upgraded in preparation for its fiftieth anniversary, also in 1987. The gardeners concentrated on refining the theme areas and displays. New areas added in 1986 included a garden of old-fashioned roses and a small Japanese-style meditation garden. The swans were returned to the small lake just outside the gift shop at the entrance to the gardens. The old tulip beds were replanted for a Tulip Festival, a tradition that dated back to the days of Harry Haverstick.

Hersheypark's tranquil season suddenly ended on Saturday,

May 23, when one of the rafts flipped on the Canyon River Rapids ride injuring its six passengers. "At about 1:00 p.m., two rafts jammed in the trough," explained Jack Silar. "A third raft piled into them, and one raft turned over," he said. The raft's six passengers bailed out before it capsized. They were treated for minor cuts and bruises, transported to the Hershey Medical Center where they were checked and released.

The park immediately did a thorough investigation. The accident occurred in a curve at the entrance to an area known as Lake II, about three-quarters of the way through the ride. The investigation concluded that the accident was caused by a section of the ride's waterway that was too wide. The wide section allowed two rafts to become wedged together and plug the watercourse. The park rebuilt the waterway in that section to make it the same width as the rest of the ride. An additional operator post was added to this area and another station moved to improve routine surveillance. A new public address system was added to allow communication with guests throughout the ride.

Park patrons jammed the Canyon River Rapids ride when it was put back in service thirteen days after the accident. "About 100 people were in line for the ride's opening Friday morning and by afternoon the line had grown to 500 people," Rich Roberts, park spokesperson, said. "The ride is doing spectacularly well," he continued. Canyon River Rapids did exceptionally well for the rest of the season.

J. Bruce McKinney, president and chief operating officer of

Hershey Gardens, which overlook the park, were upgraded in 1987.
(CHARLES J. JACQUES, JR. COLLECTION)

Filmed in action for the park's 1988 television commercial was the Toplitz family from Lancaster.
(HERSHEYPARK)

Two of the park's popular rides in the 1970's included the Skyview, and the Sky Ride.
(Charles J. Jacques, Jr. Collection)

many daily records during the summer, including fifteen attendance highs for single days and four days when attendance reached a high of 28,000. On September 27, 1987, a single-day attendance record was established as 29,686 guests visited the park.

By 1987, Candylane had become an important promotion for the park. People loved its lights, music, foods, and rides in the dull gray of winter. The event, which ran from November 16 till the end of the year, celebrated its fifth season. The park was especially appealing at night when 118,000 lights were turned on.

"Preparation for Candylane starts the day after the park closes for season, around the first half of October," said Ed Sharkey, director of entertainment. "All the work is done in-house and on volunteer time."

Gingerbread Town, Peppermint Place, Animal Crackers, Jelly Bean Junction, Sugar & Spice Passage and Sweet Street were the six Christmas Candylane theme areas. Children could visit Santa and meet Frosty the Snowman, Rudolph, and Hershey's chocolate characters. More than 40 choirs, carolers, and brass ensembles performed. The park offered merchandise purchased exclusively for Candylane. There was no admission charge for parking or to enter the park.

Horse-drawn carriage rides were a popular attraction during the Christmas celebration. (Charles J. Jacques, Jr. Collection)

HERCO, was named chief executive officer of the corporation on August 11, 1987. He replaced Edward R. Book. "What this means is that he's [McKinney's] basically responsible for the company's overall performance," a spokesperson told *Amusement Business*. McKinney was to continue to strengthen the company's Hershey-based operations.

With the help of the Canyon River Rapids, and after ten seasons of hard work and development, Hersheypark finally topped its all-time attendance record in 1987. It was a hot dry summer, just a perfect season for the introduction of the new water ride. The new attendance record was 1,729,641. The park broke

Santa Claus and his reindeer are on The Comet's lift hill.
(Photograph by Charles J. Jacques, Jr.)

Gary Chubb, assistant general manager, at Candylane in 1987.
(Gary Chubb Collection)

When the weather is warm, the lines are long for the Slidewinder and Pistol Pete's Plunge.
(CHARLES J. JACQUES, JR. COLLECTION)

At the end of the slide comes the splashdown where you might get wet. (CHARLES J. JACQUES, JR. COLLECTION)

It is more fun coming down than going up on the Frontier Chute-Out. (CHARLES J. JACQUES, JR. COLLECTION)

The park's carousel, a horse-drawn carriage, and various kiddie rides were operated on a pay-as-you-go-basis. A total of 192,500 rides were given during the festival. The weather was good and Candylane set an all-time attendance record in 1987 when an estimated 184,000 people visited.

Once the park closed in October, the maintenance department took every ride apart from its track or cable and gave it a critical inspection. The ride vehicles were disassembled, cleaned, and supports x-rayed for minor cracks or defects. Finally a fresh coat of paint was applied that matched the exact color the ride wore before (except occasionally when the color of a ride was changed as when the sooperdooperLooper was changed from tan to dark blue). In the Service Center rows of little cars sat side by side with rafts from Canyon River Rapids.

Because of the success and popularity of the Canyon River Rapids water ride, the park decided to explore other water rides on the market for the 1988 season. The park chose a ride that sent riders cascading down water-filled chutes in small rubber boats. The Frontier Chute-Out, which cost approximately $1.5

*An aerial view of the
Canyon River Rapids and
Frontier Chute-Out.*
(Charles J. Jacques, Jr. Collection)

million, was not as big an addition as the Canyon River Rapids, but it did provide more ride capacity in the popular water rides area. Its location close to the Canyon River Rapids encouraged guests to try a second water ride experience.

The ride, directly opposite Canyon River Rapids on the west side of a new midway, gave visitors a fast and refreshingly wet ride aboard a rubber boat. It consisted of four chutes which commenced from a forty-five-foot high tower; riders seated in two-person rubber rafts hydroplaned on water flowing down the slide. The water ride featured the snakelike tunnels of the Slidewinder I & II and the quick slopes of Pistol Pete's Plunge I & II. It was designed to handle between 1,000 and 1,200 riders per hour.

The Frontier Chute-Out was to be completed for Memorial Day, 1987, but because of weather-related construction delays only Pistol Pete's Plunge, the open air part of the ride, was opened by that date. The other half, the Slidewinder, which was to be enclosed in a tunnel, opened in mid-June. Because the Frontier Chute-Out was still under construction for the sneak preview, which gave some residents and the media a peek at the park before it opened, the park gave out squirt guns in honor of the new attraction.

HERCO's board of directors adopted a new mission statement in December 1987, which J. Bruce McKinney made public in early 1988. In an interview with *VSP LIFE*, an em-

ployee newsletter, McKinney said that he was not worried about eventually having all of the company's businesses concentrated in the town of Hershey because "Over the long run, that's where our strength and profitability have been. We should be concentrating on that which we do best." As an example he mentioned the Canyon River Rapids ride. "It was evaluated as a project that could produce a substantial return in a reasonable pay-back period," he said. "And look what happened—Hersheypark achieved its greatest attendance and level of profitability in history."

*One of the exhibits at the Hershey Museum is on
M.S. Hershey, The Man Behind the Chocolate Bar.*
(Hersheypark)

Hersheypark did not introduce any major new rides for the 1989 season. The park felt that the impact of the Canyon River Rapids and Frontier Chute-Out water rides was still substantial and marketable. The park put in a kiddie flume ride called Tiny Timbers, which was manufactured by Venture Ride Co. of South Carolina. The kid's ride had eight boats that could hold four children or two adults and two children. The kiddie flume cost about $300,000, which ten years earlier would have paid for a large adult ride. The Balloon Flite was relocated from an area near the Music Box Theatre to Pioneer Frontier.

Hershey Gardens was placed under the ownership and operation of the M.S. Hershey Foundation on January 1, 1989. The foundation also operated and administered the Hershey Theatre, the Hershey Community Archives, and the Hershey Museum.

Hersheypark's Christmas Candylane was expanded by adding another three acres of attractions for 1989. These included the National Marionette Company's production of *The Toy Shop* in the Music Box Theatre. There were now fourteen rides operating for the winter celebration including for the first time four kiddie rides: Earth Movers, Bizzy Bees, Lady Bugs, and the kiddie swing. The Fender Bender Skooter was also open. To prepare rides for cold weather, heaters were installed in the hydraulic systems. It took about five weeks to set up the lights and get the rides and shops ready. Two new restaurants, The Yule Tide and Santa's Sleigh Station, featured holiday food. Six

In 1989 the children got a kids' flume called Tiny Timbers.
(Charles J. Jacques, Jr. Collection)

The Balloon Flite was relocated from the Music Box Theatre area to Pioneer Frontier. (Charles J. Jacques, Jr. Collection)

The park added new Skee Ball machines to the arcade.
(Charles J. Jacques, Jr. Collection)

Whack a Mole was one of the popular games in the 1980's.
(Charles J. Jacques, Jr. Collection)

holiday shops were open featuring stocking stuffers and Christmas merchandise. A new roll of Christmas music was purchased for the Wurlitzer band organ on the carousel.

For many years the park had leased its arcade and games operation to Recreational Amusement Incorporated. At the end of the 1988 season, Hersheypark decided to take over the games from this outside company. The park purchased the operation including games and machines on the grounds from its former lessee, Recreational Amusement Incorporated. "It became more profitable for us to do it that way," McKinney told the *Hershey Chronicle*. "We take in all the revenues, but we take over all the expenses as well."

The park advertised 1989 season passes to Hersheypark for $42.50 as the "Most Splashtacular Gift Of The Season." The

The Cyclops. (CHARLES J. JACQUES, JR. COLLECTION)

slogan "Hersheypark ...Sounds Like Fun!" was adopted. The park was now using television, radio, newspapers, and billboards to reach the public. Television advertising accounted for more than 60 percent of the total media budget. Television advertisements appeared in Harrisburg, Lebanon, Lancaster, York, Baltimore, Wilkes-Barre, Scranton, Johnstown, Altoona, and Hagerstown.

The park now controlled everything inside its fence, with the exception of crafts. The late 1980's was a time when Hersheypark proved what it could do with a major new ride, Canyon River Rapids. Now that HERCO's financial problems were clearing up, J. Bruce McKinney could begin to make good on his promise to invest more substantially in Hersheypark. The future looked bright as the park entered the 1990's.

Only the lighthouse remains from the old swimming pool complex.
(CHARLES J. JACQUES, JR. COLLECTION)

CHAPTER 16

ACCELERATED GROWTH

The falcon at the top of the new ride.
(PHOTOGRAPH BY CHARLES J. JACQUES, JR.)

The Flying Falcon was erected in the new Minetown area in 1990. (PHOTOGRAPH BY CHARLES J. JACQUES, JR.)

In the 1990's, the park's map would undergo dramatic changes as old areas were renovated, major new rides were added, and several new sections developed. As the decade progressed, the rate of change would accelerate. This expansion was made possible, at least in part, because HERCO was finally able to resolve its resort hotel problems.

The park's first project in the 1990's was refurbishing the only part of the park that had not been upgraded since 1971. At a cost of $7.5 million the southeast corner of the park (Bowling Alley Hill located near the entrance of ZooAmerica and the landmark Kissing Tower) became Minetown. The centerpiece of the new area was the 105-foot-high Flying Falcon. The project also included three new kiddie rides, a new games arcade, and an air-conditioned restaurant.

"When Hersheypark became a theme park, the intention was to have a coal-mining town theme area," said Jack Silar, general manager of the park. "The Coal Cracker Flume Ride, one of

The old deer statue was relocated to a spot near the entrance of ZooAmerica. (Photograph by Charles J. Jacques, Jr.)

the most popular rides in Hersheypark, is already centered on this theme. We are developing that plan to its fullest potential." At the official opening of the new section on May 19, 1990, Jack Silar said, "Hersheypark is more beautiful than ever. The renovated area exceeds our wildest dreams, and we're sure that our guests this season will be impressed."

The Flying Falcon, which cost $1.2 million, gives fifty-six riders at a time the sensation of flying through the air as they circled around a tower and were lifted into the sky one hundred five feet aboard twenty-eight gondolas. The 300,000-pound ride was manufactured by Huss Company of Germany and could carry one thousand people per hour. J. Bruce McKinney, chairman of the board and chief operating officer of HERCO, was proud of the Falcon. "It's an exciting ride," he said. "It truly will be a landmark within Hersheypark with a great deal of

flash, and it will offer, really, a spectacular view of the park while you're riding…. Like its namesake, the flying falcon, it's a fast, high-flying ride, with a wide wingspan," McKinney explained.

A new entrance planter and walkway were created for ZooAmerica, and the entire area was resurfaced. One of the reasons the new ride was called the Falcon was to draw attention to ZooAmerica's effort to breed falcons, which were nearly extinct in Pennsylvania. Troy Stump, ZooAmerica Curator, had a program to try and breed falcons that would eventually be released into the wild near State College, Pennsylvania. "The park has successfully bred other birds, including the golden eagle and snowy owls," Stump told the *Harrisburg Patriot News*.

In the middle of the renovated area was a new 49,300-square-foot arcade and Minetown Vittles restaurant built on the site of the old arcade building. The three-story structure was designed to resemble a coal power generating plant. The restaurant could seat four hundred twenty-five indoors and had an expanded outdoor dining area which overlooked the park's Amphitheatre and Comet Hollow. The Fest Haus restaurant was renamed the Melting Pot and given a new facade.

The old arcade building was demolished because it could not be economically rehabilitated. It was built on a decaying stone foundation and was made of old timber with a limited structural strength and poor fire-safety properties. The arcade was too small to handle the crowds. Ventilation and cooling systems were outdated. The new structure, which cost $3.7 million, was made of steel structure members and reinforced concrete, with wood and grayish metal siding maintaining the coal-mining themes. The new arcade housed games of skill, such as Skee Ball and video games.

The new arcade and games building in Minetown.
(Photograph by Charles J. Jacques, Jr.)

Interior of the arcade. (Hersheypark)

The Convoy truck ride was one of the children's rides in Minetown.
(HERSHEYPARK)

The Red Baron airplane ride was located near the Flying Falcon.
(HERSHEYPARK)

Dinosaur-Go-Round was located in the Minetown children's ride area. (HERSHEYPARK)

The Himalaya and Coal Shaker were removed. J. Bruce McKinney told the *Hershey Chronicle* that "The Coal Shaker was a horribly loud ride. Before it was taken out, we had to figure out how to muffle the sound. You could hardly hear the Aquatheatre show, even with its microphone."

A kiddie section adjacent to the Flying Falcon included a Red Baron plane ride and Convoy (kiddie truck ride) both from Zamperla of Italy and the Dinosaur-Go-Round from Venture Ride Manufacturing Company of South Carolina. The park continued to scatter its kiddie rides throughout the park rather than having one section devoted exclusively to children's rides.

For 1990, Hersheypark completely overhauled all of its five shows. Allan Alberts continued to produce the park's shows. The Trailblazer Theatre was renamed the Sarsaparilla Saloon and featured a new Gay '90's can-can revue called the *Sarsaparilla Revue* that replaced *Hoedown America.* In the Melting Pot area (formerly the Fest Haus) was a new *Welcome to America* show. The German band from the Fest Haus became a Dixieland band called The Riverside Rascals that now played at the Paddleboat Cafe in Comet Hollow. *Rock 'n Roll Hershey* became the *Legend of Rock 'n Roll* in the Music Box Theatre. The rock and roll show included music from The Beatles, The Supremes, The Beach Boys, The Rolling Stones, and Aretha Franklin. Two new strolling shows, The Patchwork Players and the Buggy Kids were added. *Dance, Dance, Dance,* the flagship of

Hersheypark Entertainment, remained in the Amphitheatre. The dolphins and sea lions show continued in the Aquatheatre.

Franklin R. Shearer was named assistant vice president, sports & entertainment, by HERCO in July of 1990. He had charge of Hersheypark, Hersheypark Arena, Hersheypark Stadium, and ZooAmerica. Shearer formerly was assistant vice president, corporate operations.

The park went exclusively to paid parking in 1990. "We were one of the last amusement parks in the United States to go to paid parking," McKinney told the *Hershey Chronicle*. Prior to that time the area between the stadium and arena had been the paid parking area and the rest of the parking was free. The former paid parking area was converted to handicapped and bus parking.

In 1991, Hersheypark introduced its fourth and most terrifying roller coaster,

New for '91 was the Sidewinder coaster. (MARK WYATT/INSIDE TRACK)

At the opening of the Sidewinder, Franklin R. Shearer, vice president and general manager of the park, and Troy Stump, director of ZooAmerica, display a North American rattlesnake.
(MARK WYATT/INSIDE TRACK)

the Sidewinder. The park introduction said, "It's the single most exhilarating and frightening 90 seconds you'll live to tell about!"

The new coaster was located in the Pioneer Frontier section. It featured two lifts of one hundred five feet each and turned riders upside down a total of six times. The Sidewinder was the first coaster built at Hersheypark since the sooperdooperLooper was added in 1977.

This new boomerang coaster consisted of a 180 degree upside-down loop and a 180 degree pull out. The parabolically shaped vertical loop had a thirty-three foot diameter and reached a height of fifty-nine feet. The Sidewinder attained a speed of 50 miles per hour and featured a half loop and half-right corkscrew combination followed by a half-left corkscrew combined with a half loop. Then the train completed a 360-degree loop, and stalled for a split second

The Sidewinder turns riders upside down a total of six times.
(Charles J. Jacques, Jr. Collection)

The Sidewinder twists and turns until it seems to turn against itself. (Charles J. Jacques, Jr. Collection)

The Sidewinder's coaster train is lifted 105 feet to the top of the second hill. (Hersheypark)

The Sidewinder is a boomerang coaster that travels forward and then backward through its curves and loops.
(CHARLES J. JACQUES, JR. COLLECTION)

before plunging backward to repeat all maneuvers in reverse. One of the key features of the coaster was the sudden speed that only a coaster of this type can provide.

The Sidewinder was manufactured by Vekoma of the Netherlands and was named for the North American rattlesnake that moves in a sideways looping motion with only two parts touching the sand at any one time. The coaster, which was 876 feet long, could accommodate twenty-eight passengers per train. It had a capacity of seven hundred passengers per hour. The coaster was visible outside the park, especially from Park Avenue.

According to Franklin R. Shearer, vice president and park manager, "Our guests surveyed over the past two years have indicated a real consumer desire for a new roller coaster. The

Sidewinder is one of the most exciting rides we've ever had the opportunity to introduce to our guests. It quite simply packs more thrills per linear foot than any other coaster in the world."

In 1991, for the twelfth season in a row, Allan Alberts produced five resident shows for Hersheypark. Alberts told *Amusement Business*, "Audiences want new things. You can't get away with giving them the same show they saw last season." The New York-based director and producer did a major overhaul of all the park's shows in 1990 and again in 1991. "Fifty percent of their audience is repeat business and even though everything was new in 1990, you have to bring in new numbers to keep them coming back," Alberts said.

The park's signature show, *Dance, Dance, Dance*, featured a salute to the music of Cole Porter and incorporated live singing

187

Hotel Hershey was placed on the National Trust for Historic Preservation's list of Historic Hotels of America.
(PHOTOGRAPH BY BETTY JACQUES)

seven rooms on thirty-three landscaped acres, and Hershey Highmeadow Campground located on Route 39 just two miles west of Hersheypark had three hundred ninety-six sites on fifty-five acres. The park offered a "Barking Lot" kennel for pets at the west end of Hersheypark Stadium for a fee of three dollars per pet per day, but no overnight stays were permitted. During the dog days of Summer 1992, a special dog party day was held.

Hersheypark declared 1992 the "Year of the Family" and it lowered entrance fees by adopting a junior rate. For the first time in five years, no new rides were added. New entertainment included a strolling act called the Hersheypark Green Team, who were dressed up as environmental super heroes. They performed an ecology-theme show of juggling, magic, and comedy. The team, dressed in Astroturf shoulder pads, juggled earth balls, and visited schools before and after the season.

Anniversaries to amusement parks are like birthdays to children – the more the merrier – and 1992 was a great year because the park had three anniversaries it could celebrate. It was the eighty-fifth birthday of the park, the twentieth anniversary of its conversion to a theme park, and the fifteenth anniversary of the sooperdooperLooper roller coaster.

Hersheypark decided to become more visitor friendly in 1992. On most days, when visitors arrived in the morning they found Carl Hausman, a Berks County native, playing piano music in Tram Circle. Two or three employees were stationed at the entrance to the park to greet visitors as they arrived. At the end of the day, park employees also thanked visitors for coming.

for the first time. Another new show was *Hello America,* a first-time Americana show. The patriotic songs and red, white, and blue colors were well received, especially following the Persian Gulf War. *Rock 'n' Roll Hershey* played in the Music Box Theatre. It was a look at popular music from the 1940's to the Rolling Stones.

The Hotel Hershey continued to be recognized as one of the finest resorts in the country. It joined the ranks of sixty-four other prestigious resorts inducted into The National Trust for Historic Preservation's Historic Hotels of America Program. The program recognized quality resorts that maintain the historical ambiance and architecture. Hotel Hershey had grown to two hundred forty-one rooms and suites by 1992. The Hershey Lodge and Convention Center had four hundred fifty-

The sooperdooperLooper coaster celebrated its fifteenth birthday in 1992. (HERSHEYPARK)

The park's costume characters entertain at the entrance.
(HERSHEYPARK)

The Sky Ride was removed in 1992.
(HERSHEYPARK)

The Sky Ride, after eighteen years of service, was removed at the end of the 1992 season. (Most amusement parks in America that had a sky ride had already removed theirs.) The ride was difficult to maintain, some accidents had occurred on similar sky rides in other parks, and in the case of a shutdown the ride was extremely hard to evacuate. The park had to continually monitor the wind, because the ride could not be operated under windy conditions. The former station in Rhineland was converted into a cotton candy and Icee stand, while the Mine Town station, located near the Coal Cracker flume ride, was turned into a picnic area for overflow from the San Giorgio Pasta House.

Games remained an important part of the park. In fact, more were added after the park purchased the games concession in 1989. A new building that housed games was constructed next to The Comet.

Some of the name talent brought to the Hersheypark Amphitheatre in 1992 included Regis Philbin, The Amazing Kreskin, Mike Reid (former Penn State football star turned

country music star), Bobby Vinton, Riders in the Sky, and Eddie Rabbit.

The economy slowed in central Pennsylvania during the early 1990's, and the park's attendance dipped slightly in 1992 to 1.7 million, down from the 1.8 million visitors the previous year.

The park's warehouses, located around the park and below the museum, became overstocked and crowded with old merchandise. To remedy this, Bob Kegris, managing director of merchandise and games, had a February sale of shirts, souvenirs, gifts, collectibles, and stuffed animals. The park turned this into an annual event.

According to Kegris, "The most popular souvenir items in the 1970's were cedar wood pieces, collectibles like salt and pepper shakers, cheap glass, pennants, back scratchers and coffee mugs. Everything cost a buck or two." One of the biggest items in the 1970's and 1980's was a t-shirt with "I Survived the sooperdooperLooper" on it. "In the 1990's, it is quality wearable items, like shirts and hats," Kegris said. "People are more practical today." In twenty years Kegris had seen souvenir sales increase almost tenfold.

The Frontier Meeting House was converted into a video arcade.
(PHOTOGRAPH BY CHARLES J. JACQUES, JR.)

The Pro Shot basketball game. (PHOTOGRAPH BY CHARLES J. JACQUES, JR.)

The whole family playing the Rising Water game.

(Photograph by Charles J. Jacques, Jr.)

Stuffed animals remained the most popular prizes in the 1990's.

(Photograph by Charles J. Jacques, Jr.)

The park introduced a game also called the Sidewinder.

(Mark Wyatt/Inside Track)

Neon signs made a comeback in the 1990's.

(Photograph by Charles J. Jacques, Jr.)

A section of the park was called Music Box Way.
(Photograph by Charles J. Jacques, Jr.)

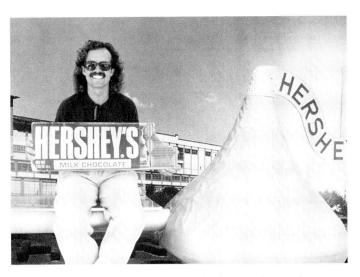

Champion driver Kyle Petty had his picture taken at the new Hersheypark Photos. (Hersheypark)

When the park took over games in 1989, Kegris was put in charge. "The most important thing in games," Kegris said, "is that they be fair and have the right prizes." The majority of people working games and souvenirs were high school students, with college people next, followed by senior citizens.

Hersheypark's slogan for 1993 remained "The Fun Starts Here!" Keeping up with the latest fads, the park added a gourmet coffee shop in Tudor Square. In addition to a wide variety of gourmet coffees, the shop offered espresso and iced cappuccino. Purchases could be made by the pound or by the cup. The park, in conjunction with the Hershey Medical Center, developed a scenic two-mile cardiovascular workout, LifeWalk. The walk began in Rhineland and had eight checkpoints, each with a tip to improve overall health.

In 1993, ZooAmerica celebrated its fifteenth anniversary by adding a new veterinary service building. The building had facilities for large and small animal quarantine and holding areas for infirm animals. Troy Stump, director/curator of the zoo said, "Any future development at the zoo hinges on

On really hot days misters give visitors another way of cooling down. (Photograph by Charles J. Jacques, Jr.)

having quality animal support facilities to provide the finest and safest care for the animals entrusted to us."

Hersheypark Amphitheatre performers in 1993 included The Lettermen, Frankie Valli, Chubby Checker, Brenda Lee, The Fabulous Greaseband, Ronnie Milsap, Jimmy Dorsey Orchestra, and others. NASCAR fans were able to meet and greet champion driver Kyle Petty on June 14 inside the park. Kyle signed autographs and posed for pictures with his fans.

Forty members of The Roller Coaster Club of Great Britain visited the park for some air time aboard the park's four roller coasters in 1993. Club members queued up for exclusive ride time aboard Hersheypark's famous Comet roller coaster and thought the park's wooden coaster was "brilliant" and "lovely."

July was a hot month in Hershey. Anything cold was selling. Park visitors wore polo shirts, shorts, bathing suits, and sunscreen. In addition to the Canyon River Rapids ride, which drenched its riders, the park added misters, sprinkler systems that sprayed cool, thin mists of

191

In 1993 the park adopted Hershey candy brands as new ride height restriction signs. (HERSHEYPARK)

Hersheypark's Family of the Day in The Sweetest Parade on Earth. (HERSHEYPARK)

The Great All-American Hersheypark Marching Band.
(PHOTOGRAPH BY CHARLES J. JACQUES, JR.)

Jeffrey Budgeon, the park's director of engineering.
(PHOTOGRAPH BY CHARLES J. JACQUES, JR.)

water into the air. Chocolate theming became more evident throughout the park in 1993 with the addition of new ride height restriction signs that corresponded to Hershey's chocolate products. "The Chocolate Characters became more important," Franklin R. Shearer told the *Hershey Chronicle.* "Families come here and if they don't see the characters, they will write me and call me."

Something new for 1993 was the *Sweetest Parade on Earth,* which was co-sponsored by Hersheypark and Hershey's Chocolate World Visitor Center. The parade wound from Chocolate World outside the park through Comet Hollow to the Frontier area. The first parade was held June 30, 1993, to help celebrate Chocolate World's twentieth anniversary. The parade consisted of a 15-piece band, jugglers and clowns, a baton twirler, and thirteen Hershey's product characters. One "Hersheypark Family of the Day" was chosen at random to participate in the event. Two parades were held daily, one in the afternoon and one in the evening.

The parade's band, called The Great All-American Hersheypark Marching Band, was reminiscent of M.S. Hershey's early park bands. It was conducted by Walter Staiton, director of orchestras at Williamsport High School in Williamsport, Pennsylvania. It was made up of fifteen high school and college students and some recent college graduates.

In September 1993, HERCO finally resolved its one remaining financial problem when the company transferred its operating lease for the Philadelphia Hilton and Towers, formerly Hershey Philadelphia Hotel, to Doubletree Hotels. "Since it opened 10 years ago, the hotel has lost money, causing HERCO to sustain substantial operating losses," McKinney told the *Lebanon Daily News.* "Philadelphia and our non-Hershey undertakings have created a tremendous cash drain on our company and have siphoned cash away from our core operations here in Hershey. Our financial commitments elsewhere have hampered our efforts here at home," he said.

For the 1994 season, HERCO announced the construction of a new water ride called TIDAL FORCE. Jeffrey W. Budgeon, park director of engineering, explained that the harsh winter had thrown off the ride's construction timetable, so crews added additional work hours and Saturdays to ensure that the ride would be completed for the Memorial Day weekend.

The $4 million ride was billed as the world's tallest and wettest splashdown ride. The ride, built in New Hampshire, was a modern shoot-the-chute ride. Its course was 935 feet long with a 100-foot lift hill. "Imagine a drop higher than that of our

Construction workers on
TIDAL FORCE.
(HERSHEYPARK)

Working on the Lighthouse entrance to TIDAL FORCE.
(HERSHEYPARK)

Construction of TIDAL FORCE. (HERSHEYPARK)

Comet roller coaster," said Franklin R. Shearer, vice president and general manager of Hersheypark. It featured a forty-three-degree angle on the drop and the boat reached the speed of over thirty miles per hour before hitting the water. The chute was only one to one and one half feet deep, but the ride held more than 200,000 gallons of water. There were three 20-foot long, 20-passenger chute boats. The attraction was built of brick and had an antique lighthouse at the entrance. It also featured a beautiful walkway on pillars and an attractive brick and wooden truss-beamed queue house.

Clowns from Ringling Bros., Barnum & Bailey Circus, who were appearing at the Hersheypark Arena, were invited to the

J. Bruce McKinney, chairman of the board of HERCO, speaks at the opening of TIDAL FORCE. (Hersheypark)

opening. They elbowed reporters and park officials out of their way so they could ride again and again. Once the clowns permitted others to ride, they stood on the bridge over the main spray area, continuing their drenching, in bathing trunks and caps. For those who wanted to take the ride in their bathing suits, a new changing room facility was built in the area. "The addition of TIDAL FORCE has drastically changed the traffic patterns in the park," Franklin R. Shearer told the *Hershey Chronicle.* "People go there [TIDAL FORCE area] immediately, when in the past they would first go to Comet Hollow."

The slogan of the new ride was "Get ready, get set, get wet." A sign at the entrance promised "You will get wet on this ride." Before getting wet, riders had to make the agonizingly slow climb to the top. From there they could see the mountains and hills that surrounded the park. Perhaps Deborah Gains, writing for the *New York Post*, best described a trip on TIDAL FORCE in her article, "Taking the plunge" that appeared on June 14, 1994:

> I was faced with the "Wile E. Coyote" portion of the ride, that split second when the boat or car is suspended in space but has not yet begun its free fall.

> "We're in for it now," muttered the woman next to me, and I realized that I was clutching the knee of a complete stranger. Then we were screaming, and the countryside with its cows and buildings spun dizzily,

At TIDAL FORCE's opening, the clowns got the first ride on the new water ride. (Hersheypark)

A boatload of clowns. (Hersheypark)

Entrance to TIDAL FORCE.
(Photograph by Charles J. Jacques, Jr.)

and the next thing we knew we were inside a solid
wall of water that rose around us like a liquid tornado.

At moments like this, language fails. The kids in the
boat, recovering sooner than the rest of us, put it best:
"Awesome!" "Beyond cool!" "Let's do it again!"

I was inclined to do it again myself, especially since the
TIDAL FORCE ride is a landmark event: the tallest,
wettest ride on earth.

(Reprinted with permission from the *New York Post*, 1994 copyright,
NYP Holdings, Inc.)

The ride also featured an observation deck where exiting
riders who wanted to could stand in the path of a huge wave as
they crossed a bridge at the bottom of the hill. The wave was
created by the next boat coming down.

Following the opening, the park had some trouble with the
wave, so it lowered the track the boats rode on to create quicker
and higher waves that generated an umbrella effect on the
bridge. In addition, warning signs were posted and an attendant
was added to tell people when they could cross without getting
wet. Later the park added plastic shields to the metal fence on
the bridge and a large rope net over the splash zone to further
diffuse the waves.

The park spent almost $150,000 restoring its 1919 Philadel-
phia Toboggan Company Carousel. The project, done in-house
during the off-season, was started in 1992 and was not com-

A boat on the way back to the loading station. (HersheyPark)

pleted until 1994. Everything on the carousel was refurbished,
including the horses, scenery, and roof.

The Amphitheatre, which had been expanded to 2,000
seats, was fully covered in 1994. Franklin R. Shearer, vice
president and general manager, commented, "The guests have
been asking us to provide a shade and rain structure for them at
the amphitheatre." The park continued to offer two concert
series. One, which was free with admission to the park, was held
at the park's amphitheatre, and the other at an additional
charge was at the Stadium.

For 1994, the park set a new attendance record of more
than 1.85 million. McKinney credited TIDAL FORCE, which
"performed beyond our expectations, had very little downtime,

Spencer Christian of Good Morning America with a Hershey's chocolate bar. (HERSHEYPARK)

and required little or no maintenance." It carried 812,479 riders during the season. "I think the combination of the excellent weather, new ride, strong destination Hershey marketing and a superb talent lineup in both the park and stadium paid off," continued McKinney. There were eleven shows in the 25,000-seat stadium and discounted tickets were offered to the park guests. The park's best year ever was topped off when ABC broadcast live from Hersheypark's Christmas Candylane on December 16, 1994.

For 1995, Jerry van Dyke, who played Luther on the ABC television series *Coach*, became the park's first spokesperson ever. Two 30-second commercials were filmed in the park showing van Dyke trying to visit the entire park, all of the rides, shows, food stands, and games, in one day and in the end falling asleep on The Comet in his pajamas.

When asked what he thought about being Hersheypark's Ambassador of Fun, van Dyke told the *Lebanon Daily News*, "I thought it would be terrific," and he added that he was an

Hersheypark – Jerry van Dyke billboards. (HERSHEYPARK)

Jerry van Dyke performs at the Amphitheatre.
(HERSHEYPARK)

An aerial view of The Comet. (Photograph by Wayne Stuber/Aerial Perspective – copyright 1996)

amusement park fan and thought Hersheypark was "one of the nicest." It did not hurt that van Dyke loved chocolate, especially Hershey's. After making the commercials van Dyke appeared on David Letterman's television show and plugged the park. McKinney commented, "He [van Dyke] already earned his money." Van Dyke's face appeared on fourteen billboards in the Harrisburg area. The main billboard was changed eight times, once every 15 days. Some of the signs were "Follow Jerry to you know where," "More fun than a barrel of Jerrys," "Jerrific Park," and "Have a Very Jerry Day."

During Hersheypark's opening weekend for the 1995 season, van Dyke entertained in the Amphitheatre. His 45-minute vaudeville-style act consisted of stories, jokes, and van Dyke's signature banjo playing accompanied by a four-piece combo, and he promised it would be a "Jerrific Year" for the park.

A Tiny Tracks train was added to the Carrousel Circle area in 1995. The ride was built by Zamperla of Italy. It was another kiddie ride that worked well both in the regular season and during Christmas Candylane. Other rides for kiddies included the carousel, Dizzy Drums, Bizzy Bees, Lollipop Line, and Dinosaur-Go-Round. Each of the park's seven sections had at

Tiny Tracks was added to Carrousel Circle in 1995.
(Hersheypark)

The Bizzy Bees in Music Box Way. (Photograph by Charles J. Jacques, Jr.)

197

least two or three kiddie rides. The Tilt-A-Whirl was moved from the Tiny Tracks location to the area formerly occupied by the Rotor, which was removed from the park.

For its fiftieth year of operation in 1995, The Comet's loading station was reconfigured to accommodate flow-through loading. (Prior to the remodeling, The Comet stopped to discharge riders, and then moved through the station to where the passengers were waiting to board.) Two new coaster trains were purchased from the Philadelphia Toboggan Coaster, Inc. The new trains cost more than the original coaster and trains had cost in 1946.

One of the old coaster cars was given to the American Coaster Enthusiasts, the largest roller coaster club in the world, for the club's coaster museum and archives, and another was given to the Derry Township Historical Society. At one time The Comet was green, a color which M.S. Hershey preferred for his rides. In 1977 it was painted white because the green blended in with the trees too much. "People thought we were toning it down and that white was more appealing," Joe Gosik, director of maintenance, told the *Harrisburg Patriot News.* "Now, being white, people can look ahead and see what they're going to experience." The coaster was computerized. "We used to apply the brakes manually, but all that is automated," Gosik said. The coaster was inspected every morning by two mechanics and two carpenters. Each year a little over one million people ride The Comet.

"Last year [1994] TIDAL FORCE was probably No. 1 for attendance, with the Coal Cracker No. 2," Gosik explained. TIDAL FORCE was popular because it was new, but The Comet showed over the years that it had real staying power. "The longevity of the ride and the nostalgia it holds for people makes it special," he said.

M.S. Hershey got a United States stamp of his own on September 13, 1995. Hershey joined authors Jack London, Sinclair Lewis, and Pearl Buck and former U.S. Chief Justice Earl Warren in the Postal Service's Great American Series. Seven thousand five hundred of his admirers packed Hersheypark Arena for the occasion, second only to the 9,000 fans who took part in the first-day ceremonies for the Elvis Presley stamp.

A new skaters light display.
(HERSHEYPARK)

In 1995, Creatures of the Night, the park's educational Halloween alternative, was expanded to six days. The highlight was observing the nocturnal activities of the animals and listening to the music they make. The guests placed luminarias (paper bags filled with sand and a lit candle) along the banks of Spring Creek, which created the perfect setting for Halloween ghost stories. A few of

Dinosaur-Go-Round in Christmas hats and scarfs. (HERSHEYPARK)

the rides were opened and specially themed for the occasion including the Transylvania Turnpike (antique cars) and Bats in the Belfry (Kissing Tower); the younger riders could enjoy the Monster Macks (Convoy) and Red Baron's Phantom Fliers. Ichabod's Train in Sleepy Hollow was new for 1995 along with live musical entertainment and a marine mammal show in the Aquatheatre.

Candylane moved into its thirteenth year with more rides open to the public. It remained on a pay as you go basis. Some days it attracted as many people as the park had during an average summer day. The Candylane Twilight Express took visitors on a seven-minute journey through Santa's Magical Forest with animated light displays including snowmen, reindeer, Colonial skaters, and snowball throwing, ice skating, and skiing bears. Returning for the second season was the Hershey Holiday Characters Pageant, which featured Rudolph, Frosty the Snowman, the Gingerbread Man, and the Hershey's product characters. In 1995, Candylane had Santa for the first time in his own house, Santa's Castle in the geodesic dome.

Hersheypark was on a hot streak. Three major new rides had been added in six years and all of them were successful. The park had continued to add the little things, kiddie rides, food stands, shops, games, and restaurants that helped to give guests a well-rounded experience. It now had the capacity both with rides and support services to break the two million mark in attendance.

A Christmas shopper in Rhineland.
(PHOTOGRAPH BY CHARLES J. JACQUES, JR)

The park's shops are beautifully decorated during Christmas Candylane. (HERSHEYPARK)

The Cat is Back!

The Wildcat. (Hersheypark)

Excitement reigned on June 30, 1995, at a press conference to announce Hersheypark's new $5.5 million roller coaster. Franklin R. Shearer, vice president and general manager of the park, presided and tried to calm a dancing Peanut Butter Cup to no avail. Shearer gave up and turned to the microphone—anticipation filled the air as he cleared his throat and shouted, "The Cat is Back!"

Shearer announced that Hersheypark was building a brand-new, but thoroughly old-fashioned wooden roller coaster to be named The Wildcat. The incredible wooden cyclone coaster would take its riders for the ride of their lives on a circuit of eleven turns, crossing through or over itself

At the bottom of the first drop.
(Photograph by Charles J. Jacques, Jr)

twenty times during the course of the ride. Shearer said, "The 90-foot lift hill will be placed here on the hill [behind Tidal Force] at the highest point in the park. The 85-foot first drop will produce speeds in excess of 45 miles per hour." The gently sloping topography of the site allowed the 90-foot-high ride to have an actual height differential of 105 feet and the top speed proved to be 49 miles per hour, but the coaster seemed to go twice as fast.

The Wildcat was Hersheypark's first new wooden roller coaster in fifty years. It attempted to reproduce one of the great cyclone-twister coasters of the late 1920's and 1930's and it was a custom, one-of-a-kind design. Although the park's first Wild Cat had been an out-and-back style coaster, Hersheypark decided to go with a twisting, cyclone coaster, because this style is generally more exciting. Also The Comet, which had just celebrated its fiftieth birthday, was an out-and-back coaster. Hersheypark executives told the designer they wanted a cyclone coaster different from The Comet and one that would fit on the site available. The coaster was designed for everyone from teenagers to older riders.

Construction workers climb The Wildcat's superstructure.
(Photograph by Jeffrey W. Budgeon)

Working on The Wildcat's structure in the snow.
(Photograph by Jeffrey W. Budgeon)

Clair Hain, Jr., president of Great Coasters, International, the builder.
(Photograph by Charles J. Jacques, Jr.)

Heavily banked turns on the new coaster.
(Photograph by Wayne Stuber)

The multimillion dollar theme project was developed in the northwest corner of the park adjoining Hersheypark Drive. The land had been the old Blue Field of the annual fall antique auto show. The Wildcat occupied nearly two acres in a new eight-acre section of the park to be called Midway America.

Construction started in August 1995 before the park closed for the season. Clair Hain, Jr., president of Great Coasters International, the builder, discovered that the site was solid limestone. It took considerable hammering to properly place the coaster's footers, which were more than three feet deep. Then the winter set in, a winter more severe, with more snow, than in decades. Two heaters were set up to keep the construction workers warm.

Hain's partner and company vice president, Mike Boodley, designed the new coaster. It was the first roller coaster built by Great Coasters International of Northumberland, Pennsylvania. Prior to his association with Great Coasters, Boodley had

designed several other coasters, as well as special effects for Universal Studios. He and Hain met in 1991. Boodley said, "This [The Wildcat] is totally unique. Nothing like it is operating anywhere. There's nothing out there like this with swooping drops and high banked turns."

Boodley joked that once the ride was running, it would snarl traffic on Hersheypark Drive. "People will be watching the trains as they reach that first drop. You know they're going to want to watch them drop!"

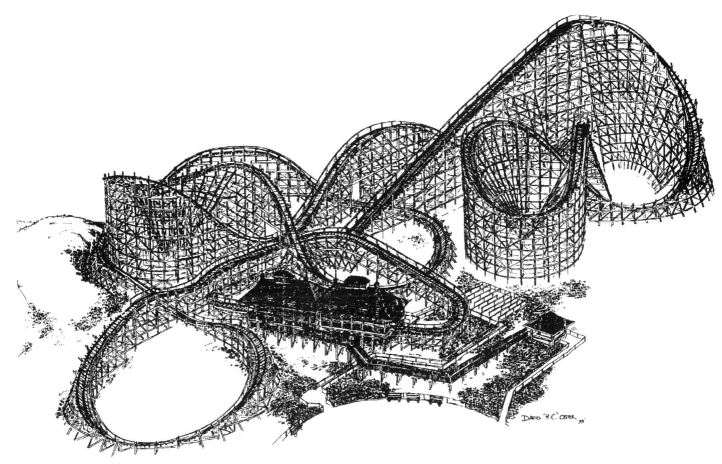

Preliminary drawing of The Wildcat.
(HERSHEYPARK)

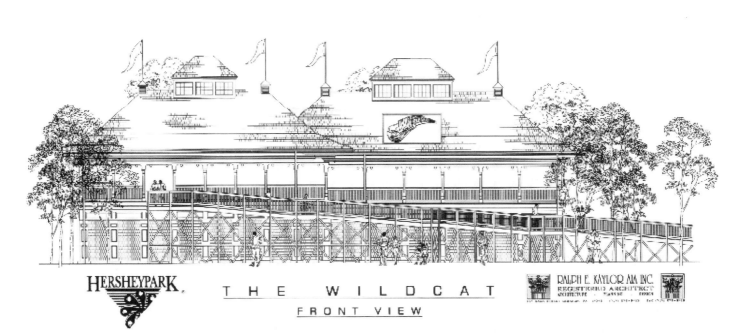

HERSHEYPARK

THE WILDCAT
FRONT VIEW

RALPH E. KAYLOR AIA INC.
REGISTERED ARCHITECT

Rendering of The Wildcat's loading station.
(BY RALPH E. KAYLOR, REGISTERED ARCHITECT)

Hain had been building coasters for ten years. In 1994, he fell fifty feet from a coaster in Indiana. He was hospitalized with broken ribs, punctured lungs, a mangled liver, a broken wrist and collarbone, and fractures of his vertebrae. He was told he would never walk again. Hain proved the doctors wrong and decided to start his own roller coaster construction business while recuperating. He said paralysis in his left side hampered his mobility, but he liked to supervise the construction personally. On The Wildcat project, Hain spent seven days a week worrying about deadlines, weather, and the health and safety of his workers.

Kathy Burrows, public relations coordinator for the park, observed that "each time we plan to put in a new ride we seem to have a severe winter." They were prevented from working only when a heavy ice storm hit the area. Jeffrey W. Budgeon, managing director of park planning, engineering, and maintenance, said that "even the equipment has to be heated slowly to get it started." About twenty Great Coaster employees were bundled against the weather. "The men worked seven days a week," Budgeon said. The coaster was built from 514,000 board feet of southern yellow pine, and at times the workers had to dig out wood from under the snow. Tracks were placed on eight layers of wood. More than one million bolts kept the coaster together. Treated wood was used thereby saving money because it did not have to be painted.

The coaster's cars were built by the Philadelphia Toboggan Coaster, Inc., Lansdale, Pennsylvania. (It was the successor company to the Philadelphia Toboggan Company.) The cars used on The Wildcat were fifty-one inches wide and seventy-two inches long; each weighed approximately 1,900 pounds. Building the cars one at a time by hand was time-consuming. The contract for Hersheypark's cars was let in September and the new coaster cars were delivered in February.

In July 1996, Brian Fauth wrote in *ACE News*, a publication of the American Coaster Enthusiasts, (the largest roller coaster club in the world with over 5,000 members) that during the construction ACE members "gawked at the convoluted curves, the intricate cross-overs, and the first drop that recalls nothing so much as the infamous Cyclone at Crystal Beach [Ontario, Canada, outside of Buffalo, New York]." The important question

Franklin R. Shearer at the opening of The Wildcat on May 25, 1996. (Photograph by Mark Wyatt/Inside Track)

The ringmaster and clowns from Ringling Bros., Barnum & Bailey at the opening. (Photograph by Mark Wyatt/Inside Track)

Elephants from Ringling Bros., Barnum & Bailey lead the way to the new coaster. (Photograph by Mark Wyatt/Inside Track)

An aerial view of The Wildcat shows how it crosses over,
through, and around itself.

(PHOTOGRAPH BY WAYNE STUBER/AERIAL PERSPECTIVE – COPYRIGHT 1996)

*Designer of The Wildcat,
Michael Boodley.*

(PHOTOGRAPH BY CHARLES J. JACQUES, JR.)

The first drop of The Wildcat.

(PHOTOGRAPH BY CHARLES J. JACQUES, JR.)

The lift hill of The Wildcat.

(PHOTOGRAPH BY CHARLES J. JACQUES, JR.)

was how would it ride? He added, "Experienced riders will be
surprised at the comfort level maintained through the course,
how each transition from swoop to swoop, overpass to underpass
feels so right."

The cyclone-style coaster cost $5.5 million including
construction, site preparation, and landscaping. Franklin R.
Shearer told *Amusement Business*, "They have put together quite
a piece." The coaster's inaugural rides on May 26, 1996, were
better than anticipated. "You might conclude I'm prejudiced," he
said, "but on a scale of 1-to-10, with 10 being spectacular, The
Wildcat is a 20! It's a marvelous ride."

"There are no dull moments in the ride," Shearer pointed
out. "After the climb to the top of the first hill, the train main-
tains a speed of at least 40 mph. It's an intense ride with steep
banking throughout with some 55-degree bends. In all, it crosses
over or under itself more than 20 times. It's fast, sleek, slick, and
has that wonderful feel of wood." The coaster was still going an
estimated 40 miles per hour when it returned to the station. The
coaster was so well-designed that no brakes were needed to slow
the trains anywhere on their trip until they reached the final
brake run. Shearer said he talked with park guests as they got off

the coaster. "It was fun hearing all the good things," he said. "One person said he counted eleven points of air time [places where a rider is lifted out of the seat]."

The Wildcat also featured a coaster loading station that was designed by architect Ralph Kaylor from nearby Lebanon, Pennsylvania. Kaylor spent several weeks in the Hershey Community Archives studying newspaper clippings, old photographs, and postcards of the original Wild Cat. "I remember the park as a young boy, and I wanted to make sure it was done correctly," he explained. The Wildcat's station was decked out with banners and flags and carnival grounds-type lighting.

The Wildcat served as the centerpiece of the new Midway America, which will be developed during the next few years as a nostalgic area, featuring the rides and attractions that existed at Hersheypark during the earlier years. Midway America developed out of a meeting of management employees in the early 1990's. The idea was to bring back some of the rides and attractions that drew people to the park in the 1930's and 1940's. The new area will recreate attractions that people remembered from the past. "We're blessed with a lot of land here in Hershey," said Shearer. "You'll see Hersheypark expanding here on land we currently have, and you'll see different configurations throughout the next century."

Originally, there was some thought to placing Midway America in Comet Hollow with the classic Comet as the centerpiece, but the frequent flooding of Spring Creek would have caused problems. Once a decision was made to build The Wildcat, developing the site into an area with old rides and games was a natural.

The Wildcat's structure silhouetted against the sky.
(PHOTOGRAPH BY CHARLES J. JACQUES, JR.)

Coming down the first hill on The Wildcat.
(PHOTOGRAPH BY CHARLES J. JACQUES, JR.)

The Wildcat as seen from the Hershey Rose Garden. (PHOTOGRAPH BY CHARLES J. JACQUES, JR.)

Opposite: The Wildcat is a hands-on coaster. (HERSHEYPARK)

A concert in the Hersheypark Stadium.
(Hersheypark)

"We'll be recreating some of the early excitement that made Hersheypark famous," Shearer said. "The two main perpendicular streets in Midway America are known as Chocolate and Cocoa Avenues, two streets in the town of Hershey." Although no timetable was set, he hoped the park would complete the area in about three years.

In 1996 only portable food and merchandise units were used in the new area, but permanent structures were planned for 1997. The only other ride in the area was the miniature train used in Kiddieland in the 1950's. It had been purchased by an employee who restored it. For the past several years, it had been set up during the park's Christmas Candylane event; now it found a summer home as well.

On June 12, 1996, the newly-constructed Star Pavilion at Hersheypark officially opened with a ribbon-cutting ceremony. Robert Lamm, singer and songwriter for Chicago, cut the ribbon. The new addition to the entertainment complex, located in the north end of the Hersheypark Stadium in a landscaped crescent, seated four thousand in the reserved section and up to three thousand in the general admission section on the grass.

The park's summer concert season in the new 7,000-seat Star Pavilion and adjacent 25,0000-seat stadium was a success. All acts were booked by Electric Factory of Philadelphia. The highlight of the concert season was on August 14-15, when Phish drew 25,000 the first night and Hootie & the Blowfish drew 23,000 the next evening. Some of the other good draws in the new Star Pavilion included The Monkees with 3,500, July 26; Meatloaf, 5,500, July 28; and James Taylor's SRO audience of 7,200, August 11.

Some of the acts that were booked into the Amphitheatre within the park included Gary Puckett, Neil Sedaka, Mary Wilson, Air Supply, Pete Fountain, and Al Hirt.

A one-day pass on September 7 to Hersheypark's Literacy Day was the reward for kids who took part in a summer reading challenge. It was sponsored by central Pennsylvania newspapers and Hersheypark. Each participant had to complete five written exercises out of ten that appeared in their paper and submit them to the paper. Michele Ridge, wife of the governor of Pennsylvania, spoke to the participants at the park on the importance of reading and told them which books her children liked the best when they were young.

Hersheypark's core market remained Harrisburg, Lebanon, Lancaster, and York, Pennsylvania. The other major markets and distances from the park were: Baltimore, 90 miles; New York City, 145 miles; Philadelphia, 90 miles; Washington, D.C., 140 miles; and Scranton, less than 100 miles.

The Wildcat was a success as the park set an all-time attendance record of over two million guests in a single season for the first time. The biggest one-day attendance record in the history of the park was set with 34,100 people on August 17, 1996. The marketing campaign of Hershey as a destination was a success.

The 1996 season was eight percent above the 1995 attendance season totals and was the third straight year that the park had set a seasonal attendance record. "We couldn't be happier with this year's results," said CEO McKinney. "Our employees are really the key to our success. Their dedication, loyalty, and commitment ensure that every visitor to Hershey receives the very best in 'Hershey Hospitality' while they are in The Sweetest Place On Earth."

For 1997 the park announced a $5.7 million plan to add a Ferris wheel approaching 100 feet in height and a re-creation of the park's original Whip ride in the Midway America theme area. The Ferris wheel will be purchased from Chance Rides, Wichita, Kansas, while the Whip will be manufactured by Rideworks, Sarasota, Florida. Other new features in the Midway America area for 1997 will include a merchandise shop and food and games buildings. "The shops and old-fashioned rides will blend the charm of the past and technology of the future," said

TIDAL FORCE at twilight. (Photograph by Charles J. Jacques, Jr.)

Kiddie Whip. (Hersheypark)

Earthmovers. (Hersheypark)

PTC Carousel #41. ((Photograph by Charles J. Jacques, Jr.)

Engine on Dry Gulch Railroad. (Hersheypark)

210

Frontier-Chute-Out. <small>(Hersheypark)</small>

Shearer. The architecture of the buildings, to be done by Ralph Kaylor, will be reminiscent of the 1930's and 1940's complete with patriotic red, white, and blue accent colors. A children's area with the Pony Parade, Granny Bugs, and miniature train rides, all relocated from other sections of the park, will be moved into the five-acre expansion of Midway America along Hersheypark Drive, just beyond the TIDAL FORCE water ride. Landscaping will replace the spots vacated by the Pony Parade and Granny Bugs. Another addition to Hersheypark for 1997 will be a 1,400-square-foot pizza restaurant between Pioneer Frontier and Midway America. The eatery will have an observation area overlooking TIDAL FORCE's splash zone. The restaurant will be built on the current miniature train site.

In all, a total of $8.2 million will be spent at Hersheypark during the 1997 season. That includes the development of Midway America and work to further enhance existing rides and attractions throughout the park.

In the fall of 1995, WITF-TV Channel 33, the public television station in Harrisburg, Pennsylvania, began production of a historical documentary chronicling the history of

TIDAL FORCE. <small>(Photograph by Mark Wyatt/Inside Track)</small>

211

Big Rig Grill.
<small>(Photograph by Charles J. Jacques, Jr.)</small>

Dolphin show. <small>(Hersheypark)</small>

Hersheypark. The hour-long special tells how the park grew from a small picnic grove to a world-class amusement park.

Executive producer Mark Samels from WITF-TV collaborated on the project with Charles J. Jacques, Jr., an amusement park historian and author. Producer Sandy Enterline began research at the Hershey Community Archives, which had a wealth of information from historic photographs to a film produced by M.S. Hershey in 1932, *The Gift of Montezuma.* Hershey Community Archivist Pamela Cassidy also found a film from 1963 featuring the park's rides in action. The station was also able to get some priceless footage shot by residents of central Pennsylvania, including children riding ponies, the Turnpike, and other kiddie rides.

A Canyon River Rapids waterfall.
<small>(Hersheypark)</small>

Phil Cousins, director/cameraman/editor of WITF's Hersheypark documentary with Ralph Spotts on right.
(Photograph by Betty Jacques)

vaudeville from Philadelphia. Huge picnics were brought in. Concert bands were engaged from all over Pennsylvania and nationally known dance bands were booked. A new, exciting electric miniature railway was built and two prestigious merry-go-rounds were purchased. A large modern convention center, an arena, and stadium were constructed. A roller coaster and Mill Chute transformed the landscape. A professional hockey team was formed and a rose garden and zoo developed.

In the 1930's Hershey commented that in the first thirty years the park had almost completely changed. The buildings were better, bigger, more substantial. "People wanted change, you know," he said. But he also had his eyes on the future.

In 1945, several weeks before his death, he called Harry Erdman, his long-time gardener, over to his hospital room to

Phil Cousins; Sandy Enterline, producer; and Charles J. Jacques, Jr. during the videotaping.
(Photograph by Betty Jacques)

Sandy Enterline interviews J. Bruce McKinney with Phil Cousins and sound recordist John Rex.
(Photograph by Charles J. Jacques, Jr.)

A number of residents from Hershey and former Hersheypark employees were interviewed. The production team included director/cameraman/editor Phil Cousins, sound recordist John Rex, production assistant Matt Murphy and other members of the WITF production staff.

Although M.S. Hershey was fifty years old when he founded Hersheypark, he was not governed by the past. What he accomplished from 1907 until his death in 1945 was truly remarkable. He turned a cornfield and some woods along Spring Creek into a marvelous amusement park.

When he officially opened Hershey Park in 1907, he did not build an old fashioned park but offered the latest and the newest. There was swimming, roller skating, dancing, and

The Brad Cassady interview took place overlooking the old site of the swimming pool complex. (Photograph by Charles J. Jacques, Jr.)

talk about planting trees around Hershey. His final words to Erdman were, "You and I may not live to see this completed, but fifty years from now people will still be enjoying it." Erdman planted the trees in the spring of 1946, and they are being enjoyed today.

So it was with Hersheypark. Many of the things M.S. Hershey did prior to his death helped Hersheypark grow and develop over the years. The excellent people he chose to lead the park, in turn, picked new management to lead into the 1970's, 1980's, and 1990's. The park now plays an important role in the life of the communities and schools that it serves. More than four million tourists enjoy a HERCO-related event each year, and the park is the very centerpiece. M.S. Hershey would be proud that fifty years after his death Hersheypark has grown into a unique and thrilling park with a sense of history.

Tudor Square.
(Photograph by Charles J. Jacques, Jr.)

Getting a picture taken with a Hershey's character.
(Hersheypark)

Spring Creek.
(Photograph by Betty Jacques)

Selected Bibliography

ACE NEWS.

Alexander, William H. "Our Hershey Heritage: The Builder, D. Paul Witmer." Hershey Rotary Club. Hershey, PA. 23 November 1992.

Amusement Business. 1960-96.

Amusement Park Management.

At The Park. 1989-96.

Billboard. 1894-1960.

Cassidy, Pamela, and Eliza Cope Harrison. *One Man's Vision: Hershey, A Model Town.* 1987.

Elizabethtown Chronicle.

Gordon, Bruce, and David Mumford. *Disneyland the Nickel Tour.* Santa Clarita, California: Camphor Tree Publishers, 1995.

Griffin, Al. *Step Right Up, Folks.* Chicago: Henry Regnery, 1974.

Harrisburg Evening News. 1854-1996.

Harrisburg Morning Telegraph.

Harrisburg Patriot. 1854-1996.

Harrisburg Patriot News. 1854-1996.

Hershey Foods Corporation. *Hershey.* 1974.

Hershey Community Archives. Pamela Cassidy, Archivist. Oral History Program. Entries for: Cyril J. Little, Terence Faul, Alma Bobb, Red McCarthy, Sarah Seavers, Dick Ulrich, Fred Mazzoli, Howard Phillippy, Kenneth V. Hatt, Edwin Zechman, Tom Guinivan, Howard Kishpaugh, Robert Reese, Robert Smith, Bill Cagnoli, Helen Cappelli, Ted Mandes, Richard Seiverling, Brent Hancock, Richard Bacastow, Howard Kishpaugh, and Monroe Stover.

Hershey Chronicle. 1985-96.

The Hershey News. 1954-62.

Hershey Press. 1909-26.

Hershey Progressive Weekly.

"Hersheypark: Sweet Memories" Producer Sandra Enterline. WITF-TV, Harrisburg, PA.

Hinkle, Samuel F. "Hershey Chocolate Corporation." 1966.

–. "Hershey Farsighted Confectioner Famous Chocolate Fine Community." 1963.

Hotel Hershey High-Lights. 1934-51.

Inside Track. 1987-96.

Kyriazi, Gary. *The Great American Amusement Park.* Secaucus, NJ: Citadel Press, 1976.

Lebanon Daily News. 1972-96.

Matthew, Milton T. "Our Hershey Heritage: The Salesman, William F. R. Murrie." Hershey Rotary Club. Hershey, PA. 9 November 1992.

"Mr. Hershey Gives Away His Fortune." *Fortune Magazine* January 1934.

Murrie, Richard Wallace. "The Story Behind a Hershey Bar." 1939.

New York Post. 1801-1996.

New York Times. 1851-1996.

The New Yorker.

Onosko, Tim. "Fun Land U.S.A." New York: Ballantine Books, 1978.

Philadelphia Bulletin.

Philadelphia Business Journal.

Philadelphia Inquirer.

Reese, Robert M. "Our Hershey Heritage: The Lawyer, John Snyder." Hershey Rotary Club. Hershey, PA. 7 Dec. 1992.

Reflections, newsletter of the Derry Township Historical Society. 1994-1996.

Rollercoaster! 1978-96.

Shippen, Katherine B., and Paul A.W. Wallace. "Milton S. Hershey." New York: Random House, 1959.

Snavely, Joseph Richard. *A Chat With Mr. Hershey.* Hershey Press, 1932.

–. *The Hershey Story.* Hershey Press, 1950.

–. *An Intimate Story of Milton S. Hershey.* Hershey Press, 1957.

–. *Meet Mr. Hershey.* Hershey Press, 1937.

–. *Milton S. Hershey, Builder.* Hershey Press, 1934.

–. *M.S. Hershey Lives On.* Hershey Press, 1947.

Steinmetz, Richard H. *Chocolate Town Trolleys: An Illustrated History of the Electric Street Railway in Hershey, Pennsylvania.* 1967.

Stoddard, Alexander. Scrapbooks and press releases. Hershey Community Archives, Hershey, PA. 1934-51.

"The Story of Hershey The Chocolate Town." 1963.

Thomas, Bob. *Walt Disney: An American Original.* New York: Simon & Schuster, 1976.

VSP LIFE. (HERCO)

Wallace, Paul A. W. "Biography of M.S. Hershey." unpublished, 1955.

INDEX

Books From Amusement Park Journal

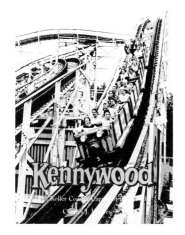

Kennywood: Roller Coaster Capital of the World by Charles J. Jacques, Jr. The history of this great traditional amusement park is told in this 212-page book. All of Kennywood's coasters including the Pippin, Speed-O-Plane, Racer, Teddy Bear, Jack Rabbit, Thunderbolt, Figure Eight and Laser Loop are covered. Many other attractions like Noah's Ark, Dentzel Carousel, circle swing, rocket ships, and many others are mentioned.

This book is available for
$24.95, plus $2.00 for postage and handling.

GOODBYE, WEST VIEW PARK, GOODBYE by Charles J. Jacques, Jr., a history of one of Pittsburgh's amusement parks from its founding by T. M. Harton in 1906 until it was closed after the 1977 season. Included in this 124 page book are many photographs of West View Park's terrific roller coasters, the Kiddie Dips, the Dips and Racing Whippet, designed by the Vettel family. Rare photographs of the carousel built by Harton with horses carved by the Muller brothers of Philadelphia, and West View Park's famous Danceland which played all of the major dance bands over the years.

This book is available for
$24.95, plus $2.00 for postage and handling.

Books soon to be published by Amusement Park Journal.
More Kennywood Memories and Idora Park - the Last Ride of Summer.

Story of Hersheypark now Available on Videocassette

"Hersheypark: Sweet Memories," a one-hour, memory-filled look at the Sweetest Place on Earth is now available.

To order call **1-800-828-4PBS.**
Produced in 1997 by WITF/Harrisburg.

The production of "Hersheypark: Sweet Memories" was made possible by a grant from:

ÆEtna
US Healthcare